PRESERVED STEAM LOCOMOTIVES OF WESTERN EUROPE

Volume 1

By the same author
On Railways at Home and Abroad
Locomotives Through the Lens
Men of the Footplate
On Engines in Britain and France
The Concise Encyclopaedia of World Railway Locomotives
(Editor and Contributor)

British Railways To-day
The Last Steam Locomotives of Western Europe
Die Letzten Dampflokomotiven Westeuropas
The World's Smallest Public Railway—RH & D
The Snowdon Mountain Railway
Last Steam Locomotives of British Railways
Southern Album
All About Photographing Trains
Ships and the Sea
The Royal Navy
Train Ferries of Western Europe
Eisenbahn-Fahren in Westeuropa

P. RANSOME-WALLIS

Preserved Steam Locomotives of Western Europe

Volume 1

LONDON

IAN ALLAN

First published 1971

SBN 7110 0196 0

Published by Ian Allan Ltd., Shepperton, Surrey and printed in the
United Kingdom by Tindal Press Ltd., London and Chelmsford

Contents

Acknowledgements

In the compilation of this book I have been greatly helped by many people in many ways. I am indebted to them all and I offer to them my sincere thanks.

Austria: Dipl. Ing. Rolf Niederhuemer, Technical Museum, Vienna.

Belgium: AMUTRA, Secretary and Members, Schepdael; Monsieur A. Vanden Eede, SNCV, Brussels; Director General SNCB, Brussels; Edgar T. Mead, Jnr., Steamtown, Bellows Falls, USA.

Denmark: W. E. Danker-Jensen, Esq., Railway Museum, Copenhagen; O. Winther Laursen, Esq., Kölding.

Finland: Igor Ahvenlahti, Esq., VR. Helsinki.

France: Monsieur Michel Doerr, Director of Railway Museum, Mulhouse; Herr A. W. Glaser, Zürich, Switzerland; N. A. Needle, Esq., London, England; J. A. Price, Esq., London, England; Monsieur C. Roche, SNCF, Paris.

West Germany: Dr. Ing. Glaser, Bundesbahndirektion, Frankfurt; Dr. Joachim, Hotz, DEGB, Karlsruhe; Dr. Pfahl, Verkehrsmuseum, Nüremberg; Herr Wolfgang Stoffels, Augsburg; Charles Walker, Esq., Hildenborough, England.

Italy: P. M. Kalla-Bishop, Esq., London, England; Sr. Carlo Saura, Leonardo da Vinci Museum, Milan.

Netherlands: Miss Marie-Anne Asselberghs, Director, Railway Museum, Utrecht; N.V. Machinefabrik, Breda; Robert Stamkot, Esq., Stichting Museum, Buurtspoorweg, Enschede.

Norway: "E.F." of the Public Relations Dept. NSB, Oslo.

Portugal: Senor Antonio Gouveia, C.P., Lisbon.

Spain: Don Senor Antonio Lago Carbello, RENFE, Madrid; Lawrence Marshall, Esq., Crawley, England; Don Señor Gustavo Reder, Madrid.

Sweden: C. A. Alrenius, Esq., SJ, Stockholm; Ulf Diehl, Esq., Lidingo; G. Ekeroth, Esq., SJ, Stockholm; L. O. Karlsson, Esq., Sollentuna; Rolf Larsson, Esq., Göteborg; Trygve Romsloe, Esq., Narvik, Norway; Erik Sundström, Esq., Karlskoga.

Switzerland: B.L.S. Publicity Department, Bern; Manfred Meier, Esq., Mettmenstetten; Herr Fr. Neuenschwander, EBT, Burgdorf; Renfer et Cie, Bienne; Herr W. Trüb, SBB, Bern; Von Moos 'schon AG; Von Roll AG, Gerlafingen; Herr Hans Wismann, Verkehrshaus, Lucerne.

The following have provided much help and information about locomotives in several countries and my thanks go to: B. M. Campbell, Esq.; D. Cole, Esq.; J. Eberstein, Esq.; R. S. Fraser, Esq.; Brian Garvin, Esq.; A. G. W. Goff, Esq.; A. J. Hart, Esq.; J. H. Price, Esq.; F. L. Pugh, Esq.; D. F. Rollins, Esq.; Trevor Rowe, Esq.; Brian Stephenson, Esq.

My old and valued friends Othmar Bamer of Vienna, Austria and Maurice Maillet of Lagny, France have once again uncomplainingly and generously given me all the support and help for which I asked. I am most grateful.

Finally, without the able assistance and information so generously given by R. G. ("Tommy") Farr, this book could never have been written. Once upon a time I thought I knew quite a lot about continental locomotives. "Tommy" Farr begins where I leave off! I can only again say "Thank you".

Photographs

The photographs in this book have come from many sources and each is acknowledged with the caption. My sincere thanks to all those who have helped in this way.

P. R-W.

Introduction

In Western Continental Europe, as in other parts of the world, the interest in the preservation of steam railway locomotives is growing apace. Rather belatedly, the various railways have begun to recognise this interest and many are now showing concern to secure for posterity representative examples of their individual steam locomotive practice.

Two major problems are common to all who try to preserve locomotives: To find adequate money to do so and to find suitable and adequate space for the purpose. Many praiseworthy efforts, both private and public, have foundered on the failure to obtain one or both of these requirements. In other cases, preservation of large tender locomotives has proved difficult to achieve and has been abandoned in favour of keeping some small and mechanically uninteresting tank locomotives.

It is the avowed intention of most countries to establish, at least one, railway museum, but the locations have not all been finalised and the space to be available for locomotives is, therefore, not known. As a result, a considerable number of locomotives which have been withdrawn from service is to be found in the sheds, yards and depots of most Western European countries. Some of these will, undoubtedly, find their ultimate homes in museums or as monuments. Others will go for scrap but which will survive has often not yet been decided. Frequent changes occur also, as more "candidates for preservation" arrive, their active lives completed.

In this book, I have had five objectives:

(1) To describe technically and historically, as far as possible, all those Continental Western European standard and broad-gauge steam locomotives which have been preserved and those which are stored for probable future preservation. I fully realise that some which are described will probably end their days as scrap metal rather than in a museum but, until the final decision has been made as to which they are to be, I have thought it better to include, rather than to neglect them. There may be some I have omitted, owing to my ignorance of their existence, but I do not think these are many. In the descriptions in this book, however, only *complete* locomotives are dealt with and the many interesting locomotive parts which are to be found in museums and technical schools have not been included.

(2) To provide as much information as possible about preserved steam locomotives from narrow gauge railways (1067 mm and less). The situation concerning these locomotives is still very fluid. In this book, an

account is given of those locomotives which are known to be preserved or which are at work on "museum railways". The roster is by no means complete and neither is the technical and historical information available.

(3) To illustrate all the classes of locomotives described I realise that this is the most important feature of the book but it has not been easy to achieve. However, for the standard and broad gauge, only in a few instances has it been impossible. Narrow gauge locomotives have proved to be much more difficult and many recorded are, unfortunately, not illustrated. No attempt is made always to show the actual preserved locomotive. A good picture of a machine of the same type and class is preferable to showing a view of the half-dismembered remains of the actual engine "stored for restoration and preservation".

(4) To afford the reader easy identification of the locomotives described. The current running number and, wherever relevant, the previous running number(s) are given. In most cases it has been possible to provide details of the builder, works number and date of construction.

(5) To give leading dimensions of each locomotive. Here, consideration of space resulted in the decision to record only cylinder diameter and stroke, coupled (or driving) wheel diameter, grate area and boiler pressure. Again, narrow gauge locomotive records are very incomplete.

The scope of this work *does NOT include industrial locomotives* which are preserved. An exception is made, however, in describing *SOME* of those which are actually working on narrow-gauge "museum railways".

The compilation of this book became something of a major research project, complicated by the inevitable author's nightmare that frequently no two "reliable" sources of information were in agreement. I am always grateful to those who write to me offering constructive criticism and informed correction.

As a result of two World Wars, many locomotives were sent away from their railways of origin and spent most of their lives on the railways of other countries. These permanent transfers were mostly of German locomotives, though many engines of Austrian origin were also to be found "away from home". In this book, all such locomotives which are preserved are included in the lists of their countries of origin. The same plan has been followed to include locomotives built away from the country of their original design. Thus, German Series 42, built in

Austria and sold to Luxembourg, is included in Germany though preserved in Luxembourg.

Finally, a word about the locations given for stored locomotives. These are in accordance with the best information available at this time. Movements of such locomotives from one depot to another are commonplace, so it is unwise to regard all the locations given as permanent. Most railways do not allow visits to depots solely occupied by locomotives in store as a regrettably large number of thefts of number plates etc., have occurred when such facilities have been made available in the past. However, it is probable that many stored locomotives may be exhibited, on a rota basis, in the museums. This principle has already been adopted in Switzerland where the locomotives in store at Vallorbe are brought, four at a time, to the Verkehrshaus at Lucerne for six-monthly periods of exhibition. Thus there is an added incentive for students of locomotive history to visit the museum each year.

December 1970   P. R-W.

Note regarding Boiler Pressures

There are differences between railways in the units
used to express boiler pressures.

Those in general use on European Railways are:
 (i) Kilograms per Square Centimetre (kg/cm^2)
        1 kg/cm^2 = 14·2 pounds per square inch (p.s.i.)
 (ii) Atmosphere (atm)
        1 atm = 1·03 kg/cm^2 = 14·7 p.s.i.
(iii) Hectopiezes (hpz)
        1 hpz = 1·02 kg/cm^2 = 14·5 p.s.i.

For all *practical* purposes these units may be regarded as equivalents.

Austrian Federal Railways

The *Österreichischen Bundesbahnen* (ÖBB) was formed in 1923 by the amalgamation of a number of comparatively small companies with the State Railways (*kaiserliche königliche Österreichische Staatsbahnen*—kkStB) which had been formed in 1884 and had, itself, absorbed many of the former independent companies. The Southern Railway (*Südbahn*) did not become a part of the ÖBB until 1924.

After the invasion of Austria by Hitler in 1938, the Austrian Railways became part of the German State Railway (*Deutsche Reichsbahn*) system and the Austrian locomotives were then numbered in the stock of the DRG.

The *Österreichischen Bundesbahnen* was reconstituted in 1945 but the Reichsbahn locomotive numbers were retained until 1952 when the system of numbering was modified.

For convenience, the *Bundesbahnen* from 1923 to 1938 is referred to as BBÖ while from 1945 until the present time it is referred to as ÖBB.

Steam Locomotion Preservation in Austria

The history of the steam locomotive in Austria is one of considerable enterprise and originality in design. Many interesting and successful locomotives were produced and the names of Haswell, Gölsdorf and Rihosek are world famous as locomotive engineers. It is, therefore, small wonder that a large number of locomotives should be "scheduled for preservation".

The first serious attempt to form a Railway Museum was made in 1891 but it was not until 1918 that the present museum was opened as part of the new Technical Museum in the Mariahilferstrasse in Vienna. Six locomotives are on display in the museum, one of which is sectioned. There is also an excellent collection of models and railway relics.

However, the popular demand to retain many other steam locomotives for posterity has led to a large number of different types being saved from the scrapheap and stored, nearly all in depots in and around Vienna.

A new Railway Museum is to be formed in the old locomotive round-house near to the Franz Josef Station in Vienna. It is not known exactly how many locomotives will be preserved and in the following pages, those which are at present (1970) stored and intended for the museum are listed and described.

AJAX in the Technical Museum, Vienna   [Technical Museum, Vienna

Beautifully restored and on exhibition in the Railway section of the Technical Museum is *AJAX*, an 0–4–2 tender engine built by Jones, Turner and Evans of Warrington, England in 1841 for the *Kaiser-Ferdinands-Nordbahn* (KFNB), as their No 37.

This locomotive is typical of English practice of the period in that it has inside cylinders, outside frames and fly-cranks with coupling rods. It is the oldest existing steam locomotive in Austria.

Dimensions: CYLINDERS: 355 × 508mm
             COUPLED WHEELS: 1560mm
             BOILER PRESSURE: 6.3atm

4–4–0 STEINBRUCK in the Technical Museum, Vienna   [Technical Museum, Vienna

Preserved in the Technical Museum at Vienna is an outside-cylinder 4–4–0 which was built in 1848 in the works of the Vienna-Gloggnitz Railway (later to become StEG) under the direction of John Haswell. It is named *STEINBRUCK* and carries works number 87. It was *Südbahn* No 827.

The valve gear is Stephenson's link motion inside the frames. The short wheelbases of both bogie and coupled wheels, the firebox situated behind the trailing coupled axle and the semi-circular backplate of the boiler all show the influence on this design of the Norris Locomotives then being built contemporaneously at the Norris Vienna Works. The enormous spark-arresting chimney is typical of the period.

The Vienna-Gloggnitz Railway became the Southern State Railway in 1853, and in 1858 the Southern Railway (*Südbahn*). In 1860 the *Südbahn* sold *STEINBRUCK* to the Graz-Köflacher Railway (GKB) who renamed it *SODING*. It operated the first train between Graz and Köflach on April 3, 1860. It was withdrawn in 1910 and presented to the Technical Museum where later, its original name was restored.

Dimensions: CYLINDERS: 369 × 790mm
COUPLED WHEELS: 1422mm
GRATE AREA: 1.0m^2
BOILER PRESSURE: 6atm

kkStB No 254, sectioned. Technical Museum, Vienna   [Technical Museum, Vienna

In the Technical Museum at Vienna is exhibited an outside-cylinder 4–4–0 which has been beautifully sectioned. This locomotive was built in 1883 for the *Kaiserin-Elisabeth-Bahn* (KEB) by Floridsdorf (works number 446). It was one of seven built to the design of the Class AR 4–4–0 of the *Kronprinz-Rudolf-Bahn* (KRB).

The *Kaiserin-Elisabeth-Bahn* was taken over by the *Kaiserliche Königliche Osterreicheische Staatsbahnen* (kkStB) in 1882 so, No 254 was always a kkStB locomotive and it later became No 1.20 in the stock of that railway.

No 254 has outside frames. The slide valves are inclined above the cylinders and are driven by outside Stephenson link motion with the eccentrics on the leading coupled axle inside the cranks. It is a good example of an express locomotive of the pre-Gölsdorf era of the State Railways.

Dimensions: CYLINDERS: 435 × 630mm

          COUPLED WHEELS: 1680mm

          GRATE AREA: 1.86m²

          BOILER PRESSURE: 11atm

No 106 FUSCH in the ÖBB Garden, Linz   [Othmar Bamer

Two 0–6–0 tender engines are preserved in the ÖBB Garden at Linz. They have been partially restored to their original condition, robbed by vandals of some interesting fittings and painted in gay colours with no regard whatsoever to historical accuracy.

No 106 *FUSCH* was built for the Kaiserin-Elisabeth Railway (KEB) as their Class B II by G. Sigl at Wiener Neustadt Works in 1868, works number 652. It was one of 69 similar locomotives constructed between 1867 and 1884, first for the KEB and then for the State Railways which took over the KEB in 1882. No 106 became No 47.17 of the kkStB and was one of three which survived long enough to be re-numbered by DR, when it became No 53.7101.

It has the enormous spark-arresting chimney so typical of the period and has outside frames and cylinders.

Dimensions: CYLINDERS: 430 × 635mm
        COUPLED WHEELS: 1257mm
        BOILER PRESSURE: 8.5atm

The main line of the KEB extended from Vienna West Station to Wörgl via Linz, Salzburg and Bischofshofen, a distance of 507km. No 106 has, therefore, a historical and geographical justification for its preservation at Linz but this is in no way true of the other two locomotives exhibited there (qv).

0–6–0 No 852 in the ÖBB Garden, Linz   [Othmar Bamer

No 852, the other 0–6–0 at Linz was built for the Austrian Southern Railway (*Südbahn*) by StEG, the Haswell works at Vienna which had become the works of the State Railways in 1855 (*Maschinen-Fabrik derr k.k. priv. österreichisehen Staatseisenbahn-Gesellschaft, Wien*). It was one of 171 locomotives of *Südbahn* Class 29 built between 1860 and 1872. These became Series 49 of the kkStB when the *Südbahn* was taken over in 1924. Five of these locomotives went to the *Graz-köflacher-Bahn* (qv), in 1925.

No 852 became kkStB No 49.28 and ÖBB No 153.7114. It carries works number 940. It was built, in 1869, without a cab. The name carried in preservation—*J. HASWELL*—is an addition made during restoration as the name was never carried during the active life of the engine.

These locomotives had long connecting rods driving the rear coupled axle. Frames, cylinders and motion were all outside the wheels.

Dimensions: CYLINDERS: 470 × 635mm
                COUPLED WHEELS: 1270mm
                BOILER PRESSURE: 7atm

It has been disclosed that Hungarian State Railways (MAV) No 333.002, a former *Südbahn* outside cylinder simple 0–6–0 of Class 32c, has been exchanged for GKB 0–6–0 No 674 previously *Südbahn* Class 29 built by StEG in 1860 (works number 507) and *Südbahn* No 1665.

Locomotives of *Südbahn* Class 32c were built between 1884 and 1900 and were Nos 1611–1683. Those remaining in Austria became BBÖ Nos 58.01–20 and DRG Series 53.7121.

16

No 333.002 will be restored and exhibited in the Railway Museum at Vienna while No 674 will go to the Railway Museum in Budapest (see also page 50).

Dimensions (Class 32c): CYLINDERS: 435 × 632mm
COUPLED WHEELS: 1258mm
GRATE AREA: 1.8m^2
BOILER PRESSURE: 10atm

The Gölsdorf Compound System

The Gölsdorf compound system was characterised by the placing of all four cylinders in line beneath the smoke-box with the low pressure cylinders outside and the high pressure inside the frames. Its distinctive feature was the fact that no starting valve was required. Instead, in the port faces of each LP cylinder were two small live-steam inlets, one at each end of the valve travel. When the engine was in full forward or backward gear, as when starting, one of the ports was uncovered and the other closed by a rib cast in the valve. So, live steam was admitted to the LP steam chest through each port in turn with the normal movement of the valve. When the engine was notched up, the travel of the valve was reduced and neither port was uncovered, the LP steam-chest receiving only the exhaust steam from the HP cylinder.

No 54.014 ex No 60.115 partly restored   [P. Ransome-Wallis

No 60.115 is a two-cylinder compound 2–6–0 of the kkStB built in 1899 at Wiener Neustadt, works number 4221. It has been restored and is at the South Depot at Vienna.

No fewer than 297 of the Class 60 engines were built during the period 1895–1910 and 30 survived in Austria to be taken into DRG stock during the Nazi occupation. No 60.115 was DRG No 54.014.

Gölsdorf's earliest two-cylinder compound engines were 0–6–0 tender freight engines with outside cylinders. These were kkStB Class 59 and 193 were built in the ten years 1893–1903. The 2–6–0s of Class 60 were a further development of Class 59, with a larger boiler and a leading pony truck to allow both greater power and faster speeds. They had Clench steam driers.

Class 60 were originally designed to work between Lemburg and Czernowitz where there was a requirement for what, to-day, would be called a mixed traffic locomotive.

Dimensions: CYLINDERS: HIGH PRESSURE: 520 × 632mm
                     LOW PRESSURE: 740 × 632mm
       COUPLED WHEELS: 1258mm
       GRATE AREA: 2.7m²
       BOILER PRESSURE: 13atm

2–6–2 No 15.13 awaiting preservation as steamheating boiler No 01.032   [R. G. Farr

In service as steam heating boiler No 01.032 at Vienna East Depot but scheduled for preservation in the Railway Museum, is the Gölsdorf four-cylinder compound 2–6–2 No 10.13 of the kkStB which became No 15.13 in the ÖBB list. This locomotive is one of a class of 19 built at Wiener Neustadt in 1909–1910 and it carries the works number 4995 of 1910.

The four cylinders are in line under the smoke-box, the high pressure cylinders between the frames and the low pressure outside. All four drive on to the second coupled axle. The engines were superheated when built and a feature common to all Gölsdorf's engines was the adequate boiler with wide firebox and large grate. The leading wheels form a Helmholz bogie with the first pair of coupled wheels, and the trailing wheels form a Bissel truck.

Dimensions: CYLINDERS: HIGH PRESSURE: 390×720mm
                           LOW PRESSURE: 630×720mm
        COUPLED WHEELS: 1780mm
        GRATE AREA: 3.7m^2
        BOILER PRESSURE: 15atm
        SUPERHEATED

AUSTRIA 2–6–4 1435mm

Gölsdorf 4-cc No 310.23 restored

[Othmar Bamer

The final form of the Gölsdorf four-cylinder compound express locomotive is seen in No 310.23 (ÖBB 16.08) which was built by StEG in 1911, works number 3791, and has been completely restored to its original condition for preservation in the Franz Josef Railway Museum.

Forty of these beautiful machines were built between 1911 and 1916. They followed ten very similar engines, Series 210 of 1908–1910, the principal difference being in the provision of a 24-element Schmidt super-heater instead of the steam drier provided in the earlier engines.

The usual Gölsdorf compound system was incorporated in the design but two large piston valves only were provided, one valve being common to each pair of HP and LP cylinders. As was usual, the leading wheels formed a Helmholz bogie with the leading coupled wheels, and the trailing wheels were in a Bissel truck.

Dimensions: CYLINDERS: HIGH PRESSURE: 390 × 720mm
LOW PRESSURE: 660 × 720mm
COUPLED WHEELS: 2100mm
GRATE AREA: 4.6m^2
BOILER PRESSURE: 15atm
SUPERHEATED

4–6–0 No 38.4103 which was identical with the preserved locomotive No 38.4101   [P. R-W

No 38.4101, which was *Südbahn* 109.13 and BBÖ 209.13, is in store at Vienna South and has been preserved for the Railway Museum. It was built at Wiener Neustadt in 1912, works number 5080.

Between 1912 and 1914, 44 powerful 4–6–0 locomotives were built for the Austrian Southern Railway (*Südbahn*). They were Nos 109.01–109.44 and although the influence of the Prussian Class P–8 is claimed to be seen in the design, the Austrian engines were much larger machines.

After World War I the mighty *Südbahn* of the Austro-Hungarian Empire was very greatly reduced; a large part of its territory was in Hungary and smaller parts became the property of the Jugoslavian Railways (JDZ) and of the Italian State Railways (FS). The *Südbahn* also found itself depleted of many of its locomotives and much of its rolling stock. Among the locomotives to go to other countries were a number of the Series 109, some of which went to Jugoslavia as Class 03, and others to Hungary to become Class 302. (Four further engines were built in Hungary to the same design.) At the end of the carve-up, the *Südbahn* was left with 32 of its Series 109 in Austria. These became Series 209 of the BBÖ and the survivors became DRG 38.4101–4117 during the Nazi occupation. These numbers were retained. Some of the engines received Giesl ejectors and the last of the class were shedded at Amstetten.

Dimensions: CYLINDERS: 550 × 660mm
             COUPLED WHEELS: 1700mm
             GRATE AREA: 3.6m²
             BOILER PRESSURE: 13 atm
             SUPERHEATED

AUSTRIA   0–8–0   1435mm

0–8–0 No 55.5720 which was identical with the preserved locomotive   [P. R-W

No 73.79 (Wiener Neustadt 3169/87) is an 0–8–0 of the kkStB which is at present at Vienna South Depot and is scheduled for preservation. It is one of a useful and successful class which was first built in 1885 and from then until 1909 no fewer than 453 were built.

They were outside cylinder machines with two simple cylinders and a huge dome with safety valves on top immediately behind the chimney after which a distinctive saddle-shaped sand-box straddled the top of the boiler. Some had a *"köbel"* (spark arrester) on the chimney and a few of them at one time were equipped for oil firing. Class 73 was to be found all over the BBÖ system and 44 survived to become Nos 55.5701–55.5744 of the *Reichsbahn*.

Dimensions: CYLINDERS: 500 × 570mm
COUPLED WHEELS: 1100mm
GRATE AREA: 2.3m²
BOILER PRESSURE: 11atm

2–8–0 No 156.3420 identical with the preserved locomotive   [P. R-W

kkStB No 270.125 (Floridsdorf 2617/20) is scheduled for preservation and is at present at Vienna South Depot. It was ÖBB No 156.3423.

Gölsdorf developed his compound freight engines from two-cylinder 0–6–0 to four-cylinder 2–12–0 and the development included a large number of very successful two-cylinder compound 2–8–0s of Class 170. Nine hundred and eight of these locomotives were built of which 50 were for the *Südbahn* and 58 for Czechoslovakia.

As so frequently happens in locomotive engineering, a change of chief mechanical engineer (or his equivalent) signals a change of policy and of design. Karl Gölsdorf died in 1916 and, although his Class 170 continued to be built for another three years, in 1917 there appeared a much more powerful and modern 2–8–0. This was Class 270 which was a superheated two-cylinder simple locomotive.

Building of Class 270 went on long after the kkStB became BBÖ in 1923 and in fact, the last of the 491 locomotives were built in 1930. Comparatively few remained in Austria. Most engines of the class were scattered around Central Europe and were to be found working on the railways of Czechoslovakia, Hungary, Italy, Jugoslavia, Poland and Rumania.

Dimensions: CYLINDERS: 570 × 632mm
         COUPLED WHEELS: 1238mm
         GRATE AREA: 3.9m^2
         BOILER PRESSURE: 13atm
         SUPERHEATED

2–8–4 No 12.10 which is preserved as No 214.10   [P. R-W

BBÖ No 214.10 is a 2–8–4 locomotive built in 1936 by Floridsdorf (works number 3101). It is to be preserved in the Railway Museum at Vienna and is, at present, stored in the Franz-Josef Depot. As No 12.10 this was the last remaining example of a class of 13 which were the largest and most powerful express locomotives in Austria.

In 1927 a Technical Commission was set up to review the future policy for the electrification of the Austrian railways. They recommended that the electrification of the main line from Vienna to Salzburg via Linz should be deferred on account of the large capital outlay involved. The traffic on the line, however, was increasing, trains of 500 tonnes tare were commonplace and, with faster schedules, these were beyond the capacity of the Gölsdorf four-cylinder compound 2–6–4 locomotives and even of the later 4–8–0s then in service.

To meet the situation, Herr Oberbaurat Lehner introduced, in 1928, the first of the powerful two-cylinder 2–8–4 locomotives of Series 214. The next year a similar locomotive appeared, Series 114, having three cylinders.

After comparative trials over three years, the two-cylinder version was accepted and in 1931, six further locomotives were put into service, Nos 214.02–214.07. In 1936 the final order for six more of these engines, Nos 214.08–214.13 was delivered and No 214.10 is one of these. The last six differed in some details from the earlier engines, most noticeably in that, to reduce the nuisance of drifting steam along the boiler, they had long and narrow smoke deflectors and a continuous casing along the top of the boiler which embraced the dome, sand dome and safety valves.

During the German occupation of Austria the locomotives were renumbered to bring them into line with the locomotive stock of the *Deutsche Reichsbahn*, Nos 214.01–214.13 becoming 12.001–12.013 and later, ÖBB 12.01–12.13.

The Rumanian Railways adopted the same design for their heavy passenger traffic and altogether 79 were built with some modifications. When, after World War II, the Austrian engines became redundant due to electrification, they were offered to the Rumanians who, however, did not purchase any of them.

As No 12.10, No 214.10 was the last of the class in service. She ended her days on the former *Südbahn* main line over the Semmering.

Dimensions: CYLINDERS: 650 × 720mm

COUPLED WHEELS: 1940mm

GRATE AREA: 4.7m^2

BOILER PRESSURE: 15atm

SUPERHEATED

The leading pony wheels and the first pair of coupled wheels form a Krauss-Helmholz bogie. Steam distribution is by Walschaerts valve gear operating Lentz o.c. poppet valves. Blast pipe is of the Kylala type.

4–8–0 No 33.121 which was identical with the preserved locomotive

[P. R-W

BBÖ No 113.02 (StEG 4694/23) which will be preserved in the Railway Museum at Franz Josef Station, Vienna, was one of 40 large 4–8–0s built for the Southern and Western main lines of the Federal Railways between 1923 and 1928. They were renumbered during the Nazi occupation and became DR Nos 33.101–33.140, which numbers they retained to the end.

The design originated in 1915 with Series 570 (DRG Series 33.001) which were the first European 4–8–0s. Similar engines were built in 1916 for the Kaschau-Oderberger Railway and, in 1924, 60 were built for the Polish Railways to become their Class Os-24. The 1923 BBÖ engines were basically similar but had Lentz o.c. poppet valves in place of the piston valves of the earlier engines. Some were later given boilers having the steam dome and the sand dome under one casing while most of the series had Giesl Ejectors fitted during their later days. Five of the engines went to Jugoslavia to become JDZ Nos 10.001–10.005, but these engines retained their single blast-pipes and were not Giesl fitted.

Dimensions: CYLINDERS: 560 × 720mm
COUPLED WHEELS: 1700mm
GRATE AREA: 4.5m^2
BOILER PRESSURE: 15atm
SUPERHEATED

No 180.01 preserved in the Technical Museum, Vienna   [Technical Museum, Vienna

No 180.01 is a two-cylinder compound 0–10–0, designed by Karl Gölsdorf and built at Floridsdorf in 1900 for the kkStB. During the next eight years, 181 of the class were built for the kkStB and 27 for the *Südbahn*. No 180.01 is exhibited, without a tender, in the Technical Museum in Vienna.

FS No 477.011 is a Gölsdorf two-cylinder compound 0–10–0 which was Austrian kkStB No 180.56. It was built in 1904 by the Erste Böhmisch-Mährische Maschinenfabrik (works number 120). This locomotive is now stored at Rome, Smistamento Depot, and awaits preservation and display.

Seventy-seven of these locomotives worked in Italy at the end of and after World War II and formed one of the 16 different classes imported from Germany, Austria and the United States to help maintain the shattered transportation system of the FS.

Class 180 was built primarily for duties on the lightly laid track of the Klostergrab—Moldau line in Bohemia where heavy coal trains were worked over severe gradients, ruling at 1 in 27 ($37^0/_{00}$). There were also curves of 200m radius (8.7°).

High power, flexibility and light axle loading were needed to meet the traffic demands. In Class 180, high power was developed by two cylinders 560 and 850mm in diameter, coupled wheels of 1258mm diameter and boiler pressure of 14atm. Flexibility was assured by providing the first, third and fifth axles with lateral movement of 28mm each side of centre.

Gölsdorf 0–10–0 two-cylinder compound as FS No 477.044 [P. R-W

A maximum axle load of 13.7 tonnes with a total engine weight of 65 tonnes all available for adhesion, fulfilled the last requirement. A Clench steam drier was fitted with a large steam pipe connecting two domes.

These locomotives proved outstandingly successful and they were ultimately used for heavy freight working all over the system. They were the forerunners of a long line of 0–10–0s, the last of which had simple cylinders, piston valves and superheaters.

Dimensions: CYLINDERS: HIGH PRESSURE: 560 × 635mm
LOW PRESSURE: 850 × 635mm
COUPLED WHEELS: 1258mm
GRATE AREA: 3.4m²
BOILER PRESSURE: 14atm

No 57.223 which was of the same class as the preserved locomotive [P. R-W

No 80.988 Class 80 is a two-cylinder simple superheated 0–10–0 which was built in 1916 for the kkStB by Wiener Neustadt (works number 5285) and which is at present at Vienna South Depot awaiting preservation in the Railway Museum.

The locomotives of Class 80 first appeared in 1911 and represent the last stage in the development of the Gölsdorf 0–10–0 type for the kkStB. Most of the class had piston valves but some of the later engines were equipped with Lentz o.c. poppet valves. On the ÖBB they were Class 57.

From 1911 until 1929 no fewer than 420 were built, many of which went to other Central European countries, notably Czechoslovakia (Class 524), Jugoslavia (Class 28), Hungary (Class 520.5), Roumania (Class 50). Poland (Class Tw 12) and Greece (Class K 6). In Austria, six went to the *Südbahn* in 1921 as Class 480.

Dimensions: CYLINDERS: 590 × 632mm
COUPLED WHEELS: 1258mm
GRATE AREA: $3.4m^2$
BOILER PRESSURE: 14atm
SUPERHEATED

No 258.917 which was identical with the preserved locomotive   [P. R-W

No 258.902, Süd No 580.03 (StEG 3826/12) is to be preserved in the Railway Museum.

Between 1912 and 1922, 37 two-cylinder 2–10–0 locomotives were built for the Austrian Southern Railway (*Südbahn*) as their Series 580. They later became ÖBB Series 258.

These engines had larger cylinders than the more modern 2–10–0s of BBÖ Series 81 (qv), but as they had a lower boiler pressure and larger coupled wheels than the later engines, the tractive effort of the two Series was comparable.

The *Südbahn* Series 580 were to be seen in the ownership of other European railways after both World Wars, notably in Jugoslavia as JDZ Nos 145.001–145.003 after the First War and in Italy as FS Group 482 after the Second. The Hellenic State Railways took the design as being suitable for their conditions and, after specifying slightly larger coupled wheels and a little more heating surface, had ten built by StEG in 1926 and 30 by Skoda in 1927. These locomotives were highly successful in working most of the main line passenger and freight services in Greece for the next 30 years and, when a crisis arose because of the failure of other more modern locomotives in 1957, a number of redundant Austrian engines of ÖBB Series 258 (*Südbahn* 580) came to the rescue and stayed in Greece for four years.

Dimensions: CYLINDERS: 610 × 720mm   GRATE AREA: 4.4m²
         COUPLED WHEELS: 1410mm   BOILER PRESSURE: 14atm
         SUPERHEATED

No 58.754 which was of the same class as No 58.744

[P. R-W

BBÖ No 81.44 is scheduled for preservation in the Railway Museum having been restored. It was one of 73 superheated 2–10–0 freight locomotives built at Wiener Neustadt between 1922 and 1924 for working over the heavily graded lines of the Arlberg, Semmering and Tauern routes. It has the works number 5754/23 and was No 58.744 in the DRG renumbering.

Designed by Johann Rihosek, these locomotives emphasised the trend after World War I towards simple rather than compound locomotives in Austria although, contemporaneously with Series 81, 27 similar locomotives were built as two-cylinder compounds (Series 181).

Locomotives of Series 81 varied in detail and the last 18 had Lentz o.c. poppet valves. Seventeen, including two with poppet valves, were sent to Jugoslavia and became JDZ Nos 29.011–29.027.

Dimensions: CYLINDERS: 590 × 632mm
COUPLED WHEELS: 1258mm
GRATE AREA: 4.1m^2
BOILER PRESSURE: 15atm
SUPERHEATED

No 69.02 showing oil fuel tank in front of the cab   [Elfried Schmidt

No 69.02 (DRG numbering) is a 2–2–2 Side Tank locomotive which was BBÖ No 12.02 and was rebuilt in 1935 from an 0–6–0 Side Tank, kkStB Class 97. It was built in 1898 by Krauss, Linz (works number 3822) and is scheduled for future preservation (see page 36).

This interesting little locomotive was rebuilt with single driving wheels, originally for working lightweight high speed trains on branch lines. It had semi-automatic controls and was equipped to burn either coal or oil fuel, the tank for the latter being placed before the cab on the boiler top.

As so rebuilt, it was the "guinea-pig" for the 2–4–2T which followed later the same year (Series 3071).

No 69.02 was later modified so that, by adjusting the spring tension of the carrying wheels, the weight on the driving wheels and hence the dynamic augment, could be altered. The locomotive has been widely used for bridge testing by many European railways and it is still in service and located at Franz-Josef Depot, Vienna.

Dimensions: CYLINDERS: 345 × 480mm

              DRIVING WHEELS: 1410mm

              GRATE AREA: 1.0m^2

              BOILER PRESSURE: 11atm

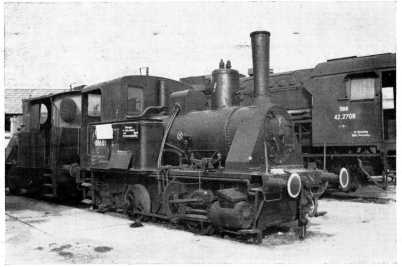

No 088.01 awaiting preservation   [Josef Hlavac

Stored at Vienna South Depot for ultimate preservation in the Railway Museum is the little 0–4–0 Well Tank engine, No 088.01. This engine was built in 1906 by Krauss, Linz (works number 5396) for the *Niederösterreichische Landes-Bahnen* (NÖLB) a lightly-laid railway system serving mainly agricultural districts in Lower Austria. It was NÖLB No 1.05 and became No 184.05 in the BBÖ roster when the NÖLB was taken over in 1922. Nine of the class were built between 1897 and 1909.

Also in store for the Railway Museum at Vienna South Depot is *Ilse*, an 0–4–0 Saddle Tank locomotive, built by Krauss, Linz in 1882 for the Vienna-Aspang Railway as their Class IIC. This locomotive was purchased by Messrs. Felton and Guilleaume AG for duties in their factory and it worked there for many years before being withdrawn and presented by the firm for the museum.

Dimensions: NOT KNOWN

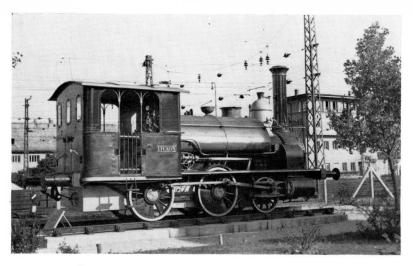

LICAON in the ÖBB Garden at Linz   [Othmar Bamer

A 2–4–0 Saddle Tank locomotive with outside cylinders named *LICAON* is preserved in the ÖBB Garden at Linz.

This locomotive was one of 34 built by Haswell between 1848 and 1853 as 2–4–0 tender freight engines for the Kaiser-Ferdinands-Northern Railway (KFNB) as their Class VII. They were all named after places and personalities in Greek mythology, the first being *ACHERON*—the River of Woe, hardly, one would have thought, a propitious class name!

They were not successful in their freight duties as they had only 20 tonnes of adhesion and, between 1868 and 1882 they were rebuilt into saddle tanks. Thus, they were more successful and they survived to become Class 289 of the kkStB when the KFNB was taken over in 1907, *LICAON* being No 289.10. (Its KFNB number was 94.)

LICAON was ultimately bought by the Stiegl Brewery in Salzburg who presented it to ÖBB for preservation. In its working life, the chimney was capped by a spark arrester.

Dimensions: CYLINDERS: 400 × 560mm
               COUPLED WHEELS: 1270mm
               GRATE AREA: 1.2m²
               BOILER PRESSURE: 7atm

No 3071.01 which was similar to the preserved locomotive   [P. R-W

No 3071.07, ex BBÖ No DT 1.07 was built in 1935 by Floridsdorf (works number 3081). It is stored at Vienna South Depot awaiting preservation.

It is a 2–4–2 Side Tank locomotive, one of 20 built between 1935 and 1937 for light, fast trains and for branch-line duties. The locomotives incorporated a baggage compartment in which also was a seat and a desk for the conductor. These engines were classed as steam railcars and originally worked alternately with petrol railcars on the Vienna-Graz and Vienna-Klagenfurt services. The 2–4–2T, hauling three coaches, provided much greater capacity than did the petrol railcars.

These locomotives were designed for one-man operation with the conductor in his compartment being able to assist at times by observing signals. The boilers had Heinl feed water pumps, were oil-fired and were superheated. Steam distribution was by oscillating cam poppet valves driven by Walschaerts valve gear. Water was carried in two side tanks and a third tank under the coal bunker.

After World War II, these lively and successful little engines were converted to coal burning and used on the more routine duties usually allocated to small tank engines.

Dimensions: CYLINDERS: 290 × 570mm
               COUPLED WHEELS: 1410mm
               GRATE AREA: 0.8m²
               BOILER PRESSURE: 16atm
               SUPERHEATED

AUSTRIA 0–6–0T 1435mm

No 89.16 which was similar to the preserved locomotive [P. R-W

No 98.703 is an outside-cylinder 0–6–0 Side Tank locomotive which is owned by the Andritzer Schleppbahn Company of Graz, and which is now preserved and is on display at the Graz-Andritz factory of the company. This locomotive was built in 1904 as No 97.236 of the kkStB by Krauss, Linz (works number 5130) and later became BBÖ No 89.236.

Between 1891 and 1911, no fewer than 254 of these useful little engines were built for kkStB. They were used for shunting and for working local trains over lightly laid tracks in rural districts. They had slide valves above the cylinders and outside Stephenson link motion.

Dimensions: CYLINDERS: 345 × 480mm
COUPLED WHEELS: 930mm
GRATE AREA: 1.0m²
BOILER PRESSURE: 11kg/cm²

On display at the Sugar Factory at Hohenau near the Czech frontier is a numberless 0–6–0T which was previously kkStB No 494.62 (Krauss, Linz 1901/87), but which originated on the Mulkreis Railway being one of five such locomotives built by Krauss in 1887–1888.

Dimensions: NOT KNOWN

No 91.09 was similar to the preserved locomotive. The steam-pipe between the domes will be noted
[P. R-W

No 91.32 is a Gölsdorf two-cylinder compound 2–6–0 Side Tank loco-motive with the high pressure cylinder on the Right and the low pressure on the Left hand side of the locomotive. It is still in service at Murzzusch-lag but is destined to be preserved in the Railway Museum.

No 91.32 was built for the kkStB as their No 99.32 by Krauss, Linz in 1900, works number 4267 and was one of 69 built between 1897 and 1908. These were smart little engines, intended for branch line duties both passenger and light freight. They had two steam domes with a connecting pipe, the system of dry steam collection much favoured by their designer.

(A number of similar locomotives was built for the *Niederösterreichische Landes-Bahnen* (NÖLB), these had larger tank and bunker capacity and boilers with single steam domes. They were NÖLB Class 102, became BBÖ Class 199 and DRG 98.13xx).

Dimensions: CYLINDERS: HIGH PRESSURE: 370 × 570mm
                      LOW PRESSURE: 570 × 570mm
       COUPLED WHEELS: 1100mm
       GRATE AREA: 1.4m^2
       BOILER PRESSURE: 13atm

No 175.804 was identical with the preserved locomotive No 175.817   [Othmar Bamer

No. 175.817 ex kkStB No. 29.22 was built in 1912 by Erste Böhmische-Mährisch Maschinenfabrik (works number 432). It is a two-cylinder compound 2–6–2 Side Tank locomotive at present used as a stationary boiler at Stadlau Depot, Vienna, but scheduled for preservation in the Railway Museum.

Karl Gölsdorf first designed two-cylinder compound 2–6–2T for the Vienna Metropolitan Railway during the last years of the nineteenth century and he followed these with 50 for the kkStB (see page 53). In 1912 the modern version of these engines appeared as Class 29 which had Schmidt superheaters and piston valves. Thirty-six of these engines were built, 33 by the First Bohemian-Moravian Engine Works at Prague and three by the Floridsdorf Works in Vienna.

Dimensions: CYLINDERS: HIGH PRESSURE: 450 × 720mm
                       LOW PRESSURE: 650 × 720mm
       COUPLED WHEELS: 1574mm
       GRATE AREA: 2.0m²
       BOILER PRESSURE: 14atm
       SUPERHEATED

kkStB No 229.222 as CSD No 354.0130 [Othmar Bamer

kkStB 229.222 (Wiener Neustadt 5444/17) is a two-cylinder compound 2–6–2 Side Tank locomotive and is one of 239 such engines built for the kkStB for suburban and branch line duties. They were developed from Class 129, a two-cylinder compound 2–6–0T and some of these were later rebuilt to Class 229.

Many locomotives of Class 229 were sent to other countries: Czechoslovakia (Class 354.0), Jugoslavia (Class 116) and Poland (Class OkI–12). No 229.222 was CSD No 354.0130 and was exchanged in 1969 for one of the GKB Class 56. It is at present in store at Vienna, Franz Josef, but is destined for the Vienna Railway Museum, while the GKB locomotive will be put on display at Böhmisch Trübau in Czechoslovakia.

Dimensions: CYLINDERS: HIGH PRESSURE: 420 × 720mm
                        LOW PRESSURE: 650 × 720mm
                COUPLED WHEELS: 1574mm
                GRATE AREA: 2.0m^2
                BOILER PRESSURE: 14atm

39

No 77.66 which is to be preserved [P. R-W

ÖBB No 77.66 ex *Südbahn* Class 629 and BBÖ No 629.101 is an outside-cylinder 4–6–2 Side Tank locomotive which was built in 1913 by StEG (works number 3883). It is scheduled for preservation in the Railway Museum but is still at work and is attached to Linz Depot.

This locomotive was the first of 100 such 4–6–2T of which the original 15 were built for the *Südbahn* between 1913 and 1915 and the remainder for the kkStB and BBÖ during the years 1917–1927. A successful and economical design.

They were two-cylinder simple superheated engines which were employed almost all over Austria on main line suburban duties and even on express passenger trains. Five were built with Caprotti valves in 1927 and 25 others had Lentz o.c. poppet valves. Many received Giesl ejectors. Some of the later engines had larger side tanks which increased the water capacity from 10.5m³ to 11m³ and they also had slightly larger bunkers.

Dimensions: CYLINDERS: 475 × 720mm
                COUPLED WHEELS: 1574mm
                GRATE AREA: 2.7m²
                BOILER PRESSURE: 13atm
                SUPERHEATED

No 78.607, shown with Giesl Ejector and German type smoke deflectors, was a sister engine to the preserved No 78.603   [P. R-W]

No 78.603 is an outside-cylinder 4–6–4 Side Tank locomotive which was BBÖ No 729.03 (Floridsdorf 3047/31) and is scheduled for preservation in the Railway Museum but, at present, is stored at Linz.

The 4–6–4T of BBÖ Class 729 first appeared in 1931 and, during the next five years, 16 were built at Floridsdorf. A further ten were built in 1938–1939 as DRG Class 78.601 during the German occupation of Austria and these had DRG pattern cabs with inward sloping sides and several modifications to boiler mountings.

The 4–6–4Ts were much larger engines than the preceding 4–6–2Ts and they had frequently been employed on express train duties. They were all built with Lentz o.c. poppet valves and all later received Giesl Ejectors.

Dimensions: CYLINDERS: 500 × 720mm
             COUPLED WHEELS: 1574mm
             GRATE AREA: 3.6m²
             BOILER PRESSURE: 13atm
             SUPERHEATED

AUSTRIA   0–8–0T   1435mm

No 92.2255 was identical to No 92.2220   [P. R-W

In store at Vienna South Depot for the Railway Museum is No 92.2220, a two-cylinder compound 0–8–0 Side Tank locomotive, which was BBÖ No 178.802 and was built by Krauss Linz in 1898 (works number 3867) for the Schneebergbahn as their Class N, No 22.

This highly successful shunting and freight tank locomotive originated in 1898 on the EWA. Gölsdorf designed it and fitted his own valve gear. The design was perpetuated on the kkStB and other private railways also had some of them. In all, 246 were built, the last one for the ÖBB in 1924. As a result of the two World Wars, they were to be found in Czechoslovakia (Class 422.0), Jugoslavia (Class 52) and Poland (Class Tkp–11). The very short coupled wheelbase no doubt contributed greatly to their success and high route availability.

Dimensions   CYLINDERS: HIGH PRESSURE: 420 × 570mm
                               LOW PRESSURE: 650 × 570mm
               COUPLED WHEELS: 1100mm
               GRATE AREA: 1.6m²
               BOILER PRESSURE: 13atm

No 392.2510 which was identical with the preserved locomotive   [P. R-W

No 392.2512 is an outside-cylinder 0–8–0 Side Tank locomotive which is still at work at Vienna East but one day will be put on display in the Railway Museum in Vienna. The engine was built by Wiener Neustadt in 1927 (works number 5783) for shunting duties on the BBÖ as their No 478.12. It became No 92.2512 of the DR and received its present identity in the 1952 renumbering of the ÖBB locomotive stock.

Fifty of Class 478 were built to the requirements of the then Chief Mechanical Engineer, Johann Rihosek, and, with a wheelbase of only 4,200mm, they have a high route availability. The two simple cylinders receive steam by way of Lentz o.c. poppet valves actuated by Walschaerts gear and the boilers have superheaters.

Dimensions: CYLINDERS: 530 × 570mm
          COUPLED WHEELS: 1100m
          GRATE AREA: 2.0m²
          BOILER PRESSURE: 14atm
          SUPERHEATED

No 95.107 which is to be preserved   [P. R-W

No. 95.107 is one of 24 two-cylinder simple 2–10–2 Side Tank locomotives, 20 of which were built in 1922 and the remainder in 1928. It was originally BBÖ No. 82.01 and was built by Wiener Neustadt (works number 5633). It is now stored at Vienna Stadlau but is scheduled for preservation in the Railway Museum in Vienna.

The Class 95 locomotives were the tank locomotive derivative of the kkStB superheated simple 0–10–0 locomotives of Class 80.900 (see page 29), and the boilers, cylinders, motion and coupled wheels are identical.

These big 2–10–2Ts were used mainly on banking and piloting duties on the northern slopes of the Semmering but they also worked freight on the steeply graded Vordernberg line. Most of them were later fitted with Giesl ejectors and some had deflector plates on either side of the wide Giesl chimney.

Dimensions: CYLINDERS: 590 × 632mm
  COUPLED WHEELS: 1258mm
  GRATE AREA: 3.4m²
  BOILER PRESSURE: 14atm
  SUPERHEATED

RACK AND ADHESION LOCOMOTIVES

The kkStB completed, in 1890, a railway to connect the open-cast iron-ore workings at Eisenerz, in Styria, with the blast furnaces of Donawitz and on, southwards, to nearby Leoben on the main line between Vienna (South) and Villach. The ore is taken from the side of a mountain about 1000m above sea level and the railway has to negotiate very severe gradients of up to 7.0 per cent, especially on the 8km section between Vordernberg and the summit of the line, 440m higher at Präbichl. On the other, northern, side of Präbichl, the line descends steeply for nearly 5km to Eisenerz. Much of this single track railway from Vordernberg to Eisenerz is operated by rack and adhesion, the Abt rack system being used.

Three classes of rack and adhesion tank locomotives have worked the line. All the locomotives have four high pressure cylinders, two outside the frames which drive the adhesion wheels in the conventional manner. Inside the frames are two more high pressure cylinders which drive the rack wheels only. There are two rack wheels which are supported by their own frames secured between the main frames of the locomotive. The rack wheels are connected by coupling rods and the cylinders drive on to the leading rack wheel through the usual system of connecting and piston rods. The rack engine is controlled by its own regulator and operates quite separately from the adhesion engine. In addition to the conventional vacuum and hand brakes these locomotives have hand brakes on the rack-wheel axles and Riggenbach counter pressure braking to all four cylinders.

One example of each of the three classes of rack and adhesion tank locomotives it to be preserved in the Railway Museum at Vienna:

No 97.207 was identical with No 97.201   [P. R-W

No 97.201 is an 0–6–2 rack and adhesion Side Tank locomotive which was kkStB No 69.01 (Floridsdorf 732/90). Eighteen of these highly successful engines were built between 1900 and 1908 and they have always done the lion's share of the work on the Eisenerz line. Most of them received Giesl Ejectors in their later years.

No 97.201 is still at work but is the locomotive chosen to represent its class in the Railway Museum.

Dimensions: CYLINDERS: (ADHESION) 480 × 500mm

(RACK) 420 × 450mm

COUPLED WHEELS: 1030mm

GRATE AREA: 2.2m²

BOILER PRESSURE: 11atm

No. 197.301 which is to be preserved. It is shown as last in service with Giesl Ejector [P. R-W

No 197.301 was kkStB No 269.01 (Floridsdorf 2090/12). This locomotive is one of three 0–12–0 rack and adhesion Side Tank locomotives designed by Gölsdorf. They are approximately twice as powerful as the previous 0–6–2T locomotives. Side play is provided for in the first, fifth and sixth axles and there is a very complete system of spring compensation. These engines were fitted with Giesl Ejectors but were never superheated. No 197.301 is scheduled for preservation but is still at work.

Dimensions: CYLINDERS: (ADHESION) 570 × 520mm

(RACK) 420 × 450mm

COUPLED WHEELS: 1030mm

GRATE AREA: 3.3m²

BOILER PRESSURE: 13atm

No 297. 401 which is to be preserved   [P. R-W

No 297.401 is one of two very powerful 2–12–2 rack and adhesion Side Tank locomotives built at Floridsdorf in 1941 when the Austrian Railways were a part of the *Deutsche Reichsbahn*. It was originally DRG No 97.401 (Floridsdorf 9100).

These two locomotives were never so successful as the preceding classes and spent much of their time in shops under repair. The locomotives had many interesting features, one of which was the welded construction of the inside cylinders which drove the rack wheels.

When working, each locomotive could take trains of 400 tonnes, unaided, over the route. This compared with 170 tonnes for Class 197 and 110 tonnes for Class 97. Maximum speeds were 30km/h on the adhesion sections of the line, and 25km/h on the rack sections.

Both locomotives are withdrawn from service and No 297.401 awaits admission to the museum. It is at present stored at Vordernberg Depot.

Dimensions: CYLINDERS: (ADHESION) 610 × 520mm
     (RACK) 400 × 500mm
  COUPLED WHEELS: 1030mm
  GRATE AREA: 3.9m^2
  BOILER PRESSURE: 16atm
  SUPERHEATED
  GIESL EJECTOR

THE GRAZ – KOFLACHEREISENBAHN UND BERBAUGESELLSCHAFT

The GKB began its long life in 1860 as a colliery line to carry soft brown coal from the open-cast mines at Köflach to the main line of the *Südbahn* at Graz. In 1873 a line was built from Lieboch to Wies-Eibiswald to exploit coal and other mineral deposits and, in 1930 the small *Sülmtalbahn* was amalgamated with the GKB. The *Südbahn* operated the GKB from 1878 until 1923 when the railway's finances had improved sufficiently for it again to become independent. To-day, GKB forms part of the nationalised Alpine-Montan mining combine.

The steam locomotive stock has always consisted of old engines from the former State Railway (kkStB) and from the *Südbahn*. The locomotive *STEINBRUCK* now in the Technical Museum at Vienna (qv) was the first locomotive to work on the GKB under the name *SODING*.

It is the intention to preserve an example of each of the interesting locomotives which have worked on the GKB over the past 70 (and more) years. Some locomotives may be exhibited at Graz.

AUSTRIA – GKB   4–4–0   1435mm

GKB LOCOMOTIVES TO BE PRESERVED

GKB No 415 which is identical to No 372   [P. R-W

GKB No 372 Class 17c is an outside cylinder 4–4–0 which was built for the Southern Railway (*Südbahn*) in 1891 by Floridsdorf (works number 768). It is at present at Vienna and is in store for the Railway Museum.

Eight of these engines were owned by the GKB and they worked the passenger services between Graz and Köflach. They had double frames and two outside cylinders placed horizontally, with slide valves above the cylinders operated by outside Stephenson link motion. The round-top boiler had two steam domes, the first, a huge affair just behind the chimney, contained the regulator and had a Salter-type safety valve on top. The second steam dome, also surmounted by a safety valve contained the feed pipe-ends for the auxiliaries.

Dimensions: CYLINDERS: 425 × 600mm
                COUPLED WHEELS: 1740mm
                GRATE AREA: 2.3m^2
                BOILER PRESSURE: 12kg/cm^2

AUSTRIA – GKB   0–6–0   1435mm

GKB No 671, the preserved locomotive   [P. R-W

GKB No 671 is an outside-cylinder 0–6–0 which was built in 1860 by StEG (works number 504) for the Southern Railway (*Südbahn*) on which it was Class 29. It was later BBÖ No 49.03, and is the oldest engine on GKB. It is (1969) still at work at Graz and is scheduled for preservation.

GKB No 674 is another outside-cylinder 0–6–0 locomotive which was built in 1860 by StEG (works number 507). This locomotive has gone to the Railway Museum at Budapest in exchange for 0–6–0 No 333.002 (see page 16).

GKB No 680 is another 0–6–0 locomotive of *Südbahn* Class 29 which was built in 1860 by StEG (works number 513). It was No 680 on the *Südbahn*, later became BBÖ No 49.10 and reverted to its original number on going to GKB in 1925. It is at present in store at Münich East Depot of the DB and is to go to the Railway Museum at Berlin when this is completed.

These engines had double frames and the slide valves above the cylinders were operated by outside Stephenson link motion. They retained their huge spark-arresting chimneys.

The GKB, at various times, owned 19 of these locomotives of which 205 were built by various Austrian firms and by Esslingen during the years 1860–1872. They were the standard freight locomotives of the *Südbahn* (Imperial and Royal Privileged Southern Railway) (see also page 16).

Dimensions: CYLINDERS: 460 × 632mm
COUPLED WHEELS: 1285mm
GRATE AREA: 1.59m²
BOILER PRESSURE: 9atm

50

GKB No 56.3268 which was identical with the preserved locomotive   [P. R-W

GKB No 56.3115 was kkStB No 170.133 and became DR and then ÖBB No 56.3115. It was built in 1914 by Floridsdorf (works number 2180) and is scheduled for preservation. It is at present at Graz.

Another engine of the same class, No 56.3255, has gone to Czechoslovakia for preservation in exchange for CSD 2–6–2T No 354.0130 (see page 39).

These engines are two-cylinder compound 2–8–0s which originated on the State Railways in 1897 and of which 796 were built for the kkStB and 54 for the *Südbahn* between then and 1918. Sixteen came to the GKB. They were large and modern locomotives for their period, weighing 69 tonnes without tender. Karl Gölsdorf was the designer and the engines were intended, primarily, for the Arlberg route. Ultimately they were to be found in Czechoslovakia (58 were built new), in Jugoslavia and in Poland. They all retained their Clench steam driers with the steampipes between two domes but most of them lost their spark arrestors.

Dimensions: CYLINDERS: HIGH PRESSURE: 540 × 632mm
                       LOW PRESSURE: 800 × 632mm
      COUPLED WHEELS: 1298mm
      GRATE AREA: 3.9m²
      BOILER PRESSURE: 13atm

GKB No 1851 which is to be preserved   [P. R-W

GKB No 1851 ex *Südbahn* No 1851 Class 32d[1] was built in 1898 by Krauss, Linz (works number 3932). It later became BBÖ 594.01. This is an 0–6–0 Side Tank locomotive, one of two used by GKB for shunting duties at Köflach. It is a two-cylinder simple machine with Walschaerts valve gear operating slide valves. During its last years in service it was provided with steel supports for both chimney and safety valves as can be seen in the photograph.

Dimensions: CYLINDERS: 310 × 480mm
           COUPLED WHEELS: 980mm
           GRATE AREA: 1.0m^2
           BOILER PRESSURE: 12 kg/cm^2

No 1 SULM which was a sister engine of the preserved locomotive   [P. R-W

GKB No 30.114 ex kkStB No 30.114 was built in 1900 by StEG (works number 2814). It is a two-cylinder compound 2–6–2 Side Tank locomotive. It is in store at Graz and is one of 13 in service at various times on the GKB having been introduced there in 1930. Two of the 13 were owned by the *Sülmtalbahn* and retained their numbers: 1 Sülm and 2 Sülm. No 2 Sülm (Wiener Neustadt 4033 of 1897) is in store at Vienna Franz Josef Depot, probably for the Railway Museum. It was originally kkStB No 30.39 and, later, GKB with the same number.

Class 30 was used on the GKB for main line freight duties before the advent of the 2–8–0s of Class 170.

These engines were originally designed by Gölsdorf and 55 were built at three different locomotive works for the Vienna Metropolitan Railway (*Wiener Stadtbahn*). They were followed by 50 for the kkStB. As built they had the large steam pipe connecting two domes, a dry steam collecting device much favoured by Gölsdorf. On the GKB, after 1947, they had more recent boilers with a top feed dome and a sandbox on the boiler top.

Dimensions: CYLINDERS: HIGH PRESSURE: 520 × 632mm
                     LOW PRESSURE: 740 × 632mm
     COUPLED WHEELS: 1298mm
     GRATE AREA: 2.1m^2
     BOILER PRESSURE: 13atm

GMUNDEN preserved in the Technical Museum, Vienna   [Othmar Bamer

Exhibited in the Technical Museum at Vienna, is an outside-cylinder 4–4–0 Side Tank locomotive No 4 *GMUNDEN* of the Lambach-Gmunden Railway which later became part of the Kaiserin Elisabeth Railway.

No 4 was designed by Johann Zek and built in 1854 by W. Günther at Wiener Neustadt Locomotive Works (works number 131). It has been in the museum since 1891.

This locomotive has several interesting peculiarities. The side tanks are placed as far forward as possible where they could have had the least possible effect upon adhesion. The cylinders are behind the bogie wheels and the slide valves above the cylinders are operated by outside Stephenson link motion. A crosshead-driven feed water pump is attached to the outer side of the Right-hand cylinder.

Dimensions: CYLINDERS: 230 × 421mm
             COUPLED WHEELS: 948mm
             GRATE AREA: 0.5m^2
             BOILER PRESSURE: 6.7atm

Narrow Gauge Railways in Austria

Austria had, at one time, 761 route kilometres of narrow gauge railways which constituted about 11 per cent of her total railway system. Early lines were laid to a gauge of 1106mm but these were later converted to 1435mm and the majority of narrow gauge railways were of 760mm gauge. Apart from three 1000mm-gauge rack railways, all the surviving narrow gauge is of 760mm.

The various private and state railways which later formed the ÖBB built and owned most of these lines many of which were, and are, of considerable importance. The extensive system based on St. Polten is a good example. Most of this line was electrified quite early (1911) but was steam operated over its main branch from Ober Grafendorf to Gresten until diesels took over. Lines of importance were built between Bregenz and Bezau and between Waidhofen and Kienberg-Gaming and there were many others. Some of those which remain open are operated partly by steam locomotives.

There were some lines which remained independent of ÖBB. Principal among these were the lines in Styria and the two best known to tourists, the *Zillertalbahn* in the Tyrol which still uses steam locomotives as well as diesels and the *Salzkammergut Lokalbahn* which ran through the lovely country between Salzburg and Bad Ischl but which is now, alas, no more.

A number of narrow gauge steam locomotives is preserved as monuments and details of these will be found in the following pages.

Narrow Gauge Steam Locomotive Preservation in Austria

At one time, the ÖBB operated nearly 550km of 760mm-gauge railways. Some of these railways have been abandoned while others are now operated by diesel and electric motive power. There were also several privately-owned narrow gauge lines of which the *Zillertalbahn* now remains as the only important survivor.

All these narrow gauge railways were, at one time, steam operated and a number of locomotives from them have been preserved and put on display as monuments in various places. It is possible that space may be found in the new Railway Museum for one or two examples from the 760mm ÖBB system.

AUSTRIA 0–4–0T 760mm

On display at Haag on the main line between St. Valentin and Amstetten, is a powerful 0–4–0T No 698.01 which was built during World War II in 1941 by Henschel (works number 25701) as No 16752 of the strategially important *Heeresfeldbahn* Military railway.

A bell-mouthed chimney, a large round topped boiler, Walschaerts operated slide valves above the cylinders, all combined to provide a locomotive of pleasing but powerful appearance.

Dimensions: CYLINDERS: 310 × 430mm
COUPLED WHEELS: 780mm
GRATE AREA: 0.8m²
BOILER PRESSURE: 12atm

0–4–0 No 2, STAINZ driven by amateurs   [Othmar Bamer

No 2 *STAINZ* is an outside-cylinder 0–4–0 Well Tank locomotive with outside link motion and Salter type safety valves on top of the dome. The sandbox is on top of the boiler behind the dome. It was built in 1892 by Krauss Linz (works number 2774) for the *Steiermärkische Landesbahnen* and worked on the Preding-Stainz section of that railway.

This locomotive is preserved in working order and is available for hire for engine-driving by amateurs. It is kept at Murau.

Dimensions: CYLINDERS: 225 × 350mm
COUPLED WHEELS: 750mm
GRATE AREA: 0.51m²
BOILER PRESSURE: 12kg/cm²

56

What has been described as the Standard Austrian Narrow Gauge locomotive is the 0–6–2 Side Tank with outside cylinders and valve gear. Slide valves are placed horizontally at an angle of 45° above the outer and upper quadrants of the cylinders. A large steam dome is immediately behind the chimney and a sand box is between the dome and the cab. This design was introduced by Krauss of Linz in the 1880s and over the years proved itself ideal for the lightly laid and often very irregular tracks of the 760mm gauge line.

The Krauss design was imitated by other builders but it has never been surpassed for reliability. Dimensional changes were made to suit the needs of the various railways for which the engines were built.

Fortunately a number of 0–6–2T, both by Krauss and by other builders, has been preserved, while others are still at work and scheduled for preservation.

Two of these came from the *Salskammergut Lokalbahn AG* (SKGLB) which operated between Salzburg and Bad Ischl, a distance of 63.2km. The line was closed in 1957 after a life of 67 years.

SKGLB No 4 at Haiden, Bad Ischl.   [P. R-W Collection

SKGLB No 4 (Krauss 2341/90) is on display at Haiden, Bad Ischl at the inn Zur Ischler-Bahn.

SKGLB No 9 (Krauss 2821/93) is on display at Mondsee. This locomotive has slightly greater tank capacity than No 4 and the boiler heating surface is greater.

Dimensions: CYLINDERS: 290 × 400mm
              COUPLED WHEELS: 800mm
              GRATE AREA: 0.8m²
              BOILER PRESSURE: 12atm

Zillertalbahn No 1 RAIMUND   [R. H. Tunstall]

Zillertalbahn No 1 *RAIMUND* is an outside-cylinder 0–6–2 Side Tank locomotive built in 1900 by Krauss, Linz (works number 4505) to the design of the kkStB Class U. It is to be preserved in the Landes Museum at Innsbruck.

Features of the design are: long side tanks extending from the cab to the front of the smokebox, Walschaerts gear operating slide valves and, immediately behind the chimney, a large dome with safety valves on top and containing the regulator operated by an external rod.

Dimensions: CYLINDERS: 290 × 400mm
    COUPLED WHEELS: 800mm
    GRATE AREA: 1.0m²
    BOILER PRESSURE: 12kg/cm²

No 298.51 ex NÖLB No U-1 built in 1897 by Krauss, Linz (works number 3709) for the *Niederösterreichische Landes-Bahn* (NÖLB) which had a 760mm system from St. Polten to Gusswerk, and lines radiating from Gmund and from Obergrafendorf.

This locomotive, one of eight Class U built for the NÖLB, is still in service at Garsten but is to be preserved probably in the Railway Museum.

Dimensions: CYLINDERS: 290 × 400mm
    COUPLED WHEELS: 800mm
    GRATE AREA: 1.0m²
    BOILER PRESSURE: 12atm

Steyrtalbahn No 298.104 a sister engine to No 298.102   [Elfreid Schmidt

No 298.102 of the *Steyrtalbahn*, whose main line extended between Klaus and Garsten, was their No 2 built by Krauss in 1888, works number 1994, with the same dimensions as No 298.51 (p.58) except for a smaller boiler with grate area 0.8m². In appearance No 298.102 and the five other engines of the same class, are quite distinctive with extended smokeboxes and much higher side tanks than the usual Krauss 0–6–2T. It is at Obergrafendorf and will probably be put on display there.

No 298.205 on display   [Alfred Luft

No 298.205 was BBÖ No Uv 5 and formerly belonged to the *Niederöster-reichische Landes-Bahn* as their No Uv 1. It was built by Krauss, Linz in

1903, works number 4785 and is now preserved and is on display at Ruprechtshofen.

This locomotive differs from the eight Class U locomotives of the NÖLB in that it is the first of three 0–6–2T which were two-cylinder compounds with, as usual, the low pressure cylinder on the left-hand side of the engine. The boiler pressure was higher and the heating surface greater, than on the simple engines.

Dimensions: CYLINDERS: HIGH PRESSURE: 320 × 400mm
LOW PRESSURE: 500 × 400mm
COUPLED WHEELS: 800mm
GRATE AREA: 1.0m²
BOILER PRESSURE: 13atm

No 398.01 which is preserved   [R. G. Farr

No 398.01 is another simple 0–6–2T which was built for the NÖLB as their No Uh 1 (Krauss, Linz 5330/05). It was BBÖ No Bh 1 and was built with an 18-element superheater and piston valves. This locomotive is at present at Obergrafendorf.

Dimensions: CYLINDERS: 340 × 400mm
COUPLED WHEELS: 800mm
GRATE AREA: 1.0m²
BOILER PRESSURE: 12atm
SUPERHEATED

60

No 498.04 a sister engine to No 498.07   [R. G. Farr

No 498.07 is at Obergrafendorf awaiting preservation. This locomotive
was built at Floridsdorf (works number 3037) for the BBÖ in 1931 as
No Uh 101. It was one of two such engines and it has a superheated
boiler and steam distribution by Caprotti valves. It is quite different from
the Krauss design and in appearance is much more modern and powerful.

These two engines were used mostly to work on the lines of the erstwhile
NÖLB which became part of the BBÖ in 1922.

Dimensions: CYLINDERS: 350 × 400mm
                COUPLED WHEELS: 800mm
                GRATE AREA: 1.1m²
                BOILER PRESSURE: 13atm
                SUPERHEATED

No Yv 1 on display at Waidhofen an der Ybbs   [Peter Schmied

Now on display at Waidhofen an der Ybbs is a small Krauss 0–6–4T restored to its original Ybbstal Railway number, Yv 1, after having been numbered 598.01 in the ÖBB list.

It was built in 1896, works number 3356, and it is a two-cylinder compound with slide valves above the cylinders and operated by Walschaerts valve gear. It is not superheated.

Dimensions: CYLINDERS: HIGH PRESSURE: 310 × 400mm
              LOW PRESSURE: 450 × 400mm
      COUPLED WHEELS: 800mm
      GRATE AREA: 1.0m²
      BOILER PRESSURE: 13atm

No 699.01 at Birkfeld, Styrian Government Railways   [Othmar Bamer

Stored at Obergrafendorf is a powerful superheated eight-coupled tender tank locomotive No 699.01 which was built for the 750mm gauge by the Soc. Franco-Belge (works number 2818) in 1944 for the German military lines. It was one of several which were converted to run on the 760mm gauge lines of the military *Heeresfeldbahn*. It has piston valves, Walschaerts valve gear and short side tanks. The four-wheeled tender is trailed behind the cab.

Another similar locomotive, built by Franco-Belge in 1944 (works number 2855) was bought by the *Salzkammergut Lokalbahn* (SKGLB) and became their No 19. On the closure of the SKGLB it was sold to the Styrian Government Railways and became their No 699.01. In 1970, it was purchased by the Welshpool and Llanfair Railway to work on their line in Wales.

Dimensions: CYLINDERS: 330 × 310mm
               COUPLED WHEELS: 630mm
               GRATE AREA: 1.0m^2
               BOILER PRESSURE: 14atm
               SUPERHEATED

63

No 199.03 identical with No 199.02   [Othmar Bamer

No 199.02 is a powerful superheated 0–8–2T built by Krauss, Linz in 1926 and their works number 1467. It was originally BBÖ No P2 and is still in traffic at Völkermarkt-Kuhnsdorf in Southern Austria, near to Klagenfurt. It will be preserved, probably in the Railway Museum.

Dimensions: CYLINDERS: 330 × 400mm
              COUPLED WHEELS: 880mm
              GRATE AREA: 1.3m^2
              BOILER PRESSURE: 13atm
              SUPERHEATED

No 399.05 a sister engine to No 399.01 [Elfreid Schmidt

No 399.01 was built for the *Niederösterreichische Landes-Bahn* (NÖLB) as their No Mh 1 by Krauss, Linz in 1906, works number 5431. It is still in service at Volkermarkt-Kuhnsdorf near Klagenfurt, on a section of the NÖLB far removed from its main line from St. Polten to Gusswerk which is south of the ÖBB east to west main line. It will be preserved in the Railway Museum.

It is probably more correct to describe this locomotive as an 0–8–0 with a four-wheeled *stütztender* this latter carrying the coal and water and being articulated with the rear end of the locomotive.

Dimensions: CYLINDERS: 410 × 450mm
COUPLED WHEELS: 900mm
GRATE AREA: 1.6m²
BOILER PRESSURE: 13atm
SUPERHEATED

Pure Rack Locomotives

A Pure Rack Locomotive is one in which the propulsion is solely by means of toothed wheels, known as rack pinions, which are driven by the steam engine cylinders and motion and which engage in the rack rail laid in the middle of the track. The carrying wheels of the locomotive are not powered and, in this, the Pure Rack Locomotive differs fundamentally from the Rack and Adhesion Locomotive (qv).

Pure Rack Locomotives are used only on the steep gradients of mountain railways and there are, in Austria, three such railways still operating. None of the locomotives from these mountain railways is at present "scheduled for preservation" but one such locomotive is on display in the Technical Museum in Vienna and this is described and illustrated.

AUSTRIA   0–4–0 Rack Tank   1000mm

0–4–0 Rack Tank No 1 in the Technical Museum, Vienna   [Technical Museum, Vienna

Exhibited in the Technical Museum in Vienna is No 1 a four-wheeled rack Side Tank locomotive built in 1886 by Kessler, Esslingen (works number 2205) for the Parsch-Gaisbergspitze mountain railway near Salzburg. The railway was operated on the Riggenbach rack system. It was opened in 1887 and closed to traffic in 1928.

Five locomotives worked on the line: they had single geared rack pinions and were fitted with Riggenbach counter pressure braking as well as band brakes.

Dimensions: CYLINDERS: 350 × 500mm
CARRYING WHEELS: 706mm
RACK PINION: 764mm
GRATE AREA: 1.3m^2
BOILER PRESSURE: 11atm

Belgian National Railways Company

This Company the *Société National des Chemins de Fer Belges* (SNCB), was formed in 1926 to take over the State Railways administration and operation. It operates all the 1435mm-gauge main lines in Belgium.

The State built and operated the first railways in Belgium but in 1842, the first concession was granted by the Government for the building of a private railway and the "period of Concessions" between 1852 and 1870 saw the building of 3136km of private railways compared with the construction of only 869km by the State.

From 1882 onwards, however, the State Railways gradually took over most of the private railways until, by 1919, only 279km remained in private hands. These railways then came into State ownership as their Concessions expired, most of them after the formation of the SNCB in 1926. The last Concession to expire was that of part of the Nord-Belge in 1948.

SNCB Steam Locomotive Preservation

At present, the only museum of the SNCB is that which is housed in the new station at Brussels North. The museum was first opened in 1951 in the old station but when that was demolished the collection was rehoused, in 1958, in the excellent new premises which it now occupies. It is possible, however, only to exhibit there one full-size locomotive, the rest of the locomotive exhibits being scale models.

It is the intention of the SNCB to open a new museum in the future in which there will be adequate space to display a dozen or so actual locomotives. A number of these have already been selected, some have been restored and most are in store at the SNCB Motive Power Depot at Louvain.

The location of this museum has not yet been finally decided.

BELGIUM   2–2–2   1435mm

Full-scale replica of LE BELGE   [SNCB

LE BELGE was an inside-cylinder 2–2–2 tender locomotive built in 1835 by John Cockerill at Seraing for the State Railway. A full-size replica has been made in wood and this is at present stored at Brussels Midi Depot of the SNCB.

LE BELGE went into service in December 1835 and was the first locomotive to be built in Belgium and the sixth to work on the newly opened State Railway. The first five were *LA FLECHE, STEPHENSON* and *L'ELEPHANT* which came from England in April 1835, *LE RAPIDE* and *L'ECLAIR* which arrived in July and August 1835 respectively and were also obtained from Robert Stephenson.

LE BELGE was obviously copied from the Stephenson 2–2–2 passenger locomotives and, like them, weighed 11 tonnes in working order.

Dimensions: CYLINDERS: 380 × 550mm
DRIVING WHEELS: 1524mm
GRATE AREA: 0.86m²
BOILER PRESSURE: 4kg/cm²

Model of L'ELEPHANT as a 2-4-0   [SNCB

L'ELEPHANT was a 2–4–0 inside-cylinder tender locomotive built in England by Tayleur in 1835. A full-size replica has been built and this is at present stored at Brussels Midi Depot of the SNCB.

The first railway in Belgium was constructed for the State and extended from Brussels (Allée-Verte) to Malines (20km). It was opened, in the presence of King Leopold and George Stephenson, on May 5, 1835, and was the first section of the trunk route from Brussels to Cologne via Liège.

L'ELEPHANT was one of three locomotives which took part in the opening ceremony of the new railway. The others were named *LA FLECHE*, a 2–2–2 which hauled the first train of seven four-wheeled coaches (some covered, others without roofs) and *STEPHENSON*, a 2–2–2 which hauled the second train of seven mixed vehicles. *L'ELE-PHANT*, then an 0–4–2, worked the third train of 16 char-à-banc coaches and, on the return journey, it hauled, unaided, all 30 of the vehicles back to Brussels.

The three locomotives were ordered from Robert Stephenson & Co but *L'ELEPHANT* was built by Tayleur under sub-contract. It was built, mainly for freight traffic, as 0–4–2 and was rebuilt as 2–4–0 and re-boilered by the Arsenal of Malines in 1849. It had two eccentrics for each valve, one for forward and the other for backward running but there was no expansion link and the engine could not be "notched up".

Dimensions: CYLINDERS: 356 × 457mm
           COUPLED WHEELS: 1372mm
           GRATE AREA: 0.8m^2
           BOILER PRESSURE: 6.5kg/cm^2

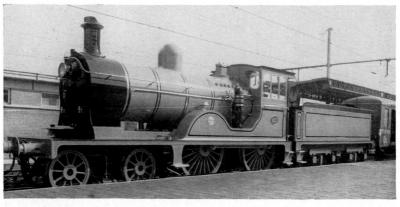

No 1805 restored　　　　　　　　　　　　　　　　　　　　　[SNCB

No 18.051 Class 18 is a saturated inside cylinder 4–4–0 which was built as SNCB No 3251 in 1905 by St. Leonard (works number 1405). It has been restored, now carries the number 1805, has an original bogie tender and is at present in store at Louvain Depot awaiting permanent preservation in the Railway Museum.

During the years from about 1898 until 1906 the Belgian State Railways adopted the designs of the Chief Mechanical Engineer of the Caledonian Railway, J. F. McIntosh (often spelled in Belgium *"McIntosch"*), for passenger, freight and mixed traffic locomotives. Although the first five engines came from Scottish builders, the remainder of the 724 McIntosh engines were constructed in Belgium.

For passenger services the 4–4–0 *DUNALASTAIR II* design was first adopted as SNCB Class 17, being modified from the original only in details such as the provision of a cab with three side windows. Ninety-five of these engines were built and they were followed in 1902 by Class 18, an improved and more powerful design which was, however, similar in appearance to Class 17.

One hundred and forty engines of Class 18 were built and the preserved locomotive was No 3251 of the 1904–5 series. Of these last engines, six (Nos 3190 and 3288–92) were built with Schmidt superheaters. They were later all fitted with standard SNCB six-wheeled tenders in place of the original McIntosh bogie tenders.

The Class 18 engines proved very successful in the operation of the "block trains" which provided a fast and frequent service between Brussels and Antwerp.

Dimensions: CYLINDERS: 482 × 660mm　　GRATE AREA: 2.2m²
　　　　COUPLED WHEELS: 1980mm　　BOILER PRESSURE: 13.5kg/cm²
(*The superheater engines had cylinders 456mm in diameter and piston valves.*)

No 12.004 in service   [P. R-W

No 12.004 (originally No 1204) is an inside-cylinder 4–4–2 (Atlantic) built in 1939 by Cockerill and at present stored at Louvain SNCB Depot. It is scheduled for preservation in the Railway Museum.

Six 4–4–2 locomotives of (new) Class 12 were designed by M. Notesse and were put into service just before the outbreak of the Second World War. They had bar frames and were air-smoothed according to the principles of Monsieur Huet, though with little sacrifice of accessibility. Four of the locomotives (including No 12.004) had Walschaerts valve gear with outside return cranks, one, No 12.005, had Dabeg rotary cam poppet valves and No 12.006 had rotary cam Caprotti valves. The boilers had copper fireboxes with arch tubes, and nickel steel barrels and they were supplied to the builders by La Société l'Energie de Marcinelle.

These locomotives were designed to work 250-tonne trains between Brussels and Ostend, 115km, in 60 minutes with a maximum speed of 140km/h. They proved themselves well able to do this but they were not always very comfortable vehicles at high speeds. The war put an end to these high-speed services and in later years the Atlantics worked mostly on the Brussels-Lille route after the Ostend line was electrified.

Dimensions: CYLINDERS: 480 × 720mm
                COUPLED WHEELS: 2100mm
                GRATE AREA: 3.7m^2
                BOILER PRESSURE: 18kg/cm^2
                SUPERHEATED

No 7.038 a sister engine to No 7.039   [P. R-W

No 7.039 Class 7/4 is a de Glehn-du Bousquet four-cylinder compound 4–6–0 built by Haine-St. Pierre in 1921 and which is at present in store at the Louvain Depot of the SNCB. It is a 1934 rebuild of No 4639, a locomotive of Class 8 *bis*, introduced in 1921.

The four-cylinder compound 4–6–0 was introduced on the Belgian State Railways in 1905 with some very successful non-superheated engines of Class 8. In 1919, an enlarged and superheated version of these engines was designed and orders for 75 of them were placed with eight Belgian firms of locomotive builders. Owing to strikes, these engines were not delivered until the period 1921–1923. They were classified 8 *bis* and had the usual divided drive and independent cut-off of the de Glehn-du Bousquet compound system.

All 75 engines survived World War I and, commencing in 1934, the rebuilding and modernisation of the class began and they were then re-classified.

The first rebuilds, in 1934, were Nos 7.016 and 7.028 in which the four compounded cylinders were placed in line and the drive was not divided. These were Class 7/1.

Class 7/2 consisted of Nos 7.062 and 7.064 in which four high pressure cylinders in line replaced the four compounded cylinders.

Class 7/3 consisted of two engines, Nos 7.018 and 7.024, each with four high pressure cylinders and divided drive, the inside cylinder being located ahead of those outside. No 7.018 was destroyed during World War II and No 7.024 was converted to Class 7/4 in 1938.

Class 7/4, to which No 7.039 belongs, consisted of the 69 remaining engines of which the rebuilding started in 1934. New Belpaire boilers and new cylinders were provided where necessary and the frames and footplating at the front end were modified. Smoke deflectors and ACFI feed-water pumps and heaters were fitted and, later, many engines received Lemaître double blast-pipes and chimneys, and others, those of the Legein type. Five of the class ran for several years with round top fireboxes.

Dimensions: CYLINDERS: HIGH PRESSURE: 400×640mm
LOW PRESSURE: 600×640mm
COUPLED WHEELS: 1800mm
GRATE AREA: 3.08m^2
BOILER PRESSURE: 16kg/cm^2
SUPERHEATED

No 10.018 is preserved

[P. R-W

No 10.018 is a four-cylinder 4–6–2 which was built as No 4518 Class 10 by a consortium of Belgian locomotive builders in 1911. It is stored at Louvain Depot for restoration and preservation in the Railway Museum.

Twenty-nine of these locomotives, designed by J. B. Flamme were put into service in 1910–1912. Their appearance was then unique and always remained so. In order to allow the inside cylinders to drive the leading coupled axle and the outside cylinders the second coupled axle, while at the same time keeping the trailing coupled axle in front of the very large firebox, it was necessary to have the inside cylinders well out in front of the bogie and this resulted in a long platform before the smokebox.

The first series of these engines was not satisfactory and in the second series of 29 engines, built in 1912–1914, a smaller firebox and modified rear-end framing helped to cure the overheating of the trailing axleboxes.

Not until the 49 engines of both series which remained after the World War I were rebuilt by F. Legein, did the Class 10 really become successful and reliable machines. Larger superheaters, Legein double blast-pipes and chimneys, ACFI feed-water pumps and heaters were the principal alterations but many other minor modifications were carried out.

Dimensions: CYLINDERS: (4) 500 × 660mm
               COUPLED WHEELS: 1980mm
               GREAT AREA (*First Series*): 4.9m²
               BOILER PRESSURE: 14kg/cm²
               SUPERHEATED

No 1.002 is the preserved locomotive of the class   [P. R-W

No 1.002, originally No 102, is a four-cylinder 4–6–2, one of 35 locomotives
of Class I, designed by Notesse and built in 1935 by five Belgian locomotive builders, No 1.002 having been built by Cockerill. It is at present
stored at Louvain Depot awaiting preservation in the Railway Museum.

These Pacifics were among the heaviest in Europe with a maximum
axle load of 23.7 tonnes. They were partly air-smoothed. The four
cylinders were in line, the inside cylinders driving the leading coupled
axle and the outside cylinders the second. Two sets of outside Walschaerts
valve gear were provided, the inside valves being driven through rocking
shafts from front extensions of the valve rods. The engines had Legein
chimneys, Kylchap double blast-pipes, ACFI feed water pumps and
heaters and two firehole doors. They had very robust bar frames and
delta trailing trucks.

Dimensions: CYLINDERS: (4): 420 × 720mm
          COUPLED WHEELS: 1980mm
          GRATE AREA: 4.9m²
          BOILER PRESSURE: 18kg/cm²
          SUPERHEATED

No 29.013 on the last official steam train in Belgium   [SNCB

No 29.013 is a 2–8–0 mixed traffic locomotive which was built for the SNCB in 1945 by the Montreal Locomotive Works (works number 74510). It worked the last official steam train in Belgium and is now stored at the Louvain depot awaiting preservation in the Railway Museum.

Three hundred of these locomotives, Nos 29.001–29.300, were supplied to SNCB in 1945–1947 and they were built by the Montreal Locomotive Works, the Canadian Locomotive Works and the American Locomotive Company (ALCO). They had bar frames, and were obviously closely related in design to the many 2–8–0s built for the U.S. Army.

Dimensions: CYLINDERS: 559 × 711mm
              COUPLED WHEELS: 1524mm
              GRATE AREA: 4.4m²
              BOILER PRESSURE: 15.8kg/cm²
              SUPERHEATED

PAYS DE WAES in the museum [SNCB

PAYS DE WAES is a 2–2–2 Saddle Tank locomotive built in Brussels in 1842 by the firm of Postula & Co. at the Renaud Works. It is preserved in the Railway Museum at Brussels North Station.

PAYS DE WAES is unquestionably one of the most interesting, as well as one of the best preserved, of all the world's historic locomotives. It was one of nine similar engines built to the design of an engineer named de Ridder

77

and was probably the first locomotive in the world to be able to use the expansive properties of steam. This was achieved by the use of two valves for each of the two cylinders. One valve admitted steam to each side of the piston alternately, and the other cut off the steam supply to the cylinders before the full extent of the piston stroke was reached. When starting, this valve was by-passed so that no expansion occurred but when the engine was at speed, the valve was brought into the steam circuit and the engine ran "notched up". Two eccentrics were provided, one for forward and the other for backward running.

A year later, Stephenson's link motion was invented and, in 1844, Walschaerts valve gear provided another method of "notching up" and reversing the engine.

PAYS DE WAES burned coke in a copper "hay-cock" firebox on top of which were a steam dome and a spring-loaded safety valve. A skid-type brake was operated through levers to bring pressure on the running rail and thus to stop the locomotive.

The locomotive was built for the 49km-long Antwerp to Ghent Railway (via Lokeren) which was the first private railway to receive a Concession from the Government to construct a railway for public use. The gauge of 1150mm was considered at the time, to be the most economical, though it was an awkward compromise between the 1435mm of the first State railways and the 1000mm gauge of the later, so-called, *Chemins de Fer Vicinaux*. Despite this, the narrow gauge Antwerp-Ghent passenger coaches were longer and more comfortable than those of the 1435mm gauge. The railway was converted to 1435mm gauge in 1896, the conversion being carried out during a single night.

PAYS DE WAES was withdrawn from service in 1890.

Dimensions: CYLINDERS: 280 × 460mm

          DRIVING WHEELS: 1500mm

          GRATE AREA: $2.7m^2$

          BOILER PRESSURE: 6atm

PRINCE DE LIEGE at Steamtown, Bellows Falls   [Edgar T. Mead, Jnr.

No 3364 *PRINCE DE LIEGE* is an outside-cylinder 0–4–0 Back Tank locomotive built in 1877 by St. Leonard (works number 466) for the Belgian State Railways. It was subsequently sold to work in a quarry in Belgium.

This locomotive has been preserved in the United States of America and is in the collection of steam locomotives on display at Steamtown, Bellows Falls, Vermont.

No 3364 has two steeply inclined cylinders with slide valves on top. The valve gear is Walschaerts. A vertical boiler with a single flu is placed centrally in the frames and is surmounted by a large flared chimney which is, however, not original.

Dimensions: CYLINDERS: 280 × 406mm
               COUPLED WHEELS: 635mm
               BOILER PRESSURE: 8kg/cm^2

No 16.052 of the same class as the preserved locomotive

[P. R-W

No 16.042 is a superheated inside-cylinder 4–4–2 Side Tank locomotive, built in 1909 by Tubize (works number 594). It is at present stored at the SNCB locomotive depot at Louvain and will be preserved in the Railway Museum.

There were two main classes of inside-cylinder 4–4–2T both of which were designed during the "McIntosh era" on the Belgian Railways (see page 70). The first engines of Class 15 appeared in 1899 and these were saturated slide-valve engines with cylinders 440 × 610mm. Later engines had larger cylinders, with piston valves, superheaters and longer fireboxes. These became Class 16 and they were introduced in 1905. During their more recent years, most of the engines of both classes had hinged chimney capouchons in an effort to keep exhaust steam and smoke well lifted no matter in which direction the engine was running.

Dimensions: CYLINDERS: 470 × 610mm
            COUPLED WHEELS: 1800mm
            GRATE AREA: 2.5m²
            BOILER PRESSURE: 12.5kg/cm²
            SUPERHEATED

No 1152 with shortened square chimney [R. G. Farr

No 1152 is an 0–6–0 Pannier Tank locomotive of Class 51 which was built in 1884 and is now in store at Louvain Depot where it will be restored for exhibition in the Railway Museum. It has been donated for preservation by its last owners, *Carbonisation Centrale SA.*

From 1865 until 1905 about 450 six-coupled pannier tanks with outside frames were built in batches as required, new engines replacing those worn out. The earlier engines had the dome immediately behind the chimney but in later engines, it was in the middle of the boiler. A number of the engines appeared with square chimneys. Basically, the design remained the same throughout the period over which they were built and they were not altered in later years. The engines were twice renumbered.

Dimensions: CYLINDERS: 380 × 460mm
COUPLED WHEELS: 1200mm
GRATE AREA: 1.5m²
BOILER PRESSURE: 8.5kg/cm²

No 53.351 is of the same class as the preserved locomotive but was built by Le Meuse   [P. R-W

No 53.320 is an 0–8–0 Side Tank locomotive which was originally No 5620 of Class 23 and which is being restored at Louvain Depot with this old number. It was built in 1906 by Boussu (works number 178) and will be preserved in the Railway Museum.

This was one of 375 locomotives of the same Class, first built in 1904 and used for shunting, banking duties at Liège and general freight working. They had a short wheelbase (4.3m) and two outside cylinders with balanced slide valves operated by Walschaerts valve gear. Maximum axle load was 17.2 tonnes.

Dimensions: CYLINDERS: 480 × 600mm
             COUPLED WHEELS: 1262mm
             GRATE AREA: 2.2m²
             BOILER PRESSURE: 12.5kg/cm²

Nord Belge No 615 which is to be preserved [R. G. Farr

Nord-Belge No 615 is an 0–8–0 Side Tank locomotive which was built in 1859 by Cockerill (works number 509). It was sold to the *SA des Charbonnages de Monceau Fontaine, Marcinelle* on whose list it was No MF 72. It is at Louvain Depot for preservation in the Railway Museum.

Twenty-three of these locomotives were built for the *Nord-Belge*, 17 by Cockerill and by Ernst Gouin (Paris) in 1859–1860, and six by Cockerill in 1884. They were Well Tank engines with domeless round-top boilers and outside Allan (?) link motion operating slide valves. They were simple, powerful and reliable machines which carried out shunting duties for many years.

Nine of the engines were rebuilt with domed boilers and side-tanks. Two of these became SNCB Type 88 in 1940, one of them went to the industrial firm (*above*) and the fate of the others is unknown.

Dimensions: COUPLED WHEELS: 1060mm
　　　　　　Other dimensions unknown

Light Railways in Belgium

In 1884, as the result of the findings of a Commission, the *Société Nationale des Chemins de Fer Vicinaux* (SNCV) was formed to develop and operate light railways in Belgium. These railways formed an extensive network all over the country, the railway tracks often being laid beside the public highway.

A few of the lines were laid to 1435mm gauge but the great majority were of 1000mm gauge. Although most of the lines were worked by steam tram locomotives, the SNCV operated the first electric railway in Belgium in 1894, and many of the steam-operated lines were later converted to electric traction.

For many years, the SNVC was a highly profitable concern, but the increasing use of road transport forced the closure of many lines and on other routes the SNCV operate omnibuses and commercial freight road vehicles.

Preservation of Light Railways Steam Locomotives

The preservation in Belgium of many interesting locomotives and much equipment of the SNCV has been well carried out by AMUTRA, the *Société National pour le Musée du Tramway*. This society works in close co-operation with SNCV and they have an excellent museum at Schepdaal, 9km from Brussels and easily accessible by tramway from the city. This museum houses a fine representative collection of steam and electric tramway motive power and rolling stock as well as much other light railway material of historic interest. It is open to the public at weekends and on public holidays from 1400–1800hrs between Easter and the end of October.

AMUTRA also operates the *Tramway Touristique de l'Aisne*, a 12km-long 1000mm-gauge railway between Pont d'Erezée and Lamormenil near Dochamps in the Ardennes. This line, which was closed by SNCV in 1955, passes through very beautiful woodland scenery and it is probable that, in the near future, the line may be extended to Dochamps.

Motive power on the line, which was never electrified, is now one Class 18 steam tram locomotive and three diesel railcars.

The line is open to the public at week-ends and on public holidays between May 1 and September 30.

0–6–0 Tram No 813 working the last train on the SNCV standard gauge line between Groenendaal and Overijse in 1957   [AMUTRA

No 813 Class 12 is an outside-cylinder 0–6–0 Tram locomotive which was built in 1906 by St. Leonard for the Groenendaal-Overijse line. It is now preserved in the Tramways Museum at Schepdaal together with two contemporary passenger coaches.

Five Class 12 locomotives were built for SNCV 1435mm lines between 1897 and 1913. These locomotives were larger and of a greater height above the rails than the previous Classes 10 and 11. They were, in fact, of the same height, 3290mm, as the passenger coaches they hauled so that the whole train was of a homogeneous appearance.

No 813 followed certain design features of the previous classes and in this it differed from other Class 12 locomotives. The drive is to the third axle and not to the second axle and the protective skirting is inclined inwards from the top. Weight in working order is 28.5 tonnes, all available for adhesion.

Dimensions: CYLINDERS: 350 × 400mm
            COUPLED WHEELS: 930mm
            GRATE AREA: 1.2m^2
            BOILER PRESSURE: 10.3kg/cm^2

0–6–0 Tram No 303   [H. Heller

No 303 Class 7 is an 0–6–0 Tram locomotive with side tanks, built in 1887 by Tubize (works number 704) for the Waremme-Oreye line of SNCV. It was sold, in 1961, to *SA des Charbonnages d'Argenteau* but was taken back by SNCV in 1965 and placed on exhibition in the Tramways Museum at Schepdaal.

Sixty-eight of these Class 7 locomotives were built between 1887 and 1915 and they were designed to work 100-tonne trains up inclines of 3 per cent (1 in 33) with curves of 100m radius. They had driving positions at each end of the locomotive which, at first, were without protective screens. The overall roof was supported by seven ornamental iron uprights. Two outside cylinders drove the third coupled axle, the coupled wheels being inside the frames. The slide valves were operated by Walschaerts valve gear. They had Belpaire boilers.

No 303 was a veteran of the class, having been in active service for nearly 75 years.

Dimensions: CYLINDERS: 350 × 360mm
              COUPLED WHEELS: 850mm
              GRATE AREA: 0.9m^2
              BOILER PRESSURE: 12.5kg/cm^2

No 1075 Class 18 in service at a coal mine

[E. Keutgens

No 1075 Class 18 was built in 1920 by Grand Hornu (works number 44). It is at present working at a coal-mine, *Charbonnages d'Argenteau,* at Trembleur, but is soon to be transferred to work on the *Tramway Touristique de l'Aisne.* Its place at the coal-mine will be taken by an autorail transferred from the Mol-Donk line of SNCV.

One hundred and twenty-six locomotives of Class 18 were built for general use on SNCV lines between 1910 and 1915, one of them being built to work on 1067mm gauge. After World War I, SNCV had virtually to re-stock its locomotive department and a further 85 locomotives of Class 18 were built in 1919–1920 and were numbered 1021 to 1105 in the SNCV list.

Class 18 had side tanks and an overall roof with driving positions, protected by glass screens, at each end of the locomotive. Two outside cylinders drove the third coupled axle, and the coupled wheels were inside the frames. They had Walschaerts valve gear. The protective skirting was fitted with four removable panels on each side so that engine maintenance could be easily carried out. All these locomotives had acetylene head lights.

No 1066 Class 18   [R. Pletinckx

No 1066 Class 18 is an 0–6–0 Tram locomotive built in 1920 by Haine St. Pierre (works number 1297). It is now preserved in the Tramways Museum at Schepdaal.

No 1076 *ELISE* Class 18 is identical with No 1066 (above) but was built in 1920 by Grand Hornu (works number 45). It is preserved in working order, by *AMUTRA*, on the *Tramways Tourstique de l'Aisne*.

Dimensions: CYLINDERS: 280 × 400mm
COUPLED WHEELS: 865mm
GRATE AREA: 0.75m²
BOILER PRESSURE: 12.4kg/cm²

No 979 Class 19 [R. Pletinckx

No 979 Class 19 is an 0–6–0 Tram locomotive with side tanks which was built in 1917 for the British Railway Operating Division by Hawthorn Leslie (works number 3228). It has been restored and is in the Tramways Museum at Schepdaal.

The Belgian light railways, known then as the Vicinal Section of the Field Railways, were of great importance to the British Army during World War I and 50 0–6–0 Tram locomotives of Class 18 were built for the ROD in 1916–1917, 30 by Robert Stephenson and 20 by Hawthorn Leslie. They differed slightly from the original Class 18 locomotives because British equivalents of metric dimensions were used and, as copper was in short supply, dome and safety valve covers were made of steel. Many of these locomotives worked in the Ypres sector and, after the war, 48 of them came into SNCV stock as Class 19. Most of them then worked in the Province of Antwerp.

They had Belpaire boilers and side tanks as did all the other classes of Belgian steam tram locomotives.

Dimensions: AS FOR CLASS 18

Danish State Railways

The *Danske Statsbaner* (DSB) came into existence in 1892 as a result of the amalgamation of the two largest railway systems, the State Railways of Jutland-Funen and the Zealand Railway Company, the latter having been taken over by the State two years previously. Some privately owned railways were also absorbed or were operated by DSB but there still remains a number of independent private railways in Denmark. None of them is now steam operated.

Steam Locomotive Preservation in Denmark

The Danish State Railways have a fine, though small, museum at Sølvgade 40, Copenhagen S and this contains a lot of interesting small relics and many excellent models but no full-size locomotives. In the future, it is intended that the Railway Museum shall be re-housed in new and much larger premises so that a number of steam locomotives can be placed on permanent display. A number of locomotives of various types is at present stored at various depots in Denmark and, from these, a selection will be made for the museum. These locomotives are listed and described.

The Technical Museum at Helsingør contains two interesting 1435mm-gauge locomotives which are described in the following pages and four narrow-gauge industrial engines which are outside the scope of the present book.

Denmark has several railway preservation societies which operate on their tracks, steam locomotives which have been obtained mostly from the private railways. The principal society is the *Danske Jernbane Klub* (Danish Railway Club) which was founded in 1962. It operates two 1435mm-gauge railways, the first of which, the Maribo-Bandholm Jernbane is a freight branch of the Lollandske Jernbane. Trains are run by the Club on Sundays in summer. The second railway is also 1435mm-gauge and is the *Mariager Handset Veteran Jernbane* which began operating in May 1970.

Smaller Societies are represented by the *Helsingør Jernbane Klub* which, at various times, steams its locomotives over the *Helsingør-Hornbaek-Gilleleje Banen* and by the *Kolding Locomotiveklub* and the *Westerhaerets Skole* at Aalborg.

It is expected that steam trains will be run on the Odsherreds Railway from Holbaek and on the Hong Tollose Railway.

Probably, most of those DSB locomotives in store will go to the Railway Museum but most of those from the private railways, which are preserved, will go to the Railway Societies or will be purchased for private preservation.

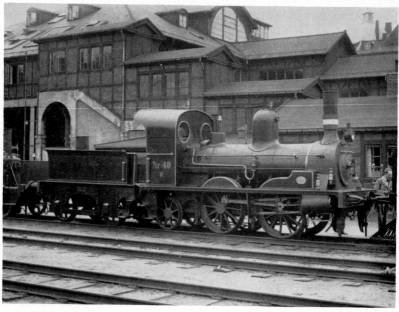

0-4-2 No 40 Class H

[DSB Museum

DSB No 40 Class H is scheduled for preservation. It is an 0-4-2 tender locomotive with inclined outside cylinders and inside link motion. When built, it was domeless but was later rebuilt with a domed boiler.

No 40 was one of six locomotives of the same class built for the Jutland-Funen State Railways by Robert Stephenson & Co. in 1868 and their works number 1900. They were intended for working light mixed trains but four were sold out of State Railways' service between 1910 and 1914. No 40 was sold to the private Vejle-Vandel-Grindsted Railway in 1914 and was withdrawn in 1946. It was then used for a short time as a stationary boiler until 1947. It was later restored and put on exhibition in the Technical Museum, Helsingør.

Dimensions: CYLINDERS: 300 × 560mm

COUPLED WHEELS: 1370mm

GRATE AREA: $0.8m^2$

BOILER PRESSURE: $8.5kg/cm^2$

0–4–2 No 246 Class Cs   [D. Trevor Rowe

DSB No 246 Class Cs was built in 1876 by Esslingen (works number 1500) as No 46 GERE of the Zealand Railway Company. Twelve of the class were built between 1875 and 1877 to work the newly-opened line between Roskilde and Kalundborg. They were built with raised fire-boxes and conical boiler barrels but these were replaced by parallel boilers about ten years later. They had four-wheeled tenders which they retained but enlarged cabs were provided when the boilers were renewed.

No 246 is at present stored at Struer but is to be preserved in the Railway Museum.

Dimensions: CYLINDERS: 410 × 560mm

COUPLED WHEELS: 1650mm

GRATE AREA: 1.3m²

BOILER PRESSURE: 10kg/cm²

(9kg/cm² with original boiler)

0–4–2 No 1 Class J   [W. E. Dancker-Jensen

DSB No 1 is an 0–4–2 of Class J which was built in 1886 by Borsig (works number 4173). It was withdrawn from service in 1954 and is at present in store at Brande awaiting preservation in the Railway Museum.

This was one of 20 engines built for the State Railways of Jutland-Funen between 1886 and 1893 to work over lightly-laid secondary lines. They were designed by O. F. A. Busse and all of them were rebuilt in the DSB shops at Copenhagen and at Aarhus between 1921 and 1927. They were then provided with larger boilers, superheaters and multiple-valve regulators. The slide valves above the cylinders and the outside Allan link motion were retained. No 1 is to be preserved in its rebuilt state.

Dimensions: CYLINDERS: 380 × 510mm
COUPLED WHEELS: 1370mm
GRATE AREA: 1.0m^2
BOILER PRESSURE: 12kg/cm^2
SUPERHEATED

2–4–0 No 45 Class B   [P. R-W

DSB No 45 Class B was built in 1869 by Robert Stephenson (works number 1923) for the State Railways of Jutland-Funen. Eleven locomotives of Class B were built and, for many years, were the main line passenger engines for the Railway. They ran in their original form until they were withdrawn, the last one lasting until 1932. As built they had one injector and a crosshead feed water pump which was ultimately replaced by a second injector.

No 45 is in store at Ryomgard and is scheduled for preservation in the Railway Museum.

Dimensions: CYLINDERS: 380 × 560mm
            COUPLED WHEELS: 1650mm
            GRATE AREA: 1.3m²
            BOILER PRESSURE: 10kg/cm²
                     (8.5kg/cm² with original boiler)

2–4–0 No 273 Class Ks

[Othmar Bamer

DSB No 273 Class Ks was built in 1886 by Schwartzkopff (works number 1502) for the State Railways of Zealand as their No 73 and was withdrawn from service in 1934. It is now stored at Esbjerg for future preservation in the Railway Museum.

Nine of these locomotives were built to the design of K. A. Weien who was Chief Mechanical Engineer of the Zealand Railways. The steam chests and slide valves driven by Walschaerts gear, were above the outside-cylinders which were placed well back between the leading wheel and the first coupled wheel. The drive was to the second coupled axle. These were heavy and powerful engines which, for their day, were very modern in concept and design.

Dimensions: CYLINDERS: 430 × 610mm
COUPLED WHEELS: 1850mm
GRATE AREA: 1.8m²
BOILER PRESSURE: 10kg/cm²

2-4-0 No 263 Class Fs   [W. E. Dancker-Jensen

DSB No 263 Class Fs is an outside-cylinder 2–4–0 which is in store at
Odense and awaiting preservation in the Railway Museum. It was built
for the State Railways of Zealand in 1888 by Hartmann (works number
1537). It was originally No 79 and was withdrawn from service in 1934.

Class Fs consisted of 14 locomotives designed originally by Esslingen
who built the first eight in 1883 and the next three in 1885. The third
batch of three engines came from Hartmann and were heavier than the
earlier machines. The boilers had Ramsbottom safety valves in addition
to Salter valves on the dome.

Class Fs took over many of the main line express services of the Zealand
Railways from earlier 0–4–2 and 2–4–0 classes.

Dimensions: CYLINDERS: 420 × 560mm
COUPLED WHEELS: 1650mm
GRATE AREA: 1.6m^2
BOILER PRESSURE: 10kg/cm^2

DENMARK   4–4–0   1435mm

4–4–0 No 159 Class A

[P. R-W

DSB No 159 Class A (Hartmann 1934/88) was withdrawn in 1956 and is at present stored at Odense awaiting preservation and display in the Railway Museum.

In 1882 the first 4–4–0 locomotive appeared in Denmark. It was designed by O.F.A. Busse for the State Railways of Jutland-Funen and became their Class A. Between 1882 and 1888, 31 of the class were built, 16 by Borsig and the rest by Hartmann; the last was not withdrawn from service until 1956.

The engine had outside cylinders and outside Allan link motion. The original boilers had the dome with Salter type safety valves on the third ring. Later boilers were without the Salter valves and had the sand-box and dome encased together. Twenty-five of the Class A locomotive were later superheated.

Dimensions: CYLINDERS: 410 × 560mm
COUPLED WHEELS: 1730mm
GRATE AREA: 1.5m²
BOILER PRESSURE: 10kg/cm²

DSB No 563 Class K was built in 1899 by Esslingen (works number 3000) for DSB. It was withdrawn in 1956 and is now in store at Skanderborg awaiting display in the Railway Museum.

4–4–0 No 546 Class K which is of the same class as the preserved locomotive [P. R-W

No 564 Class K was built in 1899 by Esslingen (works number 3001) for DSB. It was rebuilt in 1930 and sold to the Odsherred Railway (OHJ) in 1957. It now belongs to the Danish Railway Club and is at Maribo for working on their Maribo-Bandholm Railway on the Island of Lolland.

No 582 Class K was built in 1900 by Breda (works number 510), rebuilt at Aarhus in 1930 and is at present stored at Roskilde. Its future is unknown.

Numerically Class K was one of the largest classes of locomotives in Denmark. They were designed by O. F. A. Busse and between 1894 and 1902, 100 of these outside-cylinder 4–4–0s were built for DSB. With a maximum axle-load of only 13 tonnes they had a wide route availability.

The design was a development of Class A with larger cylinders and coupled wheels and a larger boiler with increased pressure. These dimensions were, in fact, the same as those used in the large 2–4–0 engines which were the last express locomotives to be built for the State Railways of Zealand. Side windows were provided in the cab. Rather surprisingly, the Salter safety valves were retained as was the outside Allan link motion.

Between 1915 and 1925 the Class K were all superheated but the slide valves were retained. However, between 1925 and 1932, 50 of the engines were drastically rebuilt with larger superheated boilers and new cylinders with piston valves. The work was carried out in the Railway's own shops at Aarhus and at Copenhagen. The Salter safety valves were replaced by pop valves and the sand-box was placed in front of the dome and under the same cover, an arrangement which was applied also to the 50 engines which remained un-rebuilt. Later alterations to all the class were the provision of air brakes in place of vacuum and the fitting of snowploughs.

The rebuilt engines were never very successful.

Dimensions (as built): CYLINDERS: 430 × 610mm
COUPLED WHEELS: 1866mm
GRATE AREA: 1.8m²
BOILER PRESSURE: 12kg/cm²
SUPERHEATED

4–4–0 No 719 Class C identical with No 715 which is preserved   [P. R-W

DSB No 715, Class C is an inside-cylinder 4–4–0 in store at Naestved for the Railway Museum. It is one of 19 engines designed by Busse for the Danish State Railways and built by Esslingen and Schwartzkopff in 1903 and 1909 respectively, No 715 being Schwartzkopff works number 4182. It was withdrawn from service in 1961.

Class C locomotives were the only inside-cylinder engines of the DSB and they were handsome and very successful express locomotives being a considerable improvement on Class K. The cylinders and coupled wheel dimensions were identical in the two classes but the Class C boiler was considerably larger. The slide valves were above the cylinders, the valve gear was Walschaerts inside the frames. Class C were all built with super-heaters and were later given sand-boxes on the boiler in front of the steam dome and air brakes.

Dimensions: CYLINDERS: 430 × 610mm
COUPLED WHEELS: 1866mm
GRATE AREA: 1.8m²
BOILER PRESSURE: 12kg/cm²
SUPERHEATED

4-cylinder compound 4–4–2 No 912. This is one of the first batch of engines but is identical in appearance with the preserved locomotive   [P. R-W

DSB four-cylinder compound 4–4–2 No 931 (Schwartzkopff 4458/10) Class P is in store at Odense and will ultimately be displayed in the Railway Museum (see also page 108).

In 1907 the Danish State Railways put into service the first large express engine ever to run in Denmark. Designated Class P it was a Vauclain four-cylinder compound 4–4–2 with the high pressure cylinders between the frames, driving the leading coupled axle and the low pressure cylinders outside, driving the second coupled axle. A single piston valve, 342mm in diameter, was common to the high pressure and to the low pressure cylinders on each side, the two piston valves for the four cylinders being operated by two sets of Walschaerts valve gear inside the frames. Bar frames of cast steel were used and, in their early days, the engines were troubled by cracked frames.

For the first time on a Danish locomotive there was a boiler of adequate size with a grate no less than 1900mm in width. Three ashpans were provided and the firehole door was divided to facilitate firing each side of the box separately. Surprisingly, the engines were not, at first, superheated but subsequently the earlier engines were so, and the later ones were built with superheaters.

The large and comfortable cab had a wedge-shaped spectacle plate and the tender was carried on eight fixed wheels.

The design of these locomotives is attributed to O. F. A. Busse and it was the last to appear under his signature before he retired. It seems highly probable, however, that his assistants had a big say in the design especially in the provision of such a very adequate boiler.

The first 19 engines were built by Hanomag in 1907–1909. The last 14 were built by Schwartzkopff in 1910 and had larger cylinders and an axle-load of 19 tonnes, which kept them strictly to main line express duties. The earlier engines with but 16½ tonnes axle-load had a much wider availability.

The Class P Atlantics were among the most beautiful steam locomotives in the world and their excellent performance and perfect riding qualities endeared them to all who knew them. Even the addition of airbrakes and of sand-boxes under the dome cover did little to mar their appearance.

The Atlantic, No 931, which is preserved, has the following dimensions:

Dimensions: CYLINDERS: HIGH PRESSURE: 360 × 640mm

LOW PRESSURE: 620 × 640mm

COUPLED WHEELS: 1984mm

GRATE AREA: 3.2m²

BOILER PRESSURE: 15kg/cm²

SUPERHEATED

0–6–0 No 64 Class G of the same class as No 78   [P. R-W

DSB No 78 Class G is an outside-cylinder o–6–o tender engine built in
1875 by Esslingen (works number 1440) for the State Railways of Jutland-
Funen. It is at present stored at Odense and will be preserved in the
Railway Museum.

    This engine was one of five of Class G which were followed by a further
four with larger cylinders, from Hanomag in 1878. They had outside
Allan link motion and these nine engines were never superheated.
Between 1884 and 1888 a further 14 engines of Class G were built for the
Jutland-Funen and from 1896 to 1901 51 were built for the Danish State
Railways. These later engines were to some extent modernised and
improved and some were later superheated.

Dimensions (of No 78): CYLINDERS: 380 × 560mm
                     COUPLED WHEELS: 1384mm
                     GRATE AREA: 1.5m^2
                     BOILER PRESSURE: 10kg/cm^2

No 602 Class G is one of the later engines built in 1896 by Esslingen,
Saronno (works number 2846) and later superheated. It is in store at
Copenhagen but it is not known if it will be preserved.

Dimensions: CYLINDERS: 410 × 560mm
            COUPLED WHEELS: 1384mm
            GRATE AREA: 1.5m^2
            BOILER PRESSURE: 10kg/cm^2
            SUPERHEATED

2–6–0 No 871 Class D-II

[W. E. Dancker-Jensen

DSB No 871 Class D-II is a superheated 2–6–0 with piston valves built by Baldwin in 1919 (works number 52434). It has air brakes and the sand-box is under the same cover as the steam dome. It is scheduled for preservation in the Railway Museum and is at present in store at Viborg.

The 2–6–0 type was introduced on the Danish State Railways by Busse in 1902 for fast mixed traffic duties. Between 1902 and 1908, 41 were built with short cabs having side windows, rather small low-pitched saturated boilers and with slide valves operated by outside Walschaerts gear. These were Class D-I. Thirteen similar engines of Class D-III with larger boilers were put into service in 1909 to compare with ten engines of Class D-II with superheaters and piston valves ordered at the same time. Ultimately, all the saturated 2–6–0s were rebuilt with superheaters though some of the earlier engines retained their slide valves. After 1910 many were further rebuilt with larger and higher-pitched superheater boilers and, by lengthening the frames at the rear end, larger and more comfortable cabs were provided. No 871, however, retains the short cab.

Between 1902 and 1922, a total of 100 2–6–0 locomotives were built for DSB being originally divided up as follows: 41 Class D-I, 46 Class D-II, 13 Class D-III. Those locomotives of Class D-I which were extensively rebuilt after 1910 became Class D-IV.

Dimensions of No 871: CYLINDERS: 460×610mm
           COUPLED WHEELS: 1404mm
           GRATE AREA: $1.7m^2$
           BOILER PRESSURE: $12kg/cm^2$
           SUPERHEATED

2–6–0 No 880 which was identical with No 885   [P. R-W

Three other DSB 2–6–0 locomotives are at present in store but they are
not officially listed for preservation and their futures are uncertain.
    These locomotives are:
No 802 Class D-I, Henschel 5982/02, rebuilt at Aarhus in 1925 and now
stored at Brande.
No 885 Class D-II Baldwin 52572/19 with lengthened frames and large cab
(Aarhus 1950) now stored at Randers.
No 900 Class D-II Frichs 41/22 with lengthened frames and large cab
(Aarhus 1949) now stored at Randers.

4–6–0 No 940 Class R-I which was a sister engine to No 942   [P. R-W

No 942 Class R-I is a two-cylinder 4–6–0 mixed traffic locomotive built for DSB in 1913 by Borsig (works number 8588). It is in store at Lunderskov for eventual preservation.

After the retirement of Busse in 1910, the firm of Borsig of Berlin designed several important main line locomotives for the DSB.

First came the mixed traffic 4–6–0 locomotives of Class R-I with two outside cylinders driving on to the leading coupled axle. Walschaerts valve gear operated piston valves above the cylinders. The locomotives had plate frames and round-top boilers without combustion chambers. They had Schmidt superheaters and all had so-called self cleaning smokeboxes with a small door below the smokebox door for the removal of ashes.

Twelve of these locomotives came from Borsig in 1912–1913 and they were very obviously a two-cylinder version of the Garbe Class S-10 design for the Prussian State Railways. They were good engines and a further eight were ordered from SLM in 1917.

Dimensions: CYLINDERS: 570 × 670mm
COUPLED WHEELS: 1866mm
GRATE AREA: 2.6m^2
BOILER PRESSURE: 12kg/cm^2
SUPERHEATED

3-cylinder 4–6–0 No 958 Class R-II which is stored awaiting preservation [P. R-W

No 958 Class R-II is a three-cylinder 4–6–0 locomotive which was built for DSB in 1921 by Borsig (works number 10915). It is in store at Viborg for future preservation.

As in the preceding Class R-I, Borsig were the designers of the three-cylinder 4–6–0 locomotives of Class R-II which were introduced in 1921.

Again, the precedent of the Prussian Class S-10 was being followed as those engines appeared also in a three-cylinder form.

The boiler of the Class R-II was identical with that of Class R-I but the smokebox was different and was not of the "self-cleaning" type.

All three cylinders drove the leading coupled axle and the piston valves, above the cylinders, were operated by three sets of Walschaerts valve gear. The eccentric movement for the inside valve was derived from a double return crank on the Left hand leading coupled wheel crank.

Borsig built five of these engines and they were followed, in 1924, by a further five from Frichs.

Dimensions: CYLINDERS (3): 470 × 670mm
        COUPLED WHEELS: 1730mm
        GRATE AREA: 2.6m^2
        BOILER PRESSURE: 12kg/cm^2
        SUPERHEATED

DENMARK 4-6-2 1435mm

4-cylinder compound 4-6-2 No 908 Class PR, which is preserved   [P. R-W

DSB No 908 Class PR is a four-cylinder compound 4-6-2 which was a reconstruction of a Class P four-cylinder compound 4-4-2 of the same number (see page 101). It was built in 1908 as a 4-4-2 by Hanomag (works number 5014) and reconstructed at the DSB works at Copenhagen in 1946. The difficult reconstruction was successfully carried out to the designs of V. Voldmester who had followed Busse as Chief Mechanical Engineer.

As a result of increasing train weights and of the introduction of the Class E Pacifics of much greater power, seven of the Class P Atlantics were reconstructed by DSB between 1943 and 1955 as four-cylinder compound Pacifics with smaller diameter coupled wheels and a maximum axle-load of 16 tonnes which gave them a much wider availability and a capacity to work heavy freight trains. The layout of cylinders and motion remained as for the original design but the bar frames were extended backwards with a plate frame extension and the boiler was extended by the insertion of a conical ring between the original front part and the new round top fire-box which was that of Class R 4-6-os.

No 908 is in store at Bramminge and will go to the Railway Museum.

Dimensions: CYLINDERS: HIGH PRESSURE: 340 × 600mm
LOW PRESSURE: 570 × 600mm
COUPLED WHEELS: 1730mm
GRATE AREA: 2.6m^2
BOILER PRESSURE: 13kg/cm^2
SUPERHEATED

3-cylinder 2–8–0 No 791 Class H-I was similar to 783 but had not a Lemaître blast-pipe   [P. R-W

No 783 Class H–II is a three-cylinder 2–8–0 freight locomotive built in 1941 for DSB by Frichs (works number 305). It is in store at Fredericks-havn awaiting preservation.

In 1923 Borsig built two three-cylinder 2–8–0 locomotives of Class H–I which were the freight-engine variant of the three-cylinder 4–6–0 of Class R–II (qv). The boilers and cylinders were identical with those of the R–II. All three cylinders drove the second coupled axle but the three sets of Walschaerts valve gear derived their eccentric movement from outside return cranks on the third coupled axle. There was one return crank on the Right and a double return crank on the Left hand side, this arrangement being identical with that used on the three-cylinder 2–8–2 locomotives of Prussian Class P–10.

The first two engines were underboiled and the next 10 built by Frichs in 1926 had the distance between tube plates increased by 300mm.

In 1941 Frichs supplied a further six engines classified H–II. They had an extra dome as a dry steam collector, Lemaître blast pipes and some modifications to the valve gear. The tenders had larger tank capacity and were of welded construction. There was some betterment in the specifications for materials for side rods which improved the running of the locomotives.

Dimensions: CYLINDERS (3): 470 × 670mm
          COUPLED WHEELS: 1404mm
          GRATE AREA: 2.6m^2
          BOILER PRESSURE: 12kg/cm^2
          SUPERHEATED

0–4–0T No L-2 Class O   [DSB Museum

DSB No L–2, Class O, is a small shunting tank engine which is preserved in the Technical Museum at Helsingør. It was one of two such locomotives built in 1869 by Alexander Chaplin and Co (works number 1162) for the State Railways of Jutland-Funen for shunting duties over a very light swing-bridge at Aarhus. Two similar locomotives were built in 1872 for working at Fredericia over the link-span serving the first Danish train ferry. This connected Fredericia with Strib (Funen) on the other side of the Little Belt.

The Class O locomotives had small water-tube vertical boilers and two vertical cylinders which drove the leading axle through gear wheels. Outside coupling rods connected the two axles. Each locomotive weighed 8 tonnes. No L–2 was withdrawn in 1884 but was restored in 1929.

Dimensions: CYLINDERS: 127 × 280mm
                COUPLED WHEELS: 915mm
                GRATE AREA: 0.4m^2
                BOILER PRESSURE: 6kg/cm^2

0–4–0WT No 372 Class Hs-I. This engine is identical with No 363 [P. R-W

No 363 Class Hs-I is an 0–4–0 Well Tank engine built in 1888 by Hartmann (works number 1539) as No 63 for the Zealand Railway.

No 368 *GUNGNER* was built in 1883 by Esslingen (works number 2017) as No 68 for the Zealand Railway and is also of Class Hs-I.

Both these locomotives are in store at Odense and Slagelse respectively and one (probably No 363) will go to the Railway Museum.

Class Hs-I consisted of 16 0–4–0 Well Tank engines with outside cylinders and Walschaerts valve gear. They were built between 1873 and 1893 and seven of them carried names. They were the first Danish shunting locomotives and formed the basis of the design of the later engines of Class Hs-II (qv).

Dimensions: CYLINDERS: 330 × 508mm
             COUPLED WHEELS: 1106mm
             GRATE AREA: 0.8m^2
             BOILER PRESSURE: 9kg/cm^2

0–4–0WT No 396 Class Hs-II which was identical with No 385 [P. R-W

DSB No 385 Class Hs-II was built in 1895 by Hartmann (works number 2110) to the order of the Danish State Railways. The design by Busse was similar to that of Class Hs-I originally built for the Zealand Railway, but provided for a more modern boiler and outside Allan Link motion instead of Walschaerts valve gear of the earlier engines. There were other minor improvements. During the eight years 1894–1902, 45 of these useful little Well Tank engines were put into service.

No 385 is now stored at Odense for future preservation in the Railway Museum.

Dimensions: CYLINDERS: 330 × 508mm
COUPLED WHEELS: 1106mm
GRATE AREA: 0.8cm²
BOILER PRESSURE: 10kg/cm²

0-4-4 Back Tank No 125 Class P   [Othmar Bamer

DSB No 125, Class P is an 0–4–4 Back Tank engine built in 1882 by Hohenzollern (works number 198) for the State Railways of Jutland-Funen. It was sold in 1906 to the Copenhagen-Slangerup Railway but was bought back again by the State Railways in 1948 for restoration to its original conditions and preservation in the Railway Museum. It is at present in store at Odense.

Twelve of these locomotives were built in 1882–1883 to the design of O. F. A. Busse who was Chief Mechanical Engineer of the State Railways of Jutland-Funen from 1881 to 1892 and, later, of the DSB from 1892 until 1910. The Class P was designed for working between Struer and Thisted, a route laid with 35lb rail and which included the Oddesund Train Ferry in its route. The locomotives had a maximum axle-load of only 7 tonnes and were of a modified Engerth type built normally to operate bunker first. This design was later patented by Busse. Outside Allan link motion operated slide valves placed above the cylinders. Water was carried in a tank beneath the bunker and supported by the bogie. The silencer for the vacuum brake ejector can be seen in the photograph immediately in front of the dome.

Dimensions: CYLINDERS: 300 × 410mm
             COUPLED WHEELS: 1067mm
             GRATE AREA: 0.7m^2
             BOILER PRESSURE: 10kg/cm^2

2–4–2T No 332 Class O which was identical with No 318 preserved   [P. R-W

DSB No 318 Class O is a 2–4–2 Side Tank locomotive built in 1898 by Borsig (works number 4650) for the Danish State Railways to the design of O. F. A. Busse, to work on the Copenhagen Suburban Services. It is at present in store at Odense for eventual display in the Railway Museum.

Thirty-six of these engines were built between 1896 and 1901, the last ten by Esslingen, Saronno, the others by Borsig. The outside cylinders and Allan link motion were standard with those of the Class K 4–4–0. All of the Class O engines were later superheated and fitted with sand-boxes behind the dome but in the same casing. All received air brakes.

Dimensions: CYLINDERS: 430 × 610mm
COUPLED WHEELS: 1730mm
GRATE AREA: 1.3m^2
BOILER PRESSURE: 12kg/cm^2
SUPERHEATED

Superheated 0–6–0WT No 428 Class F-III   [DSB

DSB No 428 Class F-III was built in 1917 by SLM (works number 2602).
It is a superheated 0–6–0 Side Tank locomotive one of eight built to work
on the Slesvig State Railways in Jutland when the DSB took over that
railway in 1920. The lines were closed in 1932 and the engines were
transferred to shunting duties and they joined the 105 non-superheater
slide-valve engines of Class F (built between 1898 and 1950).

Class F-III had piston valves operated by Walschaerts valve gear and
the sand-box and dome were combined under one cover in the usual way.

No 428 is to be preserved in the Railway Museum and is at present in
store at Padborg.

Dimensions: CYLINDERS: 406 × 610mm
             COUPLED WHEELS: 1252mm
             GRATE AREA: 1.0m²
             BOILER PRESSURE: 12kg/cm²
             SUPERHEATED

OHJ 0–6–0 No 5

[O. Winther Laursen

Odsherred Railway (OHJ) No 5 Class B was built in 1901 by the Vulcan Works in Maribo (works number 10). It is an outside-cylinder 0–6–0 identical with the Zealand Railway Class L and has inside Allan link motion with slide valves also inside the frames. It is now owned by the Danish Railway Club at Maribo on the Island of Lolland.

Dimensions: CYLINDERS: 356 × 540mm
           COUPLED WHEELS: 1194mm
           GRATE AREA: 1.0m^2
           BOILER PRESSURE: 10kg/cm^2

DENMARK (Private Rys)
2–6–0

1435mm

Fjerritslev-Frederikshaven Railway (FFJ) No 34 was built in 1916 by Henschel (works number 13965). It is at present in Aalborg at *Vesterkaerets Skole*. Thirteen of these fine superheated 2–6–os were built during the years 1910–1924, of which nine were built for the FFJ and two each for the Aalborg-Hvalpsund Railway and the Aalborg-Hadsund Railway. They had piston valve cylinders with Walschaerts valve gear. The six-wheeled tenders had tender cabs for protection of the men when the engines worked tender-first.

Dimensions: CYLINDERS: 410 × 510mm
              COUPLED WHEELS: 1168mm
              GRATE AREA: 1.1m²
              BOILER PRESSURE: 12kg/cm²
              SUPERHEATED

TKVJ 2–6–0 No 12   [O. Winther Laursen

Troldhede-Kolding-Vejen Railway (TKVJ) No 12 was built in 1916 by SLM (works number 2561). It was originally No 2 but was renumbered in 1937. It was one of four superheated piston valve engines with Walschaerts valve gear, built in 1916 for the opening of the TKVJ in 1917.

No 12 is preserved in running order by the Kolding Locomotive Club.

Dimensions: CYLINDERS: 410 × 550mm
              COUPLED WHEELS: 1245mm
              GRATE AREA: 1.5m²
              BOILER PRESSURE: 12kg/cm²
              SUPERHEATED

117

LJ 2–6–0 No 19

Lolland Railway (LJ) No 19 is a superheated 2–6–0 with outside-cylinders and piston valves, built in 1920 by Henschel (works number 17887). It was one of two engines built at that time for LJ and they were some of the largest 2–6–0s built for a Danish private railway. They had four-wheeled tenders. The leading wheels of the engine were in the frames with side-play and not in a leading pony truck.

No 19 is now owned by the Danish Railway Club for their Maribo-Bandholm Railway on the Island of Lolland.

Dimensions: CYLINDERS: 410 × 550mm
                   COUPLED WHEELS: 1245mm
                   GRATE AREA: $1.3m^2$
                   BOILER PRESSURE: $12kg/cm^2$
                   SUPERHEATED

DSB o–4–oT No 186, Class N, which was originally KB No 1   [O. Winther Laursen

Kalvehave Railway (KB) No 1 is an 0–4–0 Side Tank locomotive which was built in 1897 by Esslingen (works number 2874). Locomotives of this design were first built for the State Railways of Jutland-Funen and then for the South Funen Railway. They were Class N and three were built for the newly opened Kalvehave Railway in 1897 as their Nos 1–3. They were found to be unsuitable and were sold to DSB in 1898 becoming their Nos N 186–188. No 1 was sold in 1937 to *A/S Rangierstation, Valby* and is now owned by the Danish Railway Club for their Maribo-Bandholm Railway.

Dimensions: CYLINDERS: 300 × 510mm
COUPLED WHEELS: 1220mm
GRATE AREA: 0.7m^2
BOILER PRESSURE: 10kg/cm^2

SB 0–4–0WT No 4

[O. Winther Laursen

Skagens Railway (SB) No 4 is an 0–4–0 Well Tank locomotive which was built in 1903 for the Aalborg Private Railways (APB) as their No. 17 by Borsig (works number 5200). It was sold in 1924 to the Skagens (Skaw) Railway which had just been converted from 1000mm to 1435mm gauge. The engine is now the property of the Danish Railway Club at Maribo.
Dimensions: NOT KNOWN

Lolland Railway No 20 is an 0–4–0 Well Tank engine built in 1920 by Henschel (works number 17436). It is now the property of the Danish Railway Club and is at Maribo.
Dimensions: NOT KNOWN

DENMARK (Private Rys)
2–4–0T

1435mm

LTJ 2–4–0WT No 7   [Hans Gerner Christiansen

Lemvig-Thyborøn Railway (LTJ) No 7 is a 2–4–0 Well Tank locomotive which was built in 1909 by Henschel (works number 9482). It was one of three such locomotives which were very smart and modern engines having superheaters, piston valves, Walschaerts valve gear and a steam-turbine-driven electric generator for supplying current for train lighting.

No 7 is now the property of the Danish Railway Club for their Mariager Handset Veteran Railway (MHVJ).

Dimensions: CYLINDERS: 356 × 510mm   GRATE AREA: 0.9m²
      COUPLED WHEELS: 1066mm   BOILER PRESSURE: 12kg/cm²
      SUPERHEATED

SVJ 2–4–0T No 1   [O. Winther Laursen

Skive-West Salling Railway (SVJ) No 1 is a 2–4–0 Side Tank locomotive built in 1924 by Henschel (works number 20273). This is the survivor of three such locomotives built to operate this 37km line which opened in the same year, 1924.

No 1 is now owned by the Helsingør Railway Club and it works occasionally over the Helsingør Hornbaek Gilleleje Railway.

Dimensions: NOT KNOWN
      SUPERHEATED

OSJS 0–6–0WT No 3   [O. Winther Laursen

East Zealand Railway (ØSJS) No 3 and No 2 are two little outside-cylinder 0–6–0 Well Tank locomotives which were built in 1878 and 1879 respectively by Krauss (works numbers 759 and 761).

In this compact design, the dome is immediately behind the chimney and outside steam pipes connect it with the steam chests. The exhaust steam pipes are also outside, entering the smokebox just below the centre line of the boiler.

These engines were sold in 1910 to a sugar factory at Nykøbing Falster where they worked until recent years. They are now at Maribo and are the property of the Danish Railway Club.

Dimensions: CYLINDERS: 230 × 300mm
               COUPLED WHEELS: 770mm
               GRATE AREA: 0.5m^2
               BOILER PRESSURE: 12kg/cm^2

SNNB 0–6–0WT No 3   [O. Winther Laursen

Stubbekøbing-Nykøbing Falster-Nysted Railway (SNNB) No 3 was built
in 1910 by Maffei (works number 3173) and was one of five 0–6–0 Well
Tank engines which were among the heaviest and most powerful of this
type ever to work on the Danish private railways. They were needed
especially to work heavy trains of sugar beet and the maximum axle-load
was 12.3 tonnes. They had piston valves and were superheated. No 3 is
now privately preserved at Tollose.

Dimensions: CYLINDERS: 410 × 550mm
             COUPLED WHEELS: 1092mm
             GRATE AREA: 1.2m^2
             BOILER PRESSURE: 12kg/cm^2
             SUPERHEATED

OSJS 2–6–0WT No 7

[O. Winther Laursen

East Zealand Railway (ØSJS) No 7 is a superheated outside-cylinder 2–6–0 Well Tank locomotive which was built in 1911 by Henschel (works number 10695) as No 1 of the Kolding South Railway (KS). This was a short-lived, 56km railway, opened in 1911 and closed in 1948.

No 7 was sold to ØSJS in 1950 and is at Helsingør, owned by the Helsingør Railway Club. At times it is steamed and works over the Helsingør Hornbaek Gilleleje Railway.

Dimensions: NOT KNOWN
      SUPERHEATED

North Funen Railway No 3 is a superheated 2–6–0 Well Tank locomotive with piston valves and outside cylinders with Walschaerts valve gear. It was built in 1923 by Henschel (works number 20118) and is privately preserved at the Mansion Egeskov, Funen.

Dimensions: NOT KNOWN
      SUPERHEATED

Horsens-Odder Railway (HOJ) No L 106 and Horsens-Bryrup-Silkeborg Railway (HBS) No L 107 are superheated 2–6–0 Side Tank engines

NFJ 2-6-oWT No 3   [Hans Gerner Christiansen

built in 1928 for the Horsens Western Railway (HV) by Henschel (works numbers 21257 and 21258 respectively).

HV 2-6oT No L 106   [O. Winther Laursen

The Horsens Group of Railways was converted to 1435mm gauge from 1000mm gauge, the work being completed in 1929 and these locomotives were two of seven built to work on the newly converted lines. They were the last steam locomotives to be built for Danish private railways and they incorporated several new features. They were the first 2-6-oT to have leading Bissel trucks—previous engines of the type had the guiding wheels in the main frames but provided with side-play. They were also the first locomotives for private railways to have air, instead of vacuum brakes.

One was transferred from the Horsens Western Railway to its associated companies in 1953 and are both now privately preserved. No L107 will go to the Mariager HVR and No L106 is owned by the Brurup Veteran Railway.

Dimensions: CYLINDERS: 380 × 560mm   GRATE AREA: 1.6m²
            COUPLED WHEELS: 1300mm   BOILER PRESSURE: 12kg/cm²
            SUPERHEATED

OKMJ 2–6–2T No 14

[Hans Gerner Christiansen

Odense-Kjertemunde Martofte Railway (OKMJ) No 14 is a superheated 2–6–2 Side Tank locomotive built in 1910 by Henschel (works number 10022) as No 4 for the Odense Kjertemunde Dalby Railway (OKDJ). It is identical with six locomotives built contemporaneously by Henschel for the North-West Funen Railway (OMB). It is now privately preserved and will go to the Mariager Handset Veteran Railway of the Danish Railway Club.

An attractive-looking and very successful type of locomotive having a Bissel truck at either end. When built, the safety valves were on top of the dome.

Dimensions: CYLINDER: 344 × 546mm
COUPLED WHEELS: 1300mm
GRATE AREA: 1.0m^2
BOILER PRESSURE: 12kg/cm^2
SUPERHEATED

GDS 4-6-0T No 11

[O. Winther Laursen

Gribskov Railway (GDS) No 11 is a 4–6–0 Side Tank locomotive built in 1907 by Henschel (works number 8142) for the Helsingør-Hornbaek Railway (HHB) as their No 4 and sold in 1940.

It has outside cylinders with slide valves operated by Walschaerts valve gear and long side tanks reaching nearly to the front end of the smoke-box. It is not superheated.

It is the only engine of its type in Denmark and is now owned by the Danish Locomotive Club for their Maribo-Bandholm Railway.

Dimensions: CYLINDERS: 370 × 560mm
COUPLED WHEELS: 1194mm
GRATE AREA: 1.5m^2
BOILER PRESSURE: 12kg/cm^2

OSJS 0–8–0WT No 6 as No 2 of the Frederiksvaerk Steelworks   [O. Winther Laursen

East Zealand Railway (ØSJS) No 6 is an 0–8–0 Well Tank locomotive built in 1895 by Borsig (works number 4471). With its sister engine, ØSJS No 5, it was the first eight-coupled engine in Denmark. It has outside cylinders with slide valves above the cylinders and operated by outside Allan link motion. It is not superheated.

No 6 was out of service from 1930 to 1941 but was then completely overhauled and put back to work. It was sold as a shunting engine for the steelworks at Frederiksvaerk in 1953, and is now owned by the Danish Locomotive Club for their Maribo-Bandholm Railway.

Dimensions: CYLINDERS: 330 × 500mm
COUPLED WHEELS: 1004mm
GRATE AREA: 1.0m^2
BOILER PRESSURE: 12kg/cm^2

Finnish State Railways

Finland, until 1917, was a Grand Duchy of the Russian Empire and obtained her full independence as a result of the Bolshevik Revolution. The State Railways, *Valtionrautatiet* (VR) came into existence at that time. The gauge of the railways has remained as it was—1524mm—the Russian standard gauge.

The first railway in Finland was between Helsinki and Hameenlinna and it was opened in 1862, the first locomotive being an outside cylinder 4–4–0 named *ILMARINEN* which was built in England in 1860 by the Canada Works, Birkenhead (works number 83).

After 1875, steam locomotives were built for Finland in Sweden, Germany and USA but most were built in Finland, at first in the railway workshops at Helsinki but, since the turn of the century, by two well-known builders, Tampereen Konepaja and Lokomo Oy, both with works at Tampere. The last steam locomotive was built in 1957, a 2–8–2 No 1096 of Class Tr-1. Although the earliest locomotives showed markedly British influence, locomotive design in Finland has generally followed Scandinavian practice and, surprisingly, apart from comparatively minor details, Russian influence on design has been negligible.

Finnish locomotives were always of uncomplicated and straightforward design. There were no multicylinder engines but several early classes were two-cylinder compounds. Sand was carried in a dome on the boiler and in later classes the sand dome and steam dome were beneath the same cover (*cf* Denmark). Enclosed cabs were a necessity. All the modern locomotives had bar frames, outside cylinders with piston valves and Walschaerts valve gear. They had piston operated cylinder by-pass valves which were easily seen on the outer aspect of the cylinder block.

Soon after World War II, a new system of locomotive classification was brought into use in which the first (capital) letter indicated the duties for which the locomotive was primarily built, thus: H = Passenger; P = Suburban; S = Mixed traffic; T = Freight; V = Shunting

A second (small) letter indicates the maximum axle loading of the locomotive, thus: k = up to 11 tonnes; v = up to 14 tonnes; r = over 14 tonnes.

The maximum axle-load of any steam locomotive of the VR was the 17.5 tonnes of the American-built 2–10–0s of Class Tr 2, a class of which many were built for Russia, Finland receiving 20 of them in 1946–1947.

Until the import of Russian supplies during the last 20 years, coal has always been scarce and expensive in Finland but wood is plentiful and cheap. As a result, nearly all the early engines were wood burners, birch blocks being most favoured as fuel, having the highest calorific value. In order to burn wood in a locomotive firebox, the brick arch is removed and a spark-arresting chimney is essential. The tender is usually equipped with extra guard rails so that the wood can be stacked right up to the limit of the loading gauge. The birch blocks are fed into the firebox by hand, two at a time, the fireman wearing thick leather gloves for protection.

Until recent years, about half of the route kilometerage of the Finnish Railways was laid with rail lighter than 43.5kg/m with which most of the track in the southern part of the country was laid. This resulted in many of the steam locomotives being very lightly built and the later and more powerful machines were severely limited in their route availability. Great strides have been made in the past 7–8 years in relaying with modern track of 54kg/m and over 50 per cent of the railways are now up to this standard and some 60kg rail is now laid. This has, of course, mainly been of benefit to the design of diesel motive power though it extended the route availability of the more powerful steam locomotives during the last years in service.

Steam Locomotive Preservation on the VR

There is a small Railway Museum in the Central Station at Helsinki (entrance from Railway Square) but the steam locomotive exhibits are confined to very fine large-scale models. About 15 steam locomotives are at present stored and are scheduled for preservation in a Railway Museum which may well be established at Pasila, about 2.5km north of Helsinki Central Station. It is intended that the present freight yard at Pasila will be moved two miles further north and enlarged. The museum would be built on the site of the existing freight yard.

The stored locomotives are an interesting collection but represent mostly the older and smaller locomotives. It is to be hoped that, in the future, examples of the 4–6–2 of Class Hr I, the 2–8–2 of Class Tr I and of the suburban 2-8–2T of Class Pr I may be included for preservation.

No 58 on exhibition   [V.R.

No 58 (old) Class A–5 is an outside cylinder 4–4–0 with inside Stephenson link motion, built in 1875 for the Helsingfors-St. Petersburg Railway by the railway works at Helsingfors (works number 2). This locomotive has been restored and is to be preserved in the Railway Museum. It is at present in store at Kaipiainen.

The very large spark arrester and the guard-rails around each side of the engine are characteristic of Russian locomotive practice of the period. The head lamps burn acetylene gas. It is of interest that no cow-catcher was fitted to this locomotive.

Dimensions: CYLINDERS: 406 × 508mm
            COUPLED WHEELS: 1675mm
            GRATE AREA: 1.24m^2
            BOILER PRESSURE: 8.4kg/cm^2

A locomotive, number unknown, of Class C-1   [V.R.

No 21 (old) Class C–1 is an inside cylinder 0–6–0 with four-wheeled tender, built in 1869 by Neilson (works number 1427) for the Helsingfors-St. Petersburg Railway. This locomotive has been restored and is in store at Kaipiainen awaiting exhibition in the Railway Museum.

The large spark-arresting chimney and the air-operated bell on top of the cab are typical of Finnish steam locomotive practice but otherwise this locomotive is quite typical of many British 0–6–0s of the same period. The sand boxes were below the running plates when the engines were built but, later, they had sand domes behind the chimneys.

Details: COUPLED WHEELS: 1250mm

TRACTIVE EFFORT (75 per cent): 3200kg

WEIGHT IN WORKING ORDER: 42 tonnes

MAXIMUM SPEED: 60km/h

No 110 of Class C-5   [R. G. Farr

No 110 (old) Class C–5 is an inside cylinder 0–6–0 built in 1882 by Hanomag (works number 1477) for the Hangö-Hyvinge Railway. It has been restored and is at present in store at Kaipiainen for future preservation in the Railway Museum.

This is another 0–6–0, somewhat similar in appearance to No 21 but with a shorter wheelbase and having been built with a small sand dome on the second ring of the boiler. Inside Allan link motion is fitted. The cab is large and commodious and the air-operated bell is in its usual position on the cab roof. This locomotive was also constructed to burn wood. Its original VR number was 311.

Like the early 4–4–0s, these 0–6–0 locomotives were without cow-catchers.

Details: COUPLED WHEELS: 1120mm
TRACTIVE EFFORT (75 per cent): 4020kg
WEIGHT IN WORKING ORDER: 35.5 tonnes
MAXIMUM SPEED: 60km/h.

No 124 Class Sk I on exhibition with 2–8–2 No 1002 at Helsinki   [V.R .

No 124 Class Sk 1 (old Class G–1) is a wood-burning 2–6–0 with Salter safety valves on the dome, outside cylinders and inside Allan link motion. It was built in 1885 by SLM (works number 405) for the Helsingfors-St. Petersburg Railway. Its original VR number was 328. This locomotives is restored and is in store at Kaipiainen for the Railway Museum.

No 135 Class Sk 1 (old Class G–2) is almost identical with No 124 but was built in 1888 by the Railway Workshops at Helsingfors (works number 4). It is preserved, and is on exhibition at the VR railway works at Hyvinkää.

Class Sk 1 consisted of 68 engines built between 1886 and 1895, most of them by SLM but some by Dübs and four in the Railway Works at Helsingfors. No 198 was rebuilt to Class Sk 2.

No 315 Class Sk 2 (old Class G–9) is a 2–6–0 of similar appearance to the previous classes but with a larger boiler and cylinders of increased diameter. It was one of the first eight locomotives built by Tamperene

No 135 Class Sk 1 [V.R.

and carries their works number 2 of 1900. It was sold out of railway service to a private industrial railway but is now preserved and is exhibited in the builder's works at Tampere.

Class Sk 2 consisted of 31 engines, the first ten built by Nydquist in 1897 and the rest by Tampereen in 1900–1901.

Dimensions (Classes Sk 1 and Sk 2): CYLINDERS: 380 × 510mm
COUPLED WHEELS: 1250mm
GRATE AREA: 1.1m²
BOILER PRESSURE: 10kg/cm²

No 400 Class Sk 3 (old Class G–11) is a wood-burning two-cylinder compound 2–6–0 built in 1903 by Tampereen (works number 49). It has been restored and is in store at Hyvinkää awaiting preservation in the Railway Museum.

Class Sk 3 was the first of three classes of two-cylinder compound 2–6–0s and it consisted of 88 engines built in batches between 1898 and 1905 by SLM, Dübs, Schwartzkopff and Tampereen. The high pressure cylinder was on the Right hand side and the low pressure on the Left. A cylindrical casing on the Right hand side of the smoke-box contained the change-valve for simple to compound working.

Dimensions: CYLINDERS: HIGH PRESSURE: 400 × 600mm
LOW PRESSURE: 580 × 600mm
COUPLED WHEELS: 1250mm
GRATE AREA: 1.4mm
BOILER PRESSURE: 12.5kg/cm^2

No 451 Class Hk 2   [P. R-W

No 451 Class Hk 2 (old Class H–3) is an outside cylinder 4–6–0 with inside Stephenson link motion built in 1905 by Tampereen (works number 103). It is at present in store at Hyvinkää and will ultimately be preserved in the Railway Museum.

Twenty of the class were built between 1903 and 1906 and they were originally two-cylinder compounds. They were all rebuilt as simple expansion engines between 1929 and 1932 and, later, were superheated and three of them were provided with slightly larger boilers and classified Hk 3 (old Class H–5).

No 451 and most of her sisters, were wood burners and had acetylene headlights. The maximum axle load was 10.2 tonnes.

Dimensions: CYLINDERS: 450 × 610mm
                COUPLED WHEELS: 1575mm
                GRATE AREA: 1.4m^2
                BOILER PRESSURE: 12kg/cm^2
                SUPERHEATED

No 512 of the same class, Hk 5 as No 497 [V.R.

No 497 Class Hk 5 (old Class H–6) is an outside cylinder 4–6–0 with piston valves operated by Walschaerts valve gear. It was built in 1909 by Tampereen (works number 155) and is at present stored at Sysmäjärvi awaiting preservation in the Railway Museum.

Twenty-three of the class were built by Tampereen between 1909 and 1911. They were superheated, had small coupled wheels of 1250mm diameter and the maximum axle load was only 8.6 tonnes. They were wood burners and worked on lightly laid branch lines mostly in the north of the country.

Dimensions: CYLINDER: 430 × 510mm

COUPLED WHEELS: 1250mm

GRATE AREA: 1.4m²

BOILER PRESSURE: 10kg/cm²

SUPERHEATED

No 547 of the same class, Hv 1 as No 554   [P. R-W

No 554 Class Hv 1 (old Class H–8) is a superheated 4–6–0 with outside cylinders, piston valves, piston by-pass valves and Walschaerts valve gear. It was built in 1915 by Tampereen (works number 245) and is at present stored at Riihimäki awaiting preservation in the Railway Museum.

Between 1915 and 1941, 100 4–6–0 locomotives of Classes Hv 1 (43 in the Class), Hv 2 (33) and Hv 3 (24) were built in batches by Tampereen, Berlin and Lokomo, 12 engines of Class Hv 1 being the first locomotives to be constructed at the works of Lokomo. The classes were almost identical, there being a slight increase in tube heating surface and in adhesion weight in the last two classes compared with the first. The last 15 engines of Class Hv 3 had boiler pressure 13kg/cm² with a consequent increase in the tractive effort. The maximum axle load was 12.4 tonnes in Class Hv 1 and 12.8 tonnes in the other classes.

They were very successful engines, economical in both fuel and maintenance. They were mostly coal burners and so were seldom disfigured by the ugly spark arresting chimneys of the wood burners. They all had the standard wire-mesh spark arresters on the chimney tops.

Dimensions: CYLINDERS: 510 × 600mm
          COUPLED WHEELS: 1750mm
          GRATE AREA: 1.96m²
          BOILER PRESSURE: 12kg/cm²
          SUPERHEATED

No 760 of the same class, Hv 4 as No 742   [V.R.

No 742 Class Hv 4 (old Class H–7) is a superheated 4–6–0 with outside
cylinders, piston valves, piston by-pass valves and Walschaerts valve gear.
It was built in 1926 by Tampereen (works number 362) and is in store at
Pasila (Helsinki) for the Railway Museum.

Twenty-five of these engines were built between 1912 and 1933 by
Tampereen and Lokomo. They were mostly wood-burners and were used
for branch-line duties, the maximum axle-load being only 10.9 tonnes.

The principal dimensions of these engines are identical with those of
the earlier slide valve engines of Class Hk 3. They are slightly heavier but
the maximum axle-load is only 10.9 tonnes and would seem have
warranted a "k" rather than a "v" rating.

Dimensions: CYLINDERS: 450 × 610mm
              COUPLED WHEELS: 1575mm
              GRATE AREA: 1.4m^2
              BOILER PRESSURE: 12kg/cm^2
              SUPERHEATED

No 469 Class Tk 2 is of the same class as the two preserved locomotives   [V.R.

No 407 Class Tk 2 (old Class K–1) is a two-cylinder compound 2–8–0 built in 1903 by Tampereen (works number 53). It is stored at Myllymäki for the Railway Museum.

No 419 of the same class, Tampereen works number 69 of 1904, is preserved at the Children's Hospital, Lastenlinna Linnankeskenkatu, Helsinki.

The 2–8–0 was by far the most numerous type of locomotive in Finland having been introduced in 1900 with 20 engines from Baldwin (Class Tk 1). Thirty-four of the two-cylinder compounds were built between 1903 and 1907, all by Tampereen. With a maximum axle-load of only 8.3 tonnes they were able to work over the whole railway system. They had slide valves with inside Stephenson link motion, the low pressure cylinders being on the Right hand side of the engine. A change valve was fitted on the Right hand side of the smokebox. They were all wood-burners.

Dimensions: CYLINDERS: HIGH PRESSURE: 410 × 510mm

                 LOW PRESSURE: 590 × 510mm

     COUPLED WHEELS: 1120mm

     GRATE AREA: 1.4m^2

     BOILER PRESSURE: 12.5kg/cm^2

No 895 Class Tk 3   [V.R.

No 895 Class Tk 3 (old Class K–2) is a superheated two-cylinder simple 2–8–0 with bar frames, piston valves and Walschaerts valve gear. It was built in 1930 by Tampereen (works number 435) and it is at present in store at Pasila Depot, Helsinki, awaiting preservation in the Railway Museum.

No 859 of Class Tk 3 was built in 1929 by Lokomo (works number 89). It has been preserved by railwaymen and is to be placed on exhibition at Kouvola.

No 852 of Class Tk 3 has been withdrawn from service and is stored at Pieksamaki, a mainline junction in central southern Finland.   The locomotive will be placed on exhibition in the local museum.

Class Tk 3 was numerically by far the largest class in Finland, no fewer than 161 engines being built between 1928 and 1950, mostly by Tampereen but some also by Lokomo and a few by Frichs. With a maximum axle-load of 10.7 tonnes they had a very wide route availability and they were used on almost all classes of trains except express passenger. Many of the class were wood burners but those used on the most important duties, such as the Helsinki suburban services, burned coal. All had air brakes and electric lighting.

Dimensions: CYLINDERS: 460 × 630mm
            COUPLED WHEELS: 1270mm
            GRATE AREA: 1.6m^2
            BOILER PRESSURE: 14kg/cm^2
            SUPERHEATED

No 1305 Class Tr 2 was of the same class as No 1319 [P. R-W

No 1319 is a 2–10–0 freight locomotive of Class Tr 2 which was built in 1947 by ALCO (works number 75214). It is stored, at present, at Hyvinkää for future preservation in the Railway Museum.

Class Tr 2 was composed of 20 outside-cylinder heavy freight locomotives with a maximum axle-load of 17.5 tonnes and a tractive effort of 17,780kg. They were the heaviest and most powerful locomotives in Finland.

The round top firebox had a very wide grate and there were four circulating tubes in the firebox. All 20 engines had mechanical stokers. As might be expected in American-built locomotives, they had bar frames and the cab was supported by the boiler. A large casing on the boiler-top contained sand dome and steam dome.

The outside cylinders had piston valves above them operated by Walschaerts valve gear. Drive was to the third (or middle) coupled axle and the third pair of coupled wheels was flangeless.

These locomotives, built by Baldwin and ALCO in 1946–7, were originally part of a large order for Soviet Russia. As they were, apparently, surplus to Russian requirements they were sent to Finland.

Dimensions: CYLINDERS: 635×711mm
COUPLED WHEELS: 1320mm
GRATE AREA: $6.0m^2$
BOILER PRESSURE: $12.5kg/cm^2$
SUPERHEATED

No 68 Class Vk 4

[V.R.

No 68 Class Vk 4 is an outside-cylinder Well Tank locomotive with Walschaerts valve gear. It was built in 1910 by Borsig (works number 7858) for the Rauma Railway and later sold to the private factory, Pietarsaaren Selluloosa. It was bought from this firm by VR in June 1945 and worked as a shunting engine until July 1967 when it was withdrawn and placed on exhibition at the Kuopio Works of the State Railways.
Dimensions: CYLINDERS: 285 × 400mm
           COUPLED WHEELS: 760mm
           GRATE AREA: 0.6m²
           BOILER PRESSURE: 11kg/cm²

No 9 Class B-1 at Centenary Exhibition, Helsinki [R. G. Farr

No 9 (old) Class B–1 is an 0–4–2 Saddle Tank locomotive which was built in 1868 for the Helsingfors-St. Petersburg Railway by Beyer Peacock (works number 846). It is at present in store at Kaipiainen awaiting preservation in the Railway Museum.

No 9 has a domeless boiler and it burns wood. The back bunker has extended back and side plates to accommodate 1.6 tonnes of birch logs. Inside cylinders with Stephenson link motion, plate frames, and sandboxes below the running plate are features typical of British practice of the period.

Dimensions: CYLINDERS: 285 × 400mm
COUPLED WHEELS: 1250mm
GRATE AREA: 0.95m²
BOILER PRESSURE: 10.5kg/cm²

No 132 Class F-1

[R. G. Farr

No 132 (old) Class F–1 is a Forney outside-cylinder 0–4–4 Well Tank locomotive which was built in 1886 by SLM (works number 434) for the Helsingfors-St. Petersburg Railway.

It has been restored and is in store at Kaipiainen for future exhibition in the Railway Museum.

This engine now has a copper-topped bell-mouthed chimney in place of the large spark arrester with which it spent its wood-burning life. The extra rails on the tender are still kept, as also are the Russian-type guard rails along the left-hand side of the engine.

The trailing bogies of the Forney-type locomotives have outside bar frames and the engines can negotiate reverse curves of only 36m radii. The type was used extensively on the New York Elevated Railroad before electrification.

VR had eight Forney tank locomotives, four of which were built for the Helsingfors-St. Petersburg Railway in 1885–6 as Nos 71, 72, 226 and 227. These were re-numbered in 1888 as 115, 116, 132 and 133 respectively. The other four engines came, two from the Kerava-Porvoo Railway in 1917 (Nos 3 and 4 which became VR Nos 62 and 63 respectively) and two from the Rauma-Peipohja Railway in 1950. These were Rauma Nos 2 and 3 which became VR Nos 70 and 71 respectively. These last two were not scrapped until 1953, some 20 years after the others.

Dimensions: CYLINDERS: 310 × 510mm

           COUPLED WHEELS: 1068mm

           GRATE AREA: 0.87m²

           BOILER PRESSURE: 10.5kg/cm²

FINLAND   2–6–4T   1524mm

No 489 Class Vk 3   [R. G. Farr

No 456 Class Vk 3 is a superheated 2–6–4 Back Tank locomotive which was built in 1906 by Tampereen (works number 108), as Class I–2). It had cylinders 400mm diameter and was later known as Class Vk 2. In 1930, this locomotive was superheated and rebuilt with cylinders 420mm diameter and then became Class Vk 3. It is at present in store at Vaasa awaiting preservation in the Railway Museum.

No 489 Class Vk 3 (old Class I–3) was built in 1909 by Tampereen (works number 140) and is at present stored at the Railway Workshops at Hyvinkää. It has a tractive effort of 6,600kg compared with 5,990kg of the previous Class Vk 2, the cylinder diameter being 420mm against 400mm of the older engines.

The Finnish Railways found the 2–6–4T a useful and economical type for mixed traffic duties on the lightly laid tracks in the far north of the country. The first engines of the type were five which came to Finland from Baldwin in 1900. They were Class Vk 1 (old Class I–1) and they were bar-framed, coal-burning Back Tank locomotives. In 1906, Tampereen built Nos 454, 455, 456 of Class Vk 2 (old Class I–2) with plate-frames and inside Stephenson link motion. They were later given superheaters. A further six of these engines were built in 1909 with larger cylinders and superheaters and these were Class Vk 3 (old Class I–3). All of these classes were wood burners.

Dimensions: CYLINDERS: 420 × 600mm   GRATE AREA: 1.5m²
              COUPLED WHEELS: 1250mm   BOILER PRESSURE: 12kg/cm²
              SUPERHEATED

No 1800 Class Pr 2

[P. R-W

No 1800 Class Pr 2 (old Class N–1) is a 4–6–4 Side and Back Tank locomotive which was built in 1942 by Henschel (works number 26132) for the Estonian Railways. It is now at Hyvinkää Works and is scheduled for preservation in the Railway Museum.

Four of these locomotives came to Finland as reparations after World War II and they were put to work on the Helsinki Suburban Services. They were never popular machines and, like all 4–6–4T designs, they were prone to rolling which, on the poorly maintained track of the VR at that time, gave rise to much anxiety. They were also completely non-standard and spares were difficult to obtain for them. When the firebox crown-plate of No 1801 collapsed, killing both enginemen, the four engines were withdrawn and stored.

They had bar frames, outside-cylinders with Walschaerts valve gear and a Davies and Metcalfe exhaust steam injector was fitted on the Left hand side. They were coal burners and had a wire-mesh spark arrester on top of the chimney. Large smoke deflectors were fitted. The boiler pressure was the highest ever to be used on the VR.

Dimensions: CYLINDERS: 530 × 660mm
COUPLED WHEELS: 1830mm
GRATE AREA: 3.5m^2
BOILER PRESSURE: 16 kg/cm^2
SUPERHEATED

Narrow Gauge Railways of Finland

There were three important 750mm-gauge systems all in the southern part of the country. They were privately owned and operated, but only one now remains active.

A number of narrow gauge steam locomotives, some of them industrial are preserved, most of them as monuments in various public places.

FINLAND   750mm

The Loviisa-Lahti Railway (LLR) was a 750mm-gauge line which extended from Loviisa on the south-east coast, northwards 82km via Lahti to Niemi on Lake Wesijärvi. It was converted to 1524mm gauge in 1959–1960.

The steam locomotive stock of the Loviisa-Lahti Railway consisted of two 0–4–0 shunting tank locomotives built by Jung and eleven tender locomotives. These comprised two American-built 2–6–0s Nos 4 and 5, and one built by Tampereen, No 6, which is preserved. There were six 2–8–0s of which Nos 1, 2 and 3 were American-built, Nos 7 and 10 built by Orenstein and No 8 by Jung. No 7 is preserved. The remaining locomotives were 2–8–2s both built by Orenstein and numbered 9 and 11.

LLR No 6   [TAE

LLR No 6 is a superheated 2–8–0 with outside cylinders and Walschaerts valve gear built in 1909 by Tampereen (works number 141) and which is now preserved outside the railway station at Loviisa.

LLR No 7   [O. Winther Laursen

LLR No 7 is a superheated 2–8–0 with outside cylinders built in 1921 by Orenstein (works number 9454). It is now preserved outside the railway station at Lahti.

The Hyvinkaa-Karkkila Railway (HKR) was a 750mm-gauge line which was a subsidiary of a large commercial company. It extended from Hyvinkää, 40.5km westwards to Karkkila and the steam locomotive stock was composed of Side Tank locomotives, there being one 0–6–2T and three 2–8–2T.

HKR No 2 preserved at Tampere   [R. G. Farr

HKR No 2 is a wood-burning 0–6–2 Side Tank locomotive built in 1916 by Tampereen (works number 256) and now preserved in the

Sorsapuisto Park at Tampere. It has a spark arresting chimney and the safety valves are on the dome. Cylinders are outside with slide valves operated by outside Allan link motion.

HKR No 3 is a 2–8–2 Side Tank locomotive built in 1910 by Tampereen (works number 158). It is preserved in Karkkila, near to the bus station.

HKR No 5   [R. G. Farr

HKR No 5 is a 2–8–2 Side Tank locomotive built in 1917 by Tampereen (works number 289) and identical with No 3 (above). This locomotive has been presented to the Veturien Ystavat (Finnish Club) and it is at the Forssa Depot of the Jokioisten Railway, Humppila-Forssa.

The HKR 2–8–2Ts are impressive machines with outside cylinders and outside Allan link motion. The safety valves are on top of the dome which is in the same cover with the sandbox. The large side tanks are sloped at the front ends and the acetylene gas cylinder for the lights is carried on the Right hand tank. The engines are all wood burners.

The Humppila-Forssa Railway is a 750mm-gauge line which runs from the VR station at Humppila, northwest of Helsinki to Forssa, 23km in a south-easterly direction. This railway is still in operation for freight traffic only, passenger services having ceased in 1953. Three small diesel locomotives provide the motive power for the railway, but two outside-cylinder 2–6–2 Side Tank locomotives with outside frames, Walschaerts valve gear and a round top boiler, are kept in reserve at Humppila. These are Nos 4 and 5 which were built 1947-8 by Tubize and they may be preserved on retirement.

Riihimaki-Loppi No 3 at Riihimaki

[R. G. Farr

Preserved and on display outside the Fire Station at Riihimaki is an outside-cylinder 0–6–2 Side Tank locomotive which was built in 1912 by Tampereen (works number 188) as No 3 of the 600mm-gauge Riihimaki Loppi Railway which now no longer exists.

French National Railways Society

The *Société Nationale des Chemins de Fer Françaises* (SNCF) was formed on January 1 1938. It took over the control and operation of the six major railways and formed them into five Regions thus:

Region 1. Eastern comprising, principally, the lines of the former Est and Alsace-Lorraine Railways.

Region 2. Northern consisting mainly of the lines of the former Nord railway.

Region 3. Western which included the lines of Etat and the Ouest which railways had previously been amalgamated.

Region 4. South Western comprising the lines of the former amalgamated railways, the Paris-Orléans and the Midi.

Region 5. South Eastern which was formed from the lines of the former Paris-Lyons-Mediterranée Railway.

After the War, part of the South Western region territory was joined with part of that of the South Eastern to form a sixth region—the Mediterranean.

After 1938 there remained a considerable number of standard gauge private railways in France, most of them being in the categories of *"Chemin de Fer Economiques"* and *"Voies Ferrées d'Intérêt Local"*. Most of these have now been closed and the few which remain are either electrified or use diesel power.

The Compound Locomotive in France

France, almost alone among the countries of the world, retained compound locomotives in main line service until the end of the steam locomotive era.

The success of the compound locomotive depended, very largely, upon the exceptionally thorough training of locomotive drivers and firemen with their consequent ability to handle complicated machines with competence and understanding. Another factor was that, until recent times, all main-line locomotives in France were "machines titulaires", that is, each locomotive was driven, and largely maintained, by the same pair of men, often for many years. As a result, the very best could be obtained from each locomotive. Even so, it is very doubtful if the savings in fuel and the exceptional performances, compensated for the considerably less maintenance required by a simple machine in "common user" service with its generally greater availability.

In the following account of preserved locomotives in France, three main systems of compounding will be mentioned and, therefore, it is

153

relevant to describe, briefly, each of those systems. All refer to the four-cylinder compound arrangement.

(1) The de Glehn (and later, the de Glehn-du Bousquet) system originated on the Northern Railway (Nord) in 1886. The two high pressure cylinders were outside the frames, placed behind the centre line of the bogie and usually driving the second pair of coupled wheels. The low pressure cylinders, inside the frames, were placed further forward and drove the leading pair of coupled wheels through connecting rods of approximately equal length to those of the outside cylinders. Four sets of valve gear were provided and the cut-off was independent for high pressure and low pressure cylinders. Two regulators were provided one of which admitted live steam to the high pressure and the other to the low pressure cylinders. Intercepting valves, under the driver's control, enabled the passages between the high pressure and low pressure cylinders to be closed at will and the high pressure exhaust to pass directly into the blast-pipe. Thus the engines could be worked:

(a) as four-cylinder simples by closing the intercepting valves and opening both regulators,

(b) as two-cylinder simples with the intercepting valves closed and one or other regulator opened,

(c) as a full compound with the intercepting valves open and the high pressure regulator only opened,

(d) as a semi-compound by admitting some live steam to the low pressure cylinders by the second regulator when otherwise the engine was worked as described in (c).

These methods of working provided machines of immense flexibility for all the possible traffic conditions likely to be encountered. But they required well-trained and intelligent men to obtain the best from them.

(2) The PLM system which was originated by Monsieur A. Henry in 1888 was quite different from that of de Glehn. The high pressure cylinders were outside and the low pressure inside the frames; at first the inside cylinders were placed in rear of those outside while later, on the first PLM Pacific, the opposite was true. However, the general development of the PLM compounds was with the four cylinders in line, very short connecting rods being provided to the inside cylinders to enable them to drive the leading axle while those outside drove the second axle. When the PLM 4–8–2s were introduced in 1925, however, the low pressure cylinders were placed outside the frames with their short connecting rods still driving the leading coupled axle and the high pressure inside cylinders were placed well back over that axle to enable them to drive the second coupled axle.

PLM compounds had no intercepting valves but a reducing valve enabled the driver to admit some live steam to the low pressure cylinders when starting. Originally, four sets of Walschaerts valve gear were provided but the cut-off to high pressure and low pressure cylinders was set in a pre-determined ratio and was not independent, except in the Pacifics of Series 231 C 1–86 which became Series 231 K. Later, the inside eccentrics were done away with but the levers from the inside crossheads were retained. Their movement was combined, through rocking shafts, with that from the expansion links of the outside valve gear thus providing for constant variation of cut-off between high pressure and low pressure valves on notching up.

(3)   The Chapelon system was based on modernising and improving the de Glehn compounds of the Paris-Orléans Railway, but the principles involved and the results achieved, were so important that they influenced profoundly the design of steam locomotives both compound and simple throughout the world. Essentially, Chapelon's aims may be summarised thus:

(a) To provide a free steaming economical boiler. This was done mainly by the provision of a thermic syphon in the firebox and an efficient exhaust system. The Kylchap double blastpipe and chimney increased the smokebox vacuum by about 350 per cent without increasing the back pressure in the exhaust passages.

(b) To assist in the free-steaming of the boiler, the feed water was supplied at near boiling point through an ACFI feed water pump and heater.

(c) To provide an efficient and well designed superheater so that the steam reached the high pressure cylinders at about 750° F and was exhausted to the low pressure cylinders while still retaining a comparatively high degree of superheat (90°–110° of superheat was usual).

(d) Completely to redesign the cylinders with steam chests having wide steam passages and oscillating-cam poppet valves, to ensure completely free admission and exhaust on both the high pressure and low pressure sides. The independent cut-off was retained. By such means alone, the effective horsepower output of the low pressure cylinders was increased by as much as 300 per cent. A second regulator was retained to admit live steam to the low pressure cylinders on starting but the intercepting valve was discarded.

As the size and output of locomotives increased, it was the mechanical design and maintenance which became the Achilles heel of the compound locomotives and, although SNCF always asserted that the saving in fuel more than outweighed the increased maintenance costs of compounds over non-compounds, none other of the world's railways was convinced, though Chapelon's principles were almost universally applied to simple locomotives. André Chapelon remains the greatest steam locomotive engineer of modern times.

Locomotive Preservation in France

After years of uncertainty, it has recently been announced that the French National Railway Museum is to be established at Mulhouse. Reports at present suggest that it is to be on the grand scale and will ultimately be the largest railway museum in Europe, housing about 100 full-size locomotives with a separate hall for models and small exhibits.

Initially, however, accommodation will be provided for 30 locomotives and, as far as is known, these will all be of standard, 1435mm, gauge.

Few standard gauge locomotives are preserved in France other than in this national collection. In the following pages are described all those which at this time are scheduled for the museum and those which are kept elsewhere. It is probable that other locomotives will later be included in the collection as there is at present, for example, no representative of the 2–8–2, or Mikado, type. Both simple and compound 2–8–2s have, since World War II, worked more traffic on the SNCF than any other type of steam locomotive. The American-built engines of Series 141 R were equally at home working the "Mistral" between Marseilles and Nice as they were hauling coal trains in Northern France. One of them will, in all probability, be the last steam locomotive in scheduled service in France.

Buddicom 2–2–2 No 3 of the Paris–Rouen Railway. At the Festival of Britain 1951   [P. R-W

No 3 is a 2–2–2 locomotive with inclined outside cylinders, which was built in 1843 as No 33 *SAINT PIERRE* for the Paris-Rouen Railway by Allcard Buddicom at Chartreux, Rouen. It is to be preserved at the Railway Museum at Mulhouse.

157

This locomotive has inside gab type valve gear, the quadrant having only three positions, fore, mid and back gear. The boiler is fed by two crosshead-driven pumps, the injector fitted when it was restored in 1947, is an "essential anachronism". The design closely resembles that of the Allan 2–2–2 locomotives built at Crewe, Buddicom having been closely associated with Allan.

Forty of these engines were built in 1843–4 for the Paris-Rouen Railway which was taken over by the Western Railway who rebuilt 22 of them as 2–2–2 Well Tank locomotives and numbered them 117–138 and later, 0117–0138, No 33 becoming No 131. After 1909 when the Western became part of the State Railways, the surviving engines were numbered in the 12.001 series, and No 131 became No 12.010.

Old No 33 remained in service until 1916 when it was preserved at the Sotteville Works of the State Railways. In 1947 the SNCF restored it to its original form and a new four-wheel tender was made to the Buddicom drawings.

As No 3, it came to England in 1951 and was exhibited at the Festival of Britain. It made part of the journey under its own steam.

Dimensions: CYLINDERS: 355 × 535mm
       DRIVING WHEELS: 1720mm
       GRATE AREA: 0.9m^2
       BOILER PRESSURE: 8.5hpz

No 5, *SEZANNE*, is an outside-cylinder 2–2–2 locomotive which was built in 1846 and delivered in 1847 to the 100km long Montereau-Troyes Railway. It was built by Alfred Hallette at Arras which firm, however, went bankrupt before the order for 16 of these engines had been completed, and some were delivered un-erected. The Montereau-Troyes Railway amalgamated with the Paris-Strasbourg Railway in 1853 which, a year later, became the Eastern Railway of France. No 5 became No 291 of Series 288–299 of the Paris-Strasbourg and then of the Eastern Railway, the remaining four engines having been rebuilt as 2–4–0 Nos 300–303 of the same companies.

These engines were of the Stephenson Long-Boiler type with haycock fireboxes, cylinders horizontally placed outside the frames and gab valve gear between the frames. They had six-wheeled tenders, the handbrakes on which were the only method of stopping the locomotive.

In 1868 this engine became the first in France to be equipped for burning oil fuel. This was the work of a chemist, named Sainte-Claire-Deville. A firebox was built with vertical firebars against which the oil was fed. The heat of the firebars vaporised the oil which then became easily ignited. The bottom of the firebox was made of sheet iron covered with a refractory material and the back and sides were lined with firebrick. The experiment was very successful and the locomotive steamed exceedingly well. The scheme was abandoned because the cost of oil fuel was very much greater than that of coal.

2–2–2 No 5 SEZANNE of the Montereau–Troyes Railway [Michel Lamarche

SEZANNE was withdrawn in 1871 and was for many years kept at Chalon-sur-Marne as an object of interest. In 1926 the engine was rebuilt to its original condition and unfortunately placed on exhibition in the open at the Epernay Works of the Eastern Railway. Ultimately it was stored at Chalon-sur-Saone to await preservation in the Railway Museum.

Dimensions: CYLINDERS: 340 × 550mm
DRIVING WHEELS: 1690mm
GRATE AREA: 0.86m²
BOILER PRESSURE: 6kg/cm²

2–2–2 No 6 L'AIGLE carrying the name PIERROT at Grenoble in 1925 [P. R-W Collection

No 6, *L'AIGLE*, is an outside-cylinder 2–2–2 locomotive built in 1846 by Robert Stephenson (works number not known) for the 120km-long Avignon-Marseilles Railway which was opened to traffic (in sections) between 1847 and 1849. No 6 became No 206 of the Paris-Lyons-Mediterranean Railway (PLM) and was withdrawn from service in 1865. It is to be preserved in the Railway Museum at Mulhouse.

No 6 is one of nine locomotives built for the railway by Robert Stephenson, all of which were named after birds and which were numbered 1 to 9. They were of the Stephenson Long-Boiler type with all three axles in front of the haycock firebox. Two eccentrics were fitted for each slide valve, one for forward and one for backward running; two feed water pumps derived their motion from the backward eccentrics. These locomotives were able to haul 150-tonne trains on the level at 45km/h and their maximum speed (officially) was limited to 60km/h.

On its withdrawal from service, No 6 was used as a mobile steam boiler until 1913 after which it was restored by the works at Oullins and used for exhibition purposes. At an exhibition at Grenoble in 1925 it appeared with the name *PIERROT* (carried originally by No 1) but has later been given its proper name, *L'AIGLE* and restored completely to its original condition.

Dimensions: CYLINDERS: 330 × 610mm
COUPLED WHEELS: 1700mm
GRATE AREA: 0.8m²
BOILER PRESSURE: 6kg/cm²

Crampton 4–2–0 No 80 LE CONTINENT during the PLM Centenary Celebrations at Marseilles 1963   [P. R-W

No 80, *LE CONTINENT*, is an outside-cylinder Crampton locomotive built in 1852 by J. F. Cail (works number 187) for the Paris-Strasbourg Railway which became the Eastern Railway (*Est*) in 1854.

No 80 has been restored and is maintained in working order at a depot in Paris; it is used, hauling a train of contemporary vehicles, for various historic railway occasions and celebrations all over France. On such occasions it carries on its buffer beam, an inscription of the railway it is at that time representing and has thus apparently belonged to the PLM, the P-O and several other companies! Historical purists are inclined to blanche on seeing No 80 so bedecked but behind the paint, this is probably the finest working historical locomotive in the world.

Twelve of these engines were built by Cail, largely as a result of the successful operation of similar engines on the Northern Railway (*Nord*). Others followed later and, until 1878, all the express train services on the Est were worked by Crampton locomotives.

No 80 was withdrawn from service in 1914 and, after World War I, was restored externally and later was on exhibition at the *Gare de l'Est* in Paris. In 1946 it was taken to Epernay and restored mechanically to near its original condition. It was, however, fitted with a steel, instead of a copper, firebox and was designed to burn briquettes instead of coke. It also was given an injector (well concealed) to supplement the axle-driven feed pump. There are no brakes on the locomotive; only the tender has a hand-operated brake to all of its four wheels.

Dimensions: CYLINDERS: 400 × 560mm   GRATE AREA: 1.3m²
               DRIVING WHEELS: 2300mm   BOILER PRESSURE: 8kg/cm²

No 120 A 36 restored as Etat *No 120.036*　　　　　　　　　　[SNCF

No 120 A 36 was originally State Railways (*Etat*) 2029 *RUELLE* and then was No 120–036. It is an outside-cylinder 2–4–0 with slide valves operated by Allan link motion. It was built in 1882 by Schneider (works number 2122) and it will be preserved in the Railway Museum at Mulhouse.

　　These locomotives originated on the Vendée Railway in 1873 and when that company was amalgamated with the Charentes Railway and with other smaller companies to form the State Railways (*Etat*) in 1878, these 2–4–0s were built in considerable numbers. They were characterised by their low-pitched boilers and narrow fireboxes fitted between inside frames. They had very large driving wheels.

　　The Chief Locomotive Engineer of the State Railways in 1884 was M. Ricour and he was concerned to prevent dust and ashes being drawn into the cylinders by the lifting of the slide valves from their seats when the engines were running with steam shut off. Accordingly he designed a piston valve which had ordinary split rings and was fitted with an anti-vacuum (snifting) valve. These valves proved to be very successful and about 150 of the 2–4–0s were fitted with them between 1884 and 1894. Engines so fitted also had outside Walschaerts valve gear with a single eccentric in place of the Allan link motion. This was the first large-scale application of piston valves in Europe.

The 2–4–0s worked nearly all the *Etat* express trains for many years. They were fast and reliable but, loads in excess of 100 tonnes were difficult and over 200 tonnes, impossible to time. At high speeds (75–100km/h) they were unsteady and many were rebuilt with a trailing wheel under the cab, converting them to 2–4–2.

Dimensions: CYLINDERS: 440 × 650mm
(*as built*) COUPLED WHEELS: 2020mm
GRATE AREA: 1.33m^2
BOILER PRESSURE: 8kg/cm^2

No 121 A 340 of the Paris–Orléans Railway   [Maurice Maillet

No 121 A 340 is an outside-cylinder 2–4–2 built as No 340 for the Paris-Orleans Railway (P-O) in 1883 by Sharp-Stewart. It is to be preserved at Mulhouse in the Railway Museum.

The P-O 2–4–2s were first put into service in 1873 having been designed by the Chief Mechanical Engineer of the company, Monsieur V. Forquenot. They were direct descendents of the previous 2–4–0s which, like those of the *Etat* (qv), were found to be unstable at high speeds and had been rebuilt as 2–4–2. The P-O 2–4–2 engines continued the practice of low-pitched boilers, narrow fireboxes and outside cylinders with slide valves, but they had Gooch valve gear in place of Allan link motion.

In 1890, some of these locomotives, along with some of other types, were fitted very successfully with a form of Corless valve gear designed by Durant and Lencauchez. The primary two-eccentric drive of the Gooch gear was retained.

These engines and their many slide valve sisters, worked the Paris-Bordeaux *"rapides"* with great regularity and reliability during the period 1875–1885.

Dimensions: CYLINDERS: 440 × 650mm
           COUPLED WHEELS: 2000mm
           GRATE AREA: 1.62m^2
           BOILER PRESSURE: 10kg/cm^2

No 701 4-cylinder compound 4–2–2 of the Nord   [SNCF

No 701 of the Northern Railway (*Nord*) was the first de Glehn-du Bousquet four-cylinder compound. It was built as a 2–2–2 in 1885 by Société Alsacienne (works number 3755) and rebuilt with a leading outside-frame bogie as a 4–2–2 in 1892. It is to be preserved in the Railway Museum at Mulhouse.

These elegant machines had the high-pressure cylinders outside the frames and they drove the second driving axle while the low-pressure cylinders inside the frames drove the leading driving axle. The two driving axles were not coupled (*cf* some of F. W. Webb's three-cylinder compounds for the LNWR of the same period) and the cut-off was independent for the high-pressure and low-pressure cylinders. They had long Belpaire fireboxes and extended smokeboxes were fitted in 1899.

No 701 was shown at the Paris Exhibition of 1889.

Dimensions: CYLINDERS: HIGH PRESSURE: 330×610mm
                        LOW PRESSURE: 460×610mm
        DRIVING WHEELS: 2114mm
        GRATE AREA: 2.38m²
        BOILER PRESSURE: 11kg/cm²

PLM 4–4–0 No C 145   [Maurice Maillet

No C 145 (later No 220 A 85) is a four-cylinder compound 4–4–0 built by the Paris-Lyons-Mediterranean Railway (PLM) in their works at Arles in 1902. It is to be preserved in the Railway Museum at Mulhouse.

One hundred and twenty of these engines ("the big Cs") were built between 1899 and 1902 having been constructed in batches by various builders, including some by Wiener-Neustadt. They were Henry-Baudry compounds with high pressure cylinders outside the frames driving the second coupled axle and low pressure inside driving the leading coupled axle. They had Walschaerts valve gear and slide valves above the cylinders. Unlike the *Nord* engines (page 165) the driving wheels were coupled and the cut-off was not independent for high pressure and low pressure cylinders. The boiler pressure was comparatively high—15kg/cm². Some of the engines, including No C 145, were fitted with Stroudley speed indicators.

In an attempt to nullify the effects of the strong winds encountered in the Valley of the Rhone (notably the *Mistral*), M. Ricour, the designer, arranged a form of streamlining. The smokebox front, the leading edge of the Belpaire firebox cleading and the spectacle plate of the cab were all wedge-shaped while the space between chimneys and dome was enclosed by two steel plates. This gave the locomotives the name "COUP VENTS" or wind cutters.

These 4–4–0s were excellent and speedy machines, capable of hauling 200-tonne trains on the level at 100km/h.

Dimensions: CYLINDERS: HIGH PRESSURE: 340 × 620mm
LOW PRESSURE: 540 × 620mm
COUPLED WHEELS: 2000mm
GRATE AREA: 2.48m²
BOILER PRESSURE: 15kg/cm²

Nord *4-4-2 No 2.670*   [Michel Lamarche

No 221 A 30 was Northern Railway (*Nord*) No 2.670, a de Glehn-du Bousquet four-cylinder compound 4-4-2, built in 1903 by Cail (works number 2612). It will be preserved in the Railway Museum.

The two prototype Atlantics Nos 2641 and 2642 went into service in 1900. They were followed later the same year by the first of a further 33 engines which were delivered over the next five years. These engines were slightly modified, having a longer bogie wheelbase and driving from the Left-hand side instead of the Right.

The de Glehn-du Bousquet system has already been described (page 154) and the Nord Atlantics certainly proved its value. They were, however, at their best after rebuilding in 1912 when they were given Schmidt superheaters and piston valves for the high pressure cylinders which were larger in diameter than the previous cylinders (390mm instead of 340mm). From 1930, some of the Atlantics had Lemaître blastpipes with wide chimneys and they also had large capacity bogie tenders.

The exploits of the Nord Atlantics were, to say the least, fabulous. Their everyday work involved hauling 400-tonne trains on the level at 120km/h and their hill-climbing capabilities have probably never been excelled by any locomotive of comparable size and power.

167

No 2670 will be preserved in its rebuilt (1912) form and the dimensions given are relative to this.

Dimensions: CYLINDERS: HIGH PRESSURE: 390 × 640mm
                                LOW PRESSURE: 560 × 640mm
              COUPLED WHEELS: 2040mm
              GRATE AREA: $2.76m^2$
              BOILER PRESSURE: $16kg/cm^2$
              SUPERHEATED

PLM "BOURBONNAIS" 0–6–0 No 3 B 87   [P. R-W

No 030 A 1 was originally No 1423 of the Paris-Lyon Railway built in 1854 by Cail. It is to be preserved in the Railway Museum at Mulhouse.

    The two cylinders are outside the frames and drive the middle pair of coupled wheels. Inside Stephenson link motion actuates slide valves. The firebox is completely behind the trailing coupled axle and the total wheelbase is only 3370mm with a maximum axle-load of 14 tonnes. A large dome containing the regulator is on the first ring of the boiler and is surmounted by Salter-type safety valves. Originally the engines had no cab—only a weatherboard and brakes were only on the four wheels of the tender.

    This specification is for the 1,057 locomotives built between 1854 and 1882 though, as would be expected, details varied and boiler pressures increased from 8.5kg/cm² to 10kg/cm². Early engines were without domes. The name *"Bourbonnais"* was given collectively to this type of locomotive in France and for many years they formed the backbone of PLM freight locomotive power. More than a dozen builders shared in their construction in addition to those built in the works of the railway.

Between 1907 and 1913, 215 of these locomotives were reconstructed as 0–6–0 Side Tanks for shunting.

Dimensions: CYLINDERS: 450 × 650mm

COUPLED WHEELS: 1300mm

GRATE AREA: 1.34m²

BOILER PRESSURE: 10kg/cm²

No 030 C 581 ex Ouest *was an engine of the same class as the two preserved locomotives*   [P. R-W

No 030 C 815 was No 2.199 of the Western Railway (*Ouest*) and then, after 1909, No 030–815 of the State Railways (*Etat*). It was built in 1880, and it will be restored and placed in the Railway Museum at Mulhouse.

No 030 C 841 is identical with No 030 C 815 and has also been preserved. It is in the Canadian Railway Museum at Delson, Montreal.

Three hundred and twenty-eight of these engines were built between 1866 and 1885 by various locomotive works and many survived to come into the SNCF. The design is obviously based on the "*Bourbonnais*" engines of the PLM (qv) the main difference being that the slide valves are above the cylinders and are actuated by outside Stephenson link motion. The huge, rather ornamental domes were originally surmounted by Salter-type safety valves, but these were gradually removed in later days. The wheelbase, at 3700mm is somewhat greater than that of the PLM engines but the maximum axle-load is the same—14 tonnes.

Dimensions: CYLINDERS: 460 × 640mm

COUPLED WHEELS: 1450mm

GRATE AREA: 1.5m²

BOILER PRESSURE: 9kg/cm²

(*raised to 11kg/cm² when boilers were renewed*)

Nord *0–6–0 No 3486*   [SNCF

No 3486 was built for the Northern Railway (*Nord*) in 1890 by the
Société Alsacienne (works number 4230) and it will be preserved in the
Railway Museum.

One hundred and twelve of these locomotives were built for the Nord
between 1883 and 1891 and they were very English-looking machines
with outside frames and axle boxes, inside cylinders and slide valves
operated by Stephenson link motion. The Belpaire firebox is placed above
the trailing axle. They thus present a complete contrast to the
"*Bourbonnais*" of the PLM (qv).

These *Nord* engines were classified as "mixed traffic".

Dimensions: CYLINDERS: 480 × 610mm
               COUPLED WHEELS: 1664mm
               GRATE AREA: 2.41m^2
               BOILER PRESSURE: 10kg/cm^2

No 230 B 84 ex PLM was a sister engine of the preserved locomotive   [P. R-W

No 230 B 114 was No 2714 of the Paris-Lyon-Mediterranean Railway (PLM) and it was built in 1909 by Henschel to the design of the Chief Engineer of the PLM, Monsieur Ch. Baudry. It is to be preserved in the Railway Museum.

One hundred and sixty of these four-cylinder compound 4–6–0 locomotives were built between 1904 and 1909 as Nos 2601–2760 for express train services on the main lines of the PLM. They performed adequately until, after 1909, the new Pacifics gradually displaced them to secondary duties.

They had Belpaire fireboxes and the cylinders were in line under the smokebox, the high pressure cylinders being outside the frames. Four sets of Walschaerts valve gear operated piston valves on all four cylinders but, surprisingly, only 15 of the class were superheated.

In 1938-9, nine of these engines were rebuilt at Oullins Works with new cylinders having large steam passages, improved exhaust arrangements, ACFI feed water pumps and heaters and superheaters. These were Class 230 F and the War put an end to further rebuilding.

Dimensions: CYLINDERS HIGH PRESSURE: 340 × 650mm
                 LOW PRESSURE: 540 × 650mm
       COUPLED WHEELS: 2000mm
       GRATE AREA: 2.98m^2
       BOILER PRESSURE: 16kg/cm^2

No 230.531 of the Ouest   [Maurice Maillet

No 230 C 531 was originally No 2731 of the Western Railway (*Ouest*) and then No 230–531 of the State Railways (*Etat*) when the Western was taken over by the State Railways in 1909. The engine was built in 1904 by Batignolles (works number 1541) and it is to be preserved in the Railway Museum at Mulhouse.

This locomotive is one of 120 four-cylinder compound 4–6–0s built between 1901 and 1908 for the Western Railway, the first ten of which were the first 4–6–0 express passenger locomotives in France. They were not more powerful than the Atlantics but the additional coupled wheel gave much needed extra adhesion on heavy and fast duties. The engines had high pressure cylinders outside the frames driving the second coupled axle and the inside low pressure cylinders drove the leading coupled axle. The first 20 engines had slide valves and straight running plates. The following 98 engines of which No 2731 is an example, had piston valves and the running plates were raised above the coupled wheels. The last two engines were also superheated.

Dimensions: CYLINDERS HIGH PRESSURE: 350 × 640mm
LOW PRESSURE: 550 × 640mm
COUPLED WHEELS: 1940mm
GRATE AREA: 2.45m²
BOILER PRESSURE: 15kg/cm²

No 230 B 614 ex Midi

[Maurice Maillet

No 230 B 614 was No 1314 of the Midi Railway, built in 1902 by Société Alsacienne to the designs of Monsieur de Glehn. It is scheduled for preservation in the Railway Museum at Mulhouse.

This engine is a de Glehn four-cylinder compound 4–6–0 with high pressure outside cylinders driving the second coupled axle and inside low pressure cylinders driving the leading coupled axle. The cut-off is independent for high pressure and low pressure cylinders and Walschaerts valve gear operates the slide valves. A Belpaire boiler and outside bogie frames complete the identity between these engines and those of the Northern (*Nord*), Paris-Orleans (P-O) and of the State (*Etat*) Railways. Similar engines were also built for both Spain and Portugal.

There were two classes of these engines on the *Midi*, 30 with coupled wheels of 1600mm diameter for mixed traffic duties and 68 (of which No 1314 was one) with coupled wheels 1750mm for main line express duties. They were excellent and economical machines.

Dimensions: CYLINDERS HIGH PRESSURE: 350 × 640mm
                     LOW PRESSURE: 550 × 640mm
      COUPLED WHEELS: 1750mm
      GRATE AREA: 2.49m^2
      BOILER PRESSURE: 15kg/cm^2

No 230 G 207 ex P-O was identical with the preserved locomotive   [P. R-W

No. 230 G 352 is a two-cylinder simple superheated 4–6–0 built in 1922 by Batignolles for the Paris-Orléans Railway. It has been restored in working order and purchased by Monsieur Jean Metz, 9 Allée du Beaséjour, Tours, I. et L. It is at present in store at the SNCF Depot at Saint Pierre des Corps and its final destination is not known.

One hundred and seventy of these mixed traffic locomotives (Nos 4201–4370) were built, in batches, for the P-O between 1914 and 1922. The bogies and the Belpaire boilers were identical with those of an earlier series of 4–6–0 express locomotives (series 3200), and the design of the 4201 appeared to be a small-wheel version of the older engines. They were, however, not such good machines and, after various blast-pipe modifications, the Kylala cured their inability to steam freely. They rode badly at high speeds but were very strongly built and maintenance costs were low.

Twenty of the engines went to Morocco in 1934 and, in 1938, 51 went to the State Railways (*Etat*) where they were put to work in Brittany. On the SNCF the P-O engines were series 230 G of Region 4 while the *Etat* engines became 230 K 401–451 of Region 3.

Dimensions: CYLINDERS: 500 × 650mm
COUPLED WHEELS: 1760mm
GRATE AREA: 2.8m²
BOILER PRESSURE: 12hpz
SUPERHEATED

No 230 D 9 ex Nord

[SNCF

No 230 D 9 was No 3521 of the Northern Railway (*Nord*). It is a de Glehn-du Bousquet four-cylinder compound 4–6–0 built in 1908 at the Company's Works at La Chapelle. It is to be preserved in the Railway Museum at Mulhouse.

The Nord 3500 Class 4–6–0s first appeared in 1908 and 149 were built between then and 1912. The first 25, Nos 3513–3538 (of which No 230 D 9 is one) were built by the Nord and were saturated engines with slide valves to both high pressure and low pressure cylinders. The remainder of the class were built by private firms in 1911–12 and they had Schmidt superheaters and piston valves for the (outside) high pressure cylinders. The original engines, from 1929 on, were rebuilt to conform with these later engines. Finally, all the engines of the class were fitted with wide diameter chimneys and Lemaître blast pipes. They were the first locomotives to be fitted with the standard smokebox doors having in the centre, the small bronze medallion inscribed *NORD*.

These locomotives were designed as mixed traffic machines, with a maximum axle-load of 17 tonnes, intermediate between the Atlantic and the Pacific designs. They were highly successful and proved themselves capable of hauling fast and heavy express trains on schedules which were never envisaged at the time they were built.

Dimensions: CYLINDERS HIGH PRESSURE: 380 × 640mm
               LOW PRESSURE: 550 × 640mm
    COUPLED WHEELS: 1750mm
    GRATE AREA: 2.8m²
    BOILER PRESSURE: 16hpz
    SUPERHEATED

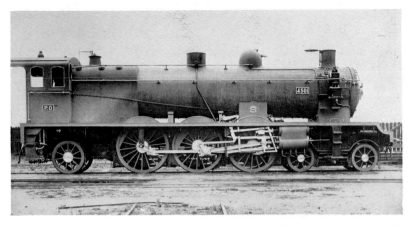

Paris–Orléans 4-cylinder compound No 4501 the first European Pacific and the first of class to which No 231 A 546 belongs [Soc. Alsacienne

No 231 A 546 was No 4546 of the Paris-Orléans Railway (P-O) and it was built in 1908 by The American Locomotive Company (ALCO), works number 42013. It is a de Glehn-du Bousquet four-cylinder compound 4–6–2 which has been restored, as nearly as possible, to its original condition and it will be preserved in the Railway Museum.

P-O Nos 4501 and 4502 were the first Pacific type locomotives in Europe. They were built by Société Alsacienne and went to Limoges Depot in 1907. They were followed, in 1908, by 68 further engines, Nos 4503–4570 of the same class and which were supplied by several different builders. These engines had certain improvements made in the boiler and the steam distribution valves as the performance of the first two had not been entirely satisfactory and they steamed badly.

All these 70 engines had piston valves to the high-pressure but slide valves to the low-pressure cylinders, and they all used saturated steam.

In 1910, a further 30 engines were put into service (Nos 4571–4600) and these were superheated and had piston valves for all four cylinders. After 1928, the original 70 engines including (No 4546) were rebuilt with piston valves to the low pressure cylinders, superheaters, trefoil or single Kylchap blast-pipes and exhaust steam injectors. They were also given smoke deflectors which brought their appearance up-to-date and matched their vastly improved performance.

Dimensions (as built): CYLINDERS HIGH PRESSURE: 390 × 650mm
LOW PRESSURE: 640 × 650mm
COUPLED WHEELS: 1850mm
GRATE AREA: 4.27m²
BOILER PRESSURE: 16kg/cm²

177

No 231 E 22 ex Nord   [Brian Garvin

No 231 E 22 was No 3.1192 of the Northern Railway (*Nord*) and it was
built in 1936 by Blanc-Misseron (works number 421). This locomotive
was to have been preserved in Switzerland by the *Association pour la
Conservation de Locomotives et de Matériel Ferroviaire.* This Society no longer
exists and No 231 E 22 is to go to the Railway Museum.

   Twenty Pacifics, Nos 3.1171–3.1190 (SNCF 231 E 1–20) were bought
by the *Nord* in 1934 from the Paris-Orléans Railway (P-O) where they
had been made redundant by electrification. They were originally engines
of the P-O series 3501–3589 which were built between 1909 and 1914 and
which were rebuilt in 1933–4 in the P-O works at Tours to the design of
Monsieur André Chapelon.

   The purchase of these engines had been preceded, in 1932–3 by a
series of comparative trials with fast and heavy trains on the Nord main
lines between Paris and Boulogne and Paris and Calais. Two Pacifics,
No 3.1289, a Nord Super Pacific and No 3715, a P-O Chapelon rebuild,
took part and they were matched against two four-cylinder compound
4–8–2s, No 241 C 1 of the PLM and No 241–003 of the Eastern Railway
(*Est*). The results outstandingly favoured the Chapelon engine.

   Twenty-eight further engines were built new for the *Nord* by Blanc-
Misseron, FAMH and Fives-Lille during 1936–7 and these 48 Pacifics
were the mainstay of the express services on the Nord main lines until they
were replaced by electric and diesel traction.

   They were four-cylinder compound 4–6–2s with the low pressure cylinders between the frames and all four cylinders had Dabeg oscillating cam poppet valves. There were four sets of Walschaerts valve gear and independent cut-off for the high pressure and the low pressure cylinders. When steam was shut off, the valves were lifted from their seatings by servo motors controlled by the main regulator handle so that there was no back pressure.

The main regulator had a ratchet quadrant enabling accurate settings to be made and kept. A second regulator handle controlled the admission of high pressure steam to the low pressure cylinders.

The Belpaire firebox had a trapezoidal grate and a single thermic syphon. A Kylchap double blast-pipe and chimney were fitted. The boiler was fed by an ACFI feed water pump with heater and a Friedmann injector.

Dimensions: CYLINDERS HIGH PRESSURE: 420 × 650mm
                LOW PRESSURE: 640 × 650mm
       COUPLED WHEELS: 1950mm
       GRATE AREA: 4.33m²
       BOILER PRESSURE: 17hpz
       SUPERHEATED

No 231 C 72 ex Nord *was identical with the preserved locomotive*   [P. R-W

No 231 C 78 was No 3.1280 of the Northern Railway (*Nord*) and was built in 1930 by Cail (works number 4142). It is to be preserved in the Railway Museum.

This is one of the famous *Nord* Super-Pacifics which were (with two exceptions) four-cylinder de Glehn-du Bousquet compounds and were

179

very complicated engines to drive. They could be worked as compound, semi-compound, or simple. The boilers had Belpaire fireboxes with long narrow grates completely between the frames. They were reasonably good engines but with the advent of the Chapelon Pacifics on the *Nord* they were largely relegated to the less important main line trains.

Different batches of *Nord* Super-Pacifics showed various modifications and alterations in the basic design and the most important of these may be summarised thus:

Nos 3.1201–3.1223 of 1923–4 had single steam domes, balanced slide valves to the low pressure cylinders and the footplating was interrupted at the front end of the cylinders, the forward part being at a lower level.

Nos 3.1224–3.1240 of 1923–4 had piston valves to all four cylinders.

Nos 3.1241–3.1248 of 1930 reverted to low pressure slide valves but they, and all subsequent engines, had two steam domes with a sand dome in between, all under a single casing. (This arrangement was later modified to a double and a single casing). The heating surfaces of the boiler were modified.

Nos 3.1249 and 3.1250 were built as two-cylinder simple engines with rotary cam poppet valves the first having Caprotti valves and No 3.1250, Dabeg. In 1934 these engines were both rebuilt with Cossart valve gear.

Nos 3.1251–3.1290, the series which includes the preserved engine, were again modified by M. de Caso. The footplating was raised in front of the outside cylinders to give access to the low pressure cylinders below the smokebox, and the engines were fitted with smoke deflectors. The low pressure cylinders were given piston valves with the large diameter of 380mm. The two steam domes were retained, the second dome containing a regulator which admitted live steam to the low pressure cylinders. The frames were strengthened and the exterior of the engine was "cleaned up" by careful locating of pumps, turbo-generator etc and covering them where possible.

All the engines were later fitted with Lemaître blastpipes and chimneys and some had Pottier glass-less spectacles. No 3.1280 was partly stream-lined and was especially painted to work the Royal Train carrying King George VI and Queen Elizabeth from Boulogne to Paris on July 19, 1938. It also worked the inaugural "Night Ferry" train between Dunkirk and Paris, being painted Wagon-Lits blue for the occasion. It had the streamline casing removed in 1946.

Dimensions: CYLINDERS HIGH PRESSURE: 440 × 660mm
 LOW PRESSURE: 620 × 690mm
 COUPLED WHEELS: 1900mm
 GRATE AREA: 3.48m^2
 BOILER PRESSURE: 17hpz
 SUPERHEATED

No 231 K 27 ex PLM at work on the Nord *main line. This locomotive was identical with 231 K 22*
[P. R-W

No 231 K 22 is a four-cylinder compound 4–6–2 of the PLM built in 1912 by Ateliers de la Loire as PLM No 6222. It has been purchased by the Lakeside Railway Estate Company Ltd of Carnforth, England where it now is preserved.

No 231 H 28 ex PLM was identical with the preserved locomotive   [P. R-W

No 231 H 8 is a four-cylinder compound 4–6–2 of the Paris-Lyons-Mediterranean Railway (PLM) which was built in 1911 as PLM No 6143

181

by Cail. It was later 231 A 43, then 231 E 43 and, in 1934, 231 H 8. It is to be preserved in the Railway Museum at Mulhouse.

To know about these locomotives it is necessary, briefly, to describe something of their ancestry.

The first PLM Pacifics went into service in 1909, two years after the first Pacific of the P-O and one year after those of the Western Railway (*Ouest*). The first two PLM engines were built in the Company's works in Paris. They were, first, No 6101, a four-cylinder simple engine with four cylinders in line and using superheated steam at a pressure of 12kg/cm². Second was No 6001, a four-cylinder compound with divided drive, the low-pressure, inside cylinders being placed further forward than the outside high-pressure cylinders. This engine used saturated steam at 16kg/cm². It later became No 231 C I. Before a final decision on the merits of each engine had been made, 70 more engines of the 6101 series had been built, 30 by Henschel in 1911 and the remainder by Cail in 1912. The 6101 engines became Nos 231 A 1–71 and they were followed by Nos 6172–6191 built by Batignolles in 1913 with superheaters and 14kg/cm² pressure. These engines became 231 B 1–20.

Starting in 1912, Henschel built 20 more four-cylinder compound engines which became 231 C and had all four cylinders in line. World War I interrupted the delivery of later engines of this series and 40 came from La Loire between 1914 and 1921 while Société Alsacienne delivered 25 between 1919 and 1921 making a total of 86 engines Nos 231 C 1–86. These engines all used superheated steam at 16kg/cm² and they had Baudry valve gear with independent cut-off for high pressure and low pressure cylinders.

Between 1922 and 1925, three French builders delivered 230 similar engines which, however, had the high-pressure and low-pressure cut-off combined in a fixed ratio and not independently under control of the driver. These were, later, Nos 231 D 1–230 and they were followed by 55 engines which had ACFI feed water pumps and heaters but which were otherwise identical. These later became Nos 231 F 231–285 but afterwards became Series 231 G.

Altogether 462 PLM Pacifics were built most of which were rebuilt or modified at least once. The main improvements were the provision of ACFI feed water pumps and heaters and the fitting of trefoil blast pipes. Later, new cylinders with greatly improved steam passages and double blast pipes and chimneys were fitted. Engines so rebuilt were re-classified, those of Series 231 D becoming 231 G and those of 231 C becoming 231 K, and of which No. 231 K 22 is one.

The four-cylinder simple engines, Nos 231 A 1–71 were rebuilt as superheated compounds during 1925–30. They had new boilers but retained their 12kg/cm² pressure. They then became Nos 231 E 1–71. Nos 231 B 1–20 were similarly rebuilt and kept their original pressure (14kg/cm²) but were not re-numbered.

Between 1934 and 1948, some engines of the Series 231 E, 231 B and one of 231 D, 30 in all, were again rebuilt. This time, the diameter of the high pressure cylinders was reduced and the boiler pressure was raised to 20kg/cm². They were, of course, superheated and the last three had Chantelot valve gear. These engines comprised Series 231 H of which No 231 H 8 is preserved.

Dimensions: *No 231 K 22*

CYLINDERS HIGH PRESSURE: 440×650mm

LOW PRESSURE: 650×650mm

COUPLED WHEELS: 2010mm

GRATE AREA: $4.3m^2$

BOILER PRESSURE: 16kg/cm²

SUPERHEATED

No 231 H 8

CYLINDERS HIGH PRESSURE: 400×650mm

LOW PRESSURE: 650×650mm

COUPLED WHEELS: 2010mm

GRATE AREA: $4.3m^2$

BOILER PRESSURE: 20kg/cm²

SUPERHEATED

No 231 D 587 ex Etat *was an identical locomotive with No 231 D 596*

No 231 D 596 was No 231–596 of the State Railways (*Etat*) built in 1921 by Batignolles-Châtillon (works number 95). This locomotive is to be preserved and will be placed in the Railway Museum.

In 1913, the *Etat* required more Pacific locomotives and their Chief Engineer, Monsieur M. Nadal decided to adopt the design of the *Paris-Orléans* Series 3551–3589.

These locomotives were superheated de Glehn-du Bousquet four-cylinder compounds and, on the P-O main lines they had been proved to be fast, reliable and economical when working some of the heaviest and fastest trains in Europe at that time. The *Etat* machines were identical in design with the exception of the firebox which was of the round-top type, with a wide grate, instead of the Belpaire firebox used on the P-O.

As a result of World War I, construction was delayed: deliveries began slowly in 1916 and the order for 283 engines (Nos 231.501–783) was not completed until 1923. The design was adopted by the Ministry of Public Works (*Travaux Publics*) and locomotives were supplied to the Alsace-Lorraine, the Northern, Eastern and Paris-Orléans Railways. (The P-O ultimately sold theirs to the *Etat* who numbered them 231–401 to 420). All the *Etat* engines became SNCF Series 3–231 C.

Good as they were in their original form, nearly all the *Etat* engines were rebuilt in various and different ways. By far the largest number (134) were rebuilt with oscillating cam Lentz-Dabeg poppet valves in place of the slide valves, for the low pressure cylinders while retaining the piston valves of the high pressure cylinders. The superheater was enlarged to provide higher steam temperatures and a single Kylchap blast-pipe with wide chimney replaced the original trefoil type. A balanced crank-axle was fitted.

These very successful rebuilds were SNCF Series 3–231 D and No 231 D 596 is one of them.

It has a tender fitted with a water scoop, the *Etat* being the only railway in France to have track-troughs.

Dimensions: CYLINDERS HIGH PRESSURE: 420×650mm

LOW PRESSURE: 640×650mm

COUPLED WHEELS: 1950mm

GRATE AREA: 4.3m^2

BOILER PRESSURE: 16hpz

SUPERHEATED

Nord No 3.1101 was the first of the two 4–6–4s of which No 3.1102 is preserved
[C. de F. du Nord

No 3.1102 of the Northern Railway (*Nord*) is a de Glehn-du Bousquet four-cylinder compound superheated 4–6–4 locomotive built in 1911 at the Company's works at La Chapelle. It has been sectioned and will be exhibited in the Railway Museum at Mulhouse.

Nord No 3.1102 as sectioned and on view at the Paris Exposition 1937   [P. R-W Collection

Two of these very large and powerful locomotives were built at La Chapelle, the first, No 3.1101 appearing in 1910. They had many interesting features one of which was the way in which the large low pressure cylinders were fitted between the frames. In order to avoid slotting, and so weakening, the frames the low pressure cylinders were "stepped", the Right hand cylinder being placed in front of the Left hand cylinder so that nearly half of the back cover of the latter was in apposition with a corresponding part of the front cover of the Right hand cylinder. The Right hand piston rod was thus the longer by an amount equal to the length of the Left hand cylinder. These low pressure cylinders had slide valves but the outside high pressure cylinders had piston valves. There were four sets of Walschaerts valve gear.

The very large boiler of No 3.1101 had a Belpaire firebox while that of No 3.1102 had a round top box of the "Du Temple" type with 623 water tubes and a combustion chamber. This boiler was built by Schneider and it was replaced by a Belpaire boiler in 1913 as it was found impossible to keep the water tubes tight.

These engines were interesting failures especially as they would never steam freely and they were probably in advance of their time. Four famous engineers were concerned in their design—Messrs du Bousquet, Demoulin, Asselin and Koechlin.

The sectioning of No 3.1102 was carried out for the 1937 Exhibition of "*Arts et Techniques*" in Paris.

Dimensions: CYLINDERS HIGH PRESSURE: 450×640mm

LOW PRESSURE: 620×730mm

COUPLED WHEELS: 2040mm

GRATE AREA: $4.28m^2$

BOILER PRESSURE: $16kg/cm^2$

SUPERHEATED

No 232 U I

[SNCF

No 232 U 1 of the Nord Region of the SNCF is a four-cylinder compound 4–6–4 which was built in 1949 by Corpet-Louvet (works number 1908) and is to be preserved in the Railway Museum.

In 1936 on the initiative of M. de Caso, Chief Mechanical Engineer of the Northern Railway (*Nord*) a study of the comparative merits of three-cylinder simple and four-cylinder compound high-power locomotives was made and the result was the building by Société Alsacienne of four three-cylinder 4–6–4 locomotives of Class 232 R and the order for four similar four-cylinder compounds (232 S). After three of the latter were completed the decision was made to complete the last one as a Ljungström turbine locomotive. The outbreak of World War II, however, stopped the project and not until 1949 was the last engine delivered.

By this time, the decision was made to complete the engine as a compound, on the same plan as the 232 S with low pressure cylinders outside the frames but having piston valves and Walschaerts valve gear with fixed ratios between the cut-off on the high pressure and low pressure cylinders instead of rotary cam poppet valves. There are roller bearings on all axles and the maximum axle load is 23 tonnes.

The boiler has a large round-top firebox with a combustion chamber and three arch tubes. It is fed by a mechanical stoker. A double blastpipe and chimney, a special and novel system of smoke deflectors and a pleasing semi-streamline fairing go to make this a machine as magnificent in appearance as it was in performance.

Dimensions: CYLINDERS HIGH PRESSURE: 446 × 700mm
                            LOW PRESSURE: 680 × 700mm
          COUPLED WHEELS: 2000m
          GRATE AREA: 5.18m^2
          BOILER PRESSURE: 20hpz
          SUPERHEATED

No 040 A 110 ex PLM was identical with the preserved locomotive   [Maurice Maillet

No 040 A 51 is an 0–8–0 with four-wheeled tender which was originally No 4052 and then 4 A 51 of the Paris-Lyon-Mediterranean Railway (PLM). It is the remaining example of 159 engines of Series 4001–4159 built in the Company's Paris Works and by Société Alsacienne between 1868 and 1887. No 4052 was built by PLM in 1873 and is to be preserved in the Railway Museum at Mulhouse.

When built these engines were equipped with tender brakes only and they had no cabs—only weatherboards. Outside Gooch valve gear operated slide valves above the cylinders but five of the class were rebuilt with piston valves and Walschaerts valve gear in 1887. The firebox is behind the fourth axle and is short and wide, having two firehole doors.

Dimensions: CYLINDERS: 540 × 660mm
                COUPLED WHEELS: 1260mm
                  GRATE AREA: 2.08m²
                BOILER PRESSURE: 10kg/cm²

No 040 B 9 ex 4 B 9 PLM which is preserved   [SNCF

No 040 B 9 was No 3219 and then 4 B 9 of the Paris-Lyon-Mediterranean
Railway (PLM). It was built in 1892 by Schneider (works number 2512)
and is to be preserved in the Railway Museum at Mulhouse.

In 1888, the PLM put into service three series of four-cylinder compound locomotives there being originally two 2–4–2 for express passenger
work, two 0–8–0 with 1270mm coupled wheels for heavy freight on
mountain lines, and two 0–8–0 with 1500mm coupled wheels for fast
freight and mixed traffic on the main line between Paris and Marseilles.

The preserved locomotive is one of 152 locomotives which were built
between 1892 and 1895 to the designs of the mixed traffic 0–8–0 and
which proved to be capable of working main line freight trains of
700 tonnes at 35km/h average on a level track.

The high pressure cylinders are between the frames and drive the third
coupled axle while the outside, low pressure cylinders drive the second
axle. There are four sets of Walschaerts valve gear. The boiler has a
Belpaire firebox.

In 1898–1900, forty of these engines were rebuilt as 4–6–0, the frames
being lengthened at the front-end to accommodate the bogie. They
became Nos 230 D 1–40.

Dimensions: CYLINDERS: HIGH PRESSURE: 360 × 650mm
LOW PRESSURE: 590 × 650mm

COUPLED WHEELS: 1510mm

GRATE AREA: 2.45m^2

BOILER PRESSURE: 15kg/cm^2

191

No 140 A 911 ex Midi, *was identical with No 140 A 908*   [P. R-W

No 140 A 908 is a four-cylinder compound 2–8–0 built in 1904 as No 4008 of the Midi Railway by Cail (works number 2598). It will be preserved in the Railway Museum at Mulhouse.

It is one of a series of 18 locomotives of which the first two, *Midi* Nos 4001 and 4002, were built by Société Alsacienne in 1901 and which were the first 2–8–0 locomotives in France. Nos 4003–4012 came out in 1904 and the last six in 1907. They were built for the freight services on the heavily graded line between Beziers and Neussargues.

The four cylinders are in line, the inside, high pressure, driving the second coupled axle and the outside, low pressure, cylinders the third. The valve gear is Walschaerts with independent cut off for high pressure and low pressure slide valves. The boiler has a Belpaire firebox and the engines were never superheated. In later years, they all had single Kylchap blast-pipes and chimneys.

Dimensions: CYLINDERS: HIGH PRESSURE: 390 × 650mm
                LOW PRESSURE: 600 × 650mm
      COUPLED WHEELS: 1400mm
      GRATE AREA: 2.8m^2
      BOILER PRESSURE: 15kg/cm^2

No 140 A 259 is a four-cylinder compound 2–8–0 which was built in 1928 by Franco-Belge as No 4319 of the Northern Railway (*Nord*). It is to be preserved in the Railway Museum at Mulhouse.

This locomotive was one of 280 which were built, in batches, between 1910 and 1929, originally to replace the 2–6–0 locomotives on the heavy

No 140 A 107 ex Nord *was identical with the preserved locomotive but had a 6-wheeled tender*
[P. R-W

coal trains between Lens and Le Bourget. They were among the most successful locomotives ever to be built in France. They had a maximum speed, officially, of 105km/h but were capable of speed considerably in excess of this and were, at times, used on heavy passenger trains. When built, the "4000" Class were the most powerful 2–8–0s in France.

Their designer was Monsieur Asselin who had succeeded Monsieur du Bousquet as Chief Mechanical Engineer of the *Nord*. The leading radial wheel was braked and was in a truck, the design of which owed much to that of the Alsace bogie. The outside, high pressure, cylinders drove the third pair of coupled wheels, the inside, low pressure, drove the second pair. All the engines were later fitted with smoke deflectors and some with Lemaître blast-pipes. All had feed water pumps and heaters, 12 of which were Worthington and the remainder, ACFI. While most of the class had bogie tenders, some had smaller, six-wheel tenders. In 1930, a further 35 engines of this class were built by Cockerill for the Nord-Belge Railway.

Dimensions: CYLINDERS: HIGH PRESSURE: 420 × 640mm
LOW PRESSURE: 570 × 700mm
COUPLED WHEELS: 1550mm
GRATE AREA: 3.27m²
BOILER PRESSURE: 17hpz
SUPERHEATED

No 140 C 225 was one of the 2–8–0 engines built for ALVF. It had a Dabeg feed-water pump
[P. R-W

No 140 C 344 is a two-cylinder simple 2–8–0 which was built in 1918 by
North British at their Atlas Works, Glasgow (works number 21581). It is
to be preserved in the Railway Museum at Mulhouse.

Three hundred and ninety-two of these engines were supplied by
British and French builders during the years 1913–20 to the order of
Artilleries Lourdes Voies Ferrées (ALVF). They were built, primarily, for
working on the State Railways (*Etat*) but 35 went to the Eastern Railway
(*Est*). A parallel construction was the supply of Robinson 2–8–0s by
various builders to the British War Department during World War I.

They were robust machines with an 18-tonne axle load and they were
among the last steam locomotives to work on SNCF. Many were fitted
with Lemaître five-jet blastpipes and wide chimneys.

Dimensions: CYLINDERS: 590 × 650mm
COUPLED WHEELS: 1450mm
GRATE AREA: 3.2m^2
BOILER PRESSURE: 13hpz on the Etat
14hpz on the Est
SUPERHEATED

Est *No 41001 now preserved*

[P. R-W

No 241 A 1 is a four-cylinder compound 4–8–2 built in 1925 by the Eastern Railway (*Est*) at their works at Epernay as *Est* No 41001 Series XIII, later Est No 241.001. It is to be preserved in the Railway Museum at Mulhouse. This was the first 4–8–2 or Mountain type locomotive in Europe, gaining this distinction by appearing a few months before that of the PLM.

No 41001 is a de Glehn-du Bousquet four-cylinder compound with the outside, high pressure, cylinders driving the second coupled axle and the inside, low pressure, cylinders the first. The maximum axle load is 20 tonnes. Piston valves for all cylinders are operated by four sets of Walschaerts valve gear, the cut-off being independent for high pressure and low pressure cylinders. (Usually, however, in service the driver maintained a predetermined ratio between each group.) The Belpaire firebox has a combustion chamber and the boiler has two domes, the forward one containing the regulator valve and the after one a perforated pipe which supplies dry steam to the regulator in the forward dome.

A backward extension of the main frames, carries the cab, American fashion, so there is no fall-plate. However, owing to the construction of the frames at the rear end, it was never possible to fit these engines with mechanical stokers and their 4.43m² of grate was always hand-fired.

The prototype locomotive was subject to intensive trials, as a result of which the low pressure cylinder diameter was increased and the high pressure steam passages improved. The boiler pressure was raised from 16hpz to 17hpz and several types of smoke deflectors were tried. In 1931 a further 40 locomotives were built for the *Est* by Fives-Lille and these had the boiler pressure raised to 20hpz. They went to work between Paris and Belfort, and Paris and Nancy but, in 1933, it was found necessary again to re-design and improve the steam passages. Feed water heaters (Worthington or ACFI) or exhaust steam injectors were fitted to all the class. One of the class, No 241 A 7 was fitted with a double blast-pipe and chimney.

Trouble was experienced with the frames and the locomotives were rather unstable at high speeds. As a result, they were limited to 105km/h later raised to 110km/h when the frames had been strengthened.

No 241 A 65 ex Etat   [courtesy Monsieur A. W. Glaser

No 241 A 65 was built in 1931 by Fives-Lille (works number 4714) for the State Railways (*Etat*) as their No 241.001. This locomotive has been restored and is preserved by Monsieur A. W. Glaser of Zurich. It is at present in store in a small locomotive shed at Sihlwald near Zurich.

In 1932–33 the State Railways (*Etat*) received from Fives-Lille 49 locomotives identical with the *Est* Series XIII. They were put to work on the Paris-Cherbourg boat trains and also worked between Le Mans and Rennes with express trains from Brittany. The *Etat* did not like them and, as and when the SNCF 141 P became available after World War II, the 4-8-2s were transferred to the Eastern Region to join the original engines of that region. The *Etat* engines all had tenders fitted with water scoops, but as the *Etat* was the only railway in France which had track-troughs, the scoops were removed when the engines were transferred during 1947–50.

Dimensions: CYLINDERS: HIGH PRESSURE: 425 × 720mm
                                 LOW PRESSURE: 660 × 720mm
            COUPLED WHEELS: 1950mm
            GRATE AREA: 4.43m²
            BOILER PRESSURE: 20hpz
            SUPERHEATED

196

No 241 P 17

No 241 P 17 is a four-cylinder compound 4–8–2 which is to be preserved in the Railway Museum at Mulhouse.

It is possible that No 241 P 11, a sister engine, may be preserved and sent to England at the instigation of a private purchaser in Altrincham, Cheshire.

The 35 four-cylinder compound 4–8–2 locomotives of Series 241 P were built by Schneider between 1948 and 1952 and were employed principally on the PLM main line between Paris and Marseilles before electrification. They then were sent, at various times, to work on all the Regions except Region 4, the South West. They are excellent machines and capable of performances which compare favourably with equivalent electric motive power.

The 241 P appeared during the period when Monsieur André Chapelon was Chief of the "Division for Studies of the Steam Locomotive" of SNCF. For various reasons, Chapelon never achieved the senior position of *"Directeur du Seine du Matériel Traction"* and this position was held by Monsieur Parmentier who came from the PLM. Thus PLM influence was often seen in post-war SNCF practice and the Series 241 P derives directly from a PLM 4–8–2.

In 1930, a four-cylinder compound 4–8–2 No 241 C 1, was introduced on the PLM. It remained always the only example of its class and it differed radically from the 145 previous 4–8–2s of that railway. Notably, whereas the previous PLM 4–8–2s had outside, low pressure cylinders driving the first coupled axle while the inside, high pressure cylinders drove the second, in No 241 C 1 the outside drive was to the second

197

coupled axle and the inside drive to the third. In the older engines, the boiler pressure was 16hpz, in No 241 C 1 it was 20hpz and the diameter of both high pressure and low pressure cylinders was reduced. The coupled wheel diameter was increased to 2010mm compared with 1800mm in the older engines.

Eighteen years later, the SNCF engines of Series 241 P were a modernised version of the PLM prototype. The frames of the 241 P were strengthened and the boilers are of welded nickel steel. Thermic syphons, Hulson mechanical stokers, double Kylchap blast-pipes, Houlet superheaters are all modern improvements on the original design. The design of the Series 241 P was carried out by the builders—Schneider and Company, and despite the creation of a modern and powerful machine it was possible to keep the maximum axle-loading to the original figure of 20 tonnes.

Dimensions: CYLINDERS: HIGH PRESSURE: 450 × 650mm

LOW PRESSURE: 680 × 700mm

COUPLED WHEELS: 2010mm

GRATE AREA: 5.1m^2

BOILER PRESSURE: 20hpz

SUPERHEATED

No 150 A 68 was identical with the preserved locomotive   [P. R-W

No 150 A 65 is a de Glehn-du Bousquet four-cylinder compound 2–10–0 which was built in 1912 by Franco-Belge (works number 2013) as No 6065 for the Paris-Orléans Railway (P-O). It is to be preserved in the Railway Museum at Mulhouse.

The 2–10–0 was introduced on the P-O and for the first time in France, by these engines which appeared in 1909. They were the second of the type in Europe, the first being those designed by Gölsdorf for the kkStB in Austria. The 70 P-O engines were built in batches between 1909 and 1913 and the first engines ran for a time with four-wheeled tenders. They were superheated engines with piston valves and had many features in common with the Pacifics of Series 4500 and 3500 of the same company. They were built for heavy freight duties on the steeply graded line between Limoges and Montauban but were also used on passenger trains on this and other difficult sections of the P-O.

In their later years, many of the engines were fitted with ACFI feed water pumps and heaters and some had Kylchap single blast-pipes. One of the class, No 150 A 30, was reconstructed by Monsieur André Chapelon into the experimental six-cylinder triple expansion 2–12–0 No. 160 A 1 in 1939–40.

Dimensions: CYLINDERS: HIGH PRESSURE: 460 × 620mm
                                LOW PRESSURE: 660 × 650mm
            COUPLED WHEELS: 1350mm   BOILER PRESSURE: 16kg/cm^2
            GRATE AREA: 3.8m^2 SUPERHEATED

No 150 P 114 was one of the series of 115 locomotives to which the preserved locomotive belonged
[P. R-W]

No 150 P 13 is a four-cylinder compound 2–10–0 built in 1941 for SNCF by Blanc Misseron (works number 442). It is to be preserved in the Railway Museum at Mulhouse.

The 115 locomotives of SNCF Series 150 P were built between 1939 and 1951. They were almost identical with the 30 engines of Series 150 B of the Northern Railway (*Nord*) which were put into service in 1933–35 and which were a development of the four-cylinder compound 2–10–0s of Series 150 A built in 1912–30. The 2–10–0s of Series 150 B and 150 P, were some of the most remarkable steam locomotives ever built and they were able to work heavy passenger trains at speeds up to 105km/h with the same facility as they worked 2000-tonne coal trains between Lens and Le Bourget. The boilers were identical with those of the *Nord* Pacifics Nos 3.1251–3.1290 but they had a higher pressure of 18hpz instead of 17hpz of the Pacifics.

The *Nord* engines were, later, all equipped with ACFI feed water pumps and heaters, Lemaître blast-pipes and mechanical stokers, the bogie tenders being modified to accommodate this feature. The SNCF Series 150 P were built new with all these features and, in addition, the riveted copper fire boxes of the *Nord* engines were replaced by welded steel fireboxes with a Nicholson thermic syphon. They had built up crank-axles.

Dimensions: CYLINDERS: HIGH PRESSURE: 490 × 640mm
LOW PRESSURE: 680 × 700mm
COUPLED WHEELS: 1550mm
GRATE AREA: 3.54m^3
BOILER PRESSURE: 18hpz
SUPERHEATED

RIMANCOURT o–6–o Side Tank as it appeared when working for Sucrerie de Nangis *as No 3032*
[R. G. Farr

RIMANCOURT is an outside-cylinder o–6–o Side Tank locomotive which is privately preserved in a garden at Thorigny near to Lagny. It carries the inscription EST on the buffer beam and the number 3032. There is no maker's plate.

This locomotive was built in 1886 by Batignolles (works number 1186) and was *Chemins de Fer Economiques* No 3032. It was later owned by the sugar factory at Nangis and retained its old number. Slide valves above the cylinders are operated by outside Allan link motion.
Dimensions: NOT KNOWN

No 030 TA 698 ex Ouest *was identical with the preserved No 030 TA 628*　　　[P. R-W

No 030 TA 628 is an outside-cylinder o–6–o Side Tank shunting locomotive built in 1870 for the Western Railway (*Ouest*) as their No 1038.
When the *Ouest* became part of the State Railways (*Etat*) this engine
became No 30.628. It is to be preserved in the Railway Museum at
Mulhouse.

This locomotive is one of 104 built by various firms for the *Ouest*
between 1867 and 1883. The dome is on the first ring of the boiler and the
safety valves, originally of the Salter type, are on the dome. The side tanks
extend back from the level of the smokebox front to the leading edges of
the third coupled wheels. Behind them are the coal bunkers loaded from
above, a practice which resulted in the firebox top frequently being
heaped high with coal or briquettes! The valve gear is outside
Stephenson link motion.

Dimensions: CYLINDERS: 420 × 600mm
　　　　　　COUPLED WHEELS: 1320mm
　　　　　　GRATE AREA: 1.1m^2
　　　　　　BOILER PRESSURE: 9.5kg/cm^2

*P-O–*Midi: *Engerth tank locomotive No 032.312 ex* Midi *No 312*
[Lucien Vilain, collection M. Maillet

No 032 TA 312 is a modified Engerth type outside-cylinder 0–6–4 Side Tank locomotive which was built in 1856 as No 312 of the Midi Railway by Kessler (works number 306) and originally named *L'ADOUR*. It will be preserved in the Railway Museum at Mulhouse.

Engerth locomotives were built, originally, to the design of the Austrian engineer Wilhelm Engerth and they were intended for working over the steep gradients of the Semmering line. The original concept was for a tank locomotive with a main frame carried on three driven axles and having a tender frame carried on two axles. The tender frame also supported the firebox and the two frames were connected by universal joints in front of the firebox. There was a gear coupling between the main axles and the tender axles so that, not only was the weight of the tender available for adhesion, but the tender wheels were also driven.

The design was impracticable and the gear couplings were dispensed with, the Engerth locomotive becoming one in which the tender was articulated with the locomotive in such a manner that much of its weight was carried by the locomotive and was thus available for adhesion.

The preserved locomotive is one of a batch built for the *Midi* by Kessler in 1856–58 and which were numbered 309–325. The tender frames were outside the wheels and the firebox was between the two tender axles and inside the frames, the front part of which was articulated to the main frames by means of lateral pivot-bearings. The engine had outside cylinders driving on to the trailing coupled axle. Outside Stephenson link motion drove slide valves above the cylinders.

The boiler seen on the preserved locomotive is of a standard Midi type with the dome on the middle ring; the cab is not original.

Many of these locomotives had very long lives, some lasting until after 1938 and being taken into SNCF stock. They worked local freight trains and occasionally were used on light passenger duties.

Dimensions: CYLINDERS: 480 × 640mm
COUPLED WHEELS: 1310mm
GRATE AREA: 1.8m^2
BOILER PRESSURE: 7.5kg/cm^2

Please also see Volume II for Engerth locomotive preserved in Switzerland.

No 040 TC 93 ex PLM was of the same class as the preserved locomotive   [P. R-W

No 040 TC 90 was No 4 DM 90 of the Paris-Lyon-Mediterranean Railway (PLM) and it will go to the Railway Museum.

It is a powerful outside-cylinder superheated 0–8–0 Side Tank locomotive which was one of 95 built for shunting duties by the Company during the period 1927–40. The construction of these locomotives included many parts from old PLM locomotives Nos 3001–3140 built in 1882–83 by Floridsdorf and Wiener Neustadt.

The coal bunker is on the Left hand side of the engine immediately in front of the cab and extending up over the top of the firebox. The cylinders have piston valves operated by Walschaerts valve gear.

Dimensions: CYLINDERS: 610 × 650mm   GRATE AREA: 2.3m²
          COUPLED WHEELS: 1310mm   BOILER PRESSURE: 10hpz
          SUPERHEATED

Hérault Railway No 70 is an outside-cylinder 0–8–0 Side Tank locomotive built in 1902 by Schneider (works number 2767). It has been beautifully restored and is on display, with three passenger coaches, at the station at Palavas.

Hérault Railway No 81 is of the same type and class as No 70 and was built in 1927 by Schneider (works number 4422). It has been similarly restored and is on display, with one passenger coach, at Montpellier.

Hérault Railway 0–8–0T No 81

[Maurice Maillet

The Hérault Railway owned 22 of these 0–8–0T locomotives, Nos 61–82, all built by Schneider. They had outside Stephenson link motion operating slide valves above the cylinders. The safety valves were above the dome and the engines all used saturated steam.

Dimensions: CYLINDERS: 400 × 540mm

COUPLED WHEELS: 1010mm

GRATE AREA: 1.53m^2

BOILER PRESSURE: 10kg/cm^2

The *Chemins de Fer d'Intérêt Local du Départment de l'Hérault* was incorporated in 1868 to serve the interests of a coastal area of South-East France west of Nîmes and with Montpellier as its focal point. At one time the Company operated 212 route kilometres of track but, especially after World War II, the activities contracted rapidly and it closed its last section of track, the 6km between Montpellier and the sea at Palavas, on October 31, 1968.

From 1928, the Hérault system was operated by the *Chemins de Fer Economiques* and, later, by the *Cie Général des Chemins de Fer et des Transports Automobiles* (CFTA).

206

No 141 TA 304 ex P-O. A locomotive of this class is to be preserved   [P. R-W

A 2–8–2 Side Tank locomotive of SNCF Series 141 TA ex Series 5300 of the Paris-Orléans Railway (P-O) is to be preserved in the Railway Museum. The actual locomotive has not yet been designated.

These husky-looking and popular engines owe their inception to a holiday in Switzerland made in 1910 by the Chief Engineer of the P-O, Monsieur P. Conte. He was, at that time, very impressed by the performance of some new superheated 2–8–2 Side Tank locomotives of Series E 4/6 of the *Thunerseebahn* which had just been outshopped by the Swiss Locomotive Company (SLM) at Winterthur. After due consideration, SLM received an order for 20 locomotives of Series 5300 for the P-O and these were delivered in 1911–12. Between 1911 and 1923 a total of 190 of these engines was supplied in batches by Fives-Lille, Batignolles, Schneider, North British and SLM, the last 80 coming to the P-O via *Travaux Publics* in 1921–23. In 1924–26, 37 were ceded to the Moroccan Railways.

These splendid machines have been most at home on the steep gradients and sharp curves of the Massif Central. The leading and trailing axles each forms a Zara truck with the leading and trailing coupled axles respectively and this undoubtedly is a major factor in the flexibility of these locomotives. The first and third domes contain sand which is delivered by the Lambert wet-sanding system. Nos 5466–5490 were fitted with feed water pumps and heaters, the first 20 had ACFI, the last five had Worthington.

COUPLED WHEELS: 1350mm
GRATE AREA: 2.73m^2
BOILER PRESSURE: 12hpz
(*this is raised to 13hpz, in some engines*)

No 141 TC 725 of the Est *was one of those which, like the preserved locomotive, later became Series 141 TD of the* Ouest Region
[P. R-W

No 141 TD 740 is a three-cylinder 2–8–2 Side Tank locomotive which was built in 1930 by Batignolles-Châtillon for the Paris Suburban Services of the Eastern Railway (*Est*). This locomotive was *Est* No 141.740 Series XII and later SNCF 1–141 TC 740. On being transferred to the *Ouest* Region is became SNCF 3–141 TD 740. It will be preserved in the Railway Museum at Mulhouse.

From 1910, the Eastern Railway (*Est*) worked its heavy suburban services with two-cylinder superheated 2–8–2T locomotives. With the increasing weight of suburban trains and the constant need for rapid acceleration, 42 three-cylinder simple 2–8–2T were put into service in 1929–30 and these were Nos 141.701–742. Three independent sets of Walschaerts valve gear operated piston valves above the cylinders. The inside cylinder was steeply inclined to drive the second coupled axle while the two horizontal outside cylinders drove the third coupled axle. The front and rear radial wheels were each in a Bissel truck.

The State Railways (*Etat*) had, for many years used suburban 2–8–2T locomotives of the same designs as those of the *Est*. In the SNCF numbering the 1910–13 two-cylinder engines of the *Est* became 141 TB while identical machines of the *Etat*, built 1921–22, were 141 TC. Similarly, the three-cylinder engines of the *Est* were 141 TC and those of the *Etat*

(40 built 1932–33) were 141 TD. As a result of electrification, some of the *Ouest* engines (including the preserved locomotive) went over to the *Etat* (SNCF Region 3) and became 141 TD but kept their original running numbers.

Dimensions: CYLINDERS (3): 510 × 660mm
COUPLED WHEELS: 1410mm
GRATE AREA: 2.8m²
BOILER PRESSURE: 16hpz
(*The Etat engines had boiler pressure reduced to 13.8hpz*)
SUPERHEATED

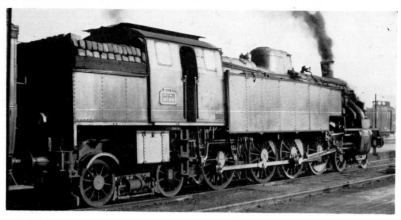

PLM No 242 AT 19 was of the same series as No 242 TA 6 [P. R-W

No 242 TA 6 is a four-cylinder compound 4–8–4 Side Tank locomotive of the former Paris-Lyon-Mediterranean Railway (PLM) and which was built as No 242 AT 6 in 1927 by Blanc Misseron (works number 227). It will go to the Mulhouse Railway Museum.

The PLM introduced the four-cylinder compound 4–8–4T in 1927 and the first 120, Series 242 AT, were built during the next two years. Between 1929 and 1935 another 131 were built with some modifications. Those engines of PLM Series 242 BT and 242 DT had oscillating cam poppet valves. (These engines became 242 TB and 242 TD of the SNCF.)

The four cylinders were in line in all the engines, the outside, high pressure, cylinders driving the second coupled axle while the inside, low pressure, cylinders drove the first. The valves were driven by Walschaerts valve gear, but as the cut-off was not independent, the valve gear of the inside low pressure cylinders was modified, a single outside die-block sufficing for the high pressure and low pressure cylinders on each side. The boilers all had Belpaire fireboxes and the sand-dome was placed ahead of the steam dome but under the same cover.

Built originally for heavy suburban traffic around Paris and other cities, many of these big tank engines were displaced by electrification and sent to other Regions of the SNCF notably the Nord and the Est. Some were equipped for push-and-pull working.

Dimensions: CYLINDERS: HIGH PRESSURE: 420 × 650mm
LOW PRESSURE: 630 × 650mm
COUPLED WHEELS: 1660mm
GRATE AREA: 3.1m²
BOILER PRESSURE: 16kg/cm²
SUPERHEATED

Narrow Gauge Steam Locomotive Preservation in France

Until about the year 1930, a very extensive network of narrow gauge railways existed in France. After having developed as agricultural or as feeder lines, many of the narrow gauge railways before World War I, became grouped into two large companies—the *Compagnie des Chemins de Fer Départmentaux* and the *Société Générale des Chemins de Fer Economiques*, both of which extended their "empires" until road competition made the concept of the narrow gauge railway uneconomic in all but a few isolated areas.

The fascinating and complicated history of French narrow gauge railway systems is far beyond the scope of this book but is excellently dealt with by W. J. K. Davies in his book *French Minor Railways*. All the surviving locomotives from these railways, with two exceptions, run on the 1000mm or on the 600mm gauge. The exceptions are working on the 700mm gauge of the *Chemin de Fer Forestier d'Abreschviller*.

Many locomotives from Industrial Concerns are privately preserved or exist as monuments and these are not included in this book. Others of non-industrial origins are described and these are, for the most part, in enthusiast museums or working on "Museum Railways". Two of the most important museums are at Verneuil (Marne) where a deserted railway station has been converted to museum premises, and at Paris where the Malakoff Museum houses a number of interesting exhibits under the auspices of *l'Association pour le Musée des Transports Urbains, Interurbains et Ruraux* (AMTUIR).

France has four very active Museum Railways:
1. *Chemin de Fer Touristique de Meyzieu* (CFTM): 600mm gauge
2. *Chemin de Fer du Vivarais* (owned and operated by CFTM): 1000mm gauge
3. *Association de Musée des Transports de Pithiviers:* 600mm gauge
4. *Chemins de Fer Forestier d'Abreschviller:* 700mm gauge.

These systems and their motive power are described even though some of the locomotives have industrial origins.

All the remaining narrow gauge railways in France which are commercially operated now exclusively use diesel motive power.

FRANCE
CHEMIN DE FER TOURISTIQUE DE MEYZIEU

This 600mm-gauge railway extends 1.4km between Meyzieu-Le Carreau 13km east of Lyon, and a popular beauty spot on the Grand Large, an artificial reservoir. It was founded in 1960 by Monsieur Jean Arrivetz of the Omnibus et Tramways de Lyon (OTL) who managed to obtain the status of *Chemin de Fer d'Iterêt Local* for his railway. His private organisation has operated the line since 1962, running steam trains every Sunday afternoon and, in summer, on Saturdays and Sunday mornings as well. The railway will also exhibit on its premises the historical road transport vehicles which are to be preserved by OTL.

At present, the railway owns eight steam locomotives which are listed below:

CFTM No 1 COQUETTE [M. Geiger

No 1 *COQUETTE*, is an outside-cylinder 0–4–0 Side Tank locomotive built in 1912 by Decauville for the Tarare Quarry near Lyon. This was one of the first two locomotives to be owned by and to work on CFTM. No 3 *BEAUJOLAIS* is an outside-cylinder 0–6–0 Side Tank locomotive built in 1928 by Decauville and formerly owned by the Tarare Quarry, near Lyon.

212

[SODEP

No 2 *CHAMPAGNE*, is an outside-cylinder 0–6–0 Side Tank locomotive with a Belpaire boiler and outside frames. It formerly belonged to the *Société Sucrerie Agricole de Maizy* and was built in 1910 by Couillet (works number 1586).

No 7 is an outside-cylinder 0–6–0 Side Tank locomotive built in 1918 by Decauville (works number 1797). It was owned by the Quarry Company at Moulins Neuf, Nievre until 1963.

No 8 *CHABLAIS*, is an outside-cylinder 2–6–0 Side Tank locomotive, built in 1938 by La Meuse (works number 3932). It was owned by *Société Sucrerie Agricole de Maizy* until 1966.

No. 4 *BOURGOGNE*, is an outside-cylinder 0–8–0 Side Tank locomotive with inside frames built in 1916 by Krauss (works number 6999) for the German Military Railways (DFB). It carries, in error, the maker's plate "Orenstein and Koppel 8607 of 1918". This locomotive formerly belonged to *Lambert, Frères et Cie, Grand Tuilleries de Bourgogne, Chagny.*

No 4–13 *RHONE*, is an outside-cylinder 0–8–0 Side Tank locomotive with piston valves, built in 1944 by Franco-Belge (works number 2844) for the German Military Railways (DFB). This is a modern superheated tank locomotive with frames inside the wheels and coal carried in a bunker behind the cab. It was built for the 750mm gauge and is quite unlike the

213

CFTM No 4-13 RHONE

[JFLC

earlier *Deutsches Heeresfeldbahnen* 0–8–0T of which No 4 (above) is an example. No 4–13 was owned, after the War, by a sugar factory and later by the *Tramway de Pithiviers à Toury*.

CFTM No 5 as TPT No 22-5

[R. G. Farr

No 5 *LOIRET*, was No 22–5 of the *Tramway de Pithiviers à Toury*. It is a Mallet compound 0–4–4–0 Side Tank locomoitve, built in 1905 by Orenstein and Koppel (works number 1769).

This locomotive has slide valves above the cylinders and they are operated by four sets of Hackworth valve gear.

MTP No 1

[M. Geiger

The premises of the Museum of Transport, Pithiviers are situated within the confines of the SNCF station of Pithiviers (Loiret). This was originally the terminus of the 600mm-gauge Departmental Railway, *Tramway Pithiviers-Toury* (TPT) which extended 35km to Toury. The railway was constructed by the Decauville Company and was opened for passenger and freight traffic in 1892. After 1952, passenger traffic ceased and the principal revenue of the line was from the transport of sugar-beet to the sugar factories at Toury and Pithiviers-le-Viel. In 1964 the line closed completely.

A group of railway enthusiasts, however, decided to open a Museum of Industrial Locomotives and they achieved their purpose in 1966. Later, they re-opened 4km of the original railway from Pithiviers to Orme and now steam-hauled passenger trains are operated on Sundays from May 1 to October 30 each year.

The museum now owns 11 steam locomotives, with one exception, all 600mm gauge. Most of the 600mm-gauge locomotives are in working order and are used from time to time "on the line".

215

Although it is not strictly within the scope of the present book, a list of locomotives is given below:

Type	Builder	Works No	Date	MTP No	Name	Origin
0–6–0T	Couillet	1576	1910	1	—	Maizy Sugar Factory
0–8–0T	Hartmann	4126	1918	2	*Jacqueline*	DFB
0–6–0T	Decauville	1834	1925	3	—	Toury Sugar Factory, Type 17
0–6–2T	Decauville	360	1902	4	*La Martroy*	Coucy Sugar Factory, Type 10
0–6–0T	Blanc Misseron	282	1902	5	*Le Minihic*	TPT No 3–5
0–6–0T	Decauville	945	1913	8	*Colette*	ETP *Villeneuve la Guyard*
2–6–0T	La Meuse	3931	1938	9	*Les Fontenelles*	Maizy Sugar Factory
0–4–0T	Decauville	431	1908	10	—	Type 3 *T.P. Vandewalle*
0–8–0T	Franco Belge	2843	1944	12	*Pithiviers*	TPT No 4–12
0–4–0T	Schneider	1347	1870	—	—	Ets Boigues à Decize*
0–6–0T	Schneider	4321	1925	—	—	No 103 of CGB*†

* *Not in working order.*

† *1435mm gauge.*

All the above are Side Tank locomotives with outside cylinders.

MTP No 2 JACQUELINE

[M. Geiger

MTP No 3   [M. Geiger

MTP No 4 LA MARTROY   [M. Geiger

MTP No 5 LE MINIHIC [M. Geiger

MTP No 9 LES FONTENELLES [M. Geiger

MTP No 10   [M. Geiger

MTP No 12 as TPT No 4–12

[R. G. Farr

Schneider 0–4–0T as MTP No 2 (since removed) on the occasion of the 100th "birthday" of this locomotive in 1970

[M. Geiger

No 3–23 is an outside-cylinder 2–6–2 Side Tank locomotive which was No 1265, built in 1916 by ALCO (works number 57156) for the British Railway Operating Division (ROD) in France. It is now preserved in working order and is owned by the Festiniog Railway in Wales and is named *MOUNTAINEER*.

One hundred of these little engines were built for the ROD and, after World War I, No 1265 worked on the Tramway Pithiviers-Toury as their No 3–23 until the line was closed in 1964. It went to Wales in 1967. It has Walschaerts valve gear with slide valves above the cylinders. The leading and trailing wheels is each in a Bissel truck.

Dimensions: CYLINDERS: 230 × 355mm

             COUPLED WHEELS: 685mm

             GRATE AREA: 0.7m^2

             BOILER PRESSURE: 12kg/cm^2

TPT No 5–3 with Luttermoller axles

[R. G. Farr

No 5–3 is an 0–10–0 Side Tank locomotive which was built in 1917 by Orenstein and Koppel (works number 8285) for the German Military Railways (DFB). After World War I, it went to the *Regie Départmentale CF d'Intérêt Local de Pithiviers à Toury* (Tramway Pithiviers–Toury). It is, at present, owned by a Monsieur Bayon but its location is not known.

This locomotive has piston valves above the outside cylinders and Walschaerts valve gear. It is not superheated. The frames are outside the wheels and the first and fifth driving axles are free to move laterally and radially in relation to them. These movements are achieved by those axles being driven from the second and fourth coupled axles respectively through totally enclosed gear trains and there are no coupling rods to the first and fifth axles. This is the well-known Luttermöller principle which was developed during World War I to overcome the limitations of the Klien-Lindner axle for narrow gauge locomotives working over irregular and severely curved track.

Dimensions: CYLINDERS: 270 × 300mm

COUPLED AND DRIVING WHEELS: 600mm

GRATE AREA: 2.86m²

BOILER PRESSURE: 14kg/cm²

No 3 of the *Tramways Départmenteaux des Deux Sèvres* is an 0–6–0 Tram locomotive which was built in 1896 by Blanc Misseron (works number 152). It was later sold to the *Société des Usines de Melle* and it is at present stored at Melle for probable preservation.
No further information is available.

No 51 *FOULLETOURTE* is an 0–6–0 Tram locomotive which was built in 1898 by Blanc Misseron (works number 176) for the Tramways de la Sarthe. It was sold to the *Société de Fonderie Usine Radiateurs*, Sarthe in 1947 and is now preserved in the *Musee de l'Automobile*, Le Mans.
No further information is available.

CF Cotes du Nord No 36   [P. R-W

No 36 is an 0–6–0 Side Tank locomotive with outside cylinders which was built in 1925 by Corpet Louvet (works number 1679) for the *Société Générale des Chemins de Fer Economiques, Chemin de Fer des Côtes du Nord*. It is preserved near the SNCF Station at St Brieuc.

This little engine is fairly typical of many of the same type which worked over the 1000mm gauge tracks of the various reseaux of the *C de F Economiques*. Slide valves above the cylinders are operated by Walschaerts valve gear and the coal bunker is behind the large Right hand side tank.
Dimensions: NOT KNOWN

The following are outside cylinder 0–6–0 Side Tank locomotives which are preserved but about which full information is not available:

CAMBRAI, built in 1888 by Corpet Louvet (works number 493) is at present preserved in the Narrow Gauge Railway Museum at Towyn, Wales. It was built for the *Chemin de Fer du Cambrésis* on which it was No 5 *CLARY*. It was sold to Messrs Thomas W. Ward in 1936 who in turn sold it to the Loddington Ironstone Company. This concern passed it on to the Eastwell and Waltham Ironstone Company of Eaton in Leicestershire with whom it finished its working life.

Dimensions: CYLINDERS: 300 × 450mm
COUPLED WHEELS: 900mm
GRATE AREA: 0.84m²
BOILER PRESSURE: 10kg/cm²

No 75 of the *Tramway à Vapeur d'Ille et Villaine* was built in 1909 by Corpet Louvet (works number 1234). It worked for a time as No 5 of the quarries of Lambert Frères et Compagnie at Vajours in the Valley of the Oise and is now preserved in the Malakoff Transport Museum in Paris.

No 4 of the *Tramways de la Corrèze* was built in 1912 by Piguet and is now preserved in the Malakoff Transport Museum in Paris.

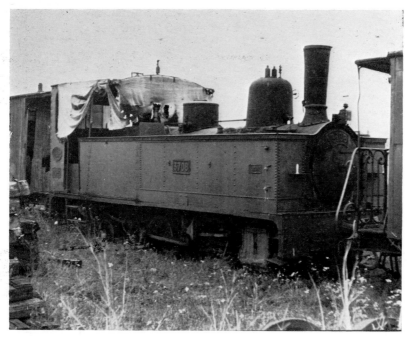

CF Nangis a Jouy-le-Chattel *No 3708 which was similar to the preserved locomotive No 3714*
[R. G. Farr

No 3714 is an outside-cylinder 0–6–2 Side Tank locomotive which was built in 1910 by Robatel and Buffault for the *Chemins de Fer Economiques, Chemin de Fer Nangis à Jouy le Chattel*. It is at present in the museum at Verneuil.

No further details are known.

FRANCE   2–6–0T   1000mm

The following are outside-cylinder 2–6–0 Side Tank locomotives which are preserved but about which complete information is not known:

No 77 was built in 1895 by Cail (works number 2458) for the *Chemins de Fer Départmenteaux, Charantes à Deux Sévres*. In 1952 it was sold to the Société des Usines de Melle and it is now in the museum at Verneuil.

No 1 *AISNE* was built by Corpet Louvet (works number 1097) for *Chemins de Fer Secondaires du Nord-Est*. It was sold to the *Régie Départmentale des Transports de l'Aisne* in 1921 and is now preserved in the museum at Verneuil.

No 15 of the VFIL St Just à Froissy   [R. G. Farr

No 15 was built in 1920 by Haine St. Pierre (works number 1316) for the *Voies Ferrées d'Interêt Local., St. Just à Froissy*. It is now in the FACS Depot at Jouy for possible preservation.

No 13 of the VFIL St Just à Froissy   [R. G. Farr

No 13 was built in 1924 by Société Alsacienne (works number 7381) for the *Voies Ferrées d'Interêt Local, St. Just à Froissy.* It is, like No 15, in store at Jouy.

RB No E 332 now owned by CF Blonay–Chamby   [R. Gottschall]

No E.332 is an outside-cylinder 4–6–0 Side Tank locomotive which was built in 1909 for the *Réseau Breton* by Fives, Lille (works number 3587). It has been purchased by the 1000mm-gauge Blonay-Chamby Tourist Railway near Vevey in Switzerland. It is in working order and operates trains for its new owners.

No E 327 is a 4–6–0 Side Tank locomotive which was built in 1909 by Fives, Lille (works number 3582) for the *Réseau Breton*. It is preserved in working order by the *Société de Chemin de Fer Touristique de Meyzieu* for duties on the Tournon-Lamastre section (33km) of the *Chemin de Fer du Vivarais*.

The *Réseau Breton* had 12 of these engines which were designed by Fives, Lille, to haul 150-tonne trains at 20km/h up a gradient of $20^0/_{00}$. Their maximum speed was limited (probably by the track) to 55km/h.

The first five engines, Nos E.321–325 were built in 1904 by Franco-Belge and the last seven came from Fives in 1908–9, No E.332 being the last of the series. They were smart little engines, having Walschaerts valve gear driving slide valves angled outwards above the cylinders.

The prefix E before the number indicated that, prior to the days of SNCF, the *Réseau Breton* was owned and operated by the State Railways (*Etat*).

Dimensions: CYLINDERS: 400 × 460mm
              COUPLED WHEELS: 1230mm
              GRATE AREA: 1.0m²
              BOILER PRESSURE: 12hpz

FRANCE   1000mm
CHEMINS DE FER DU VIVARAIS

This line which is now open between Tournon and Lamastre is but a
small part of what was once a very considerable 1000mm-gauge system,
second only, in France, to the *Réseau Breton*. Its main line extended from
La Voute S. Loire to Le Cheylard where the line divided, one branch
going north east to reach the Rhône at Tournon while the other pursued
a more southerly course again reaching the Rhône at La Voulte.
Cheylard was the headquarters of the line. The *Réseau de Vivarais*
operated 203 route-kilometers of track through very beautiful but
difficult and mountainous country.

The Mallet Side Tank locomotives proved their worth on this line and
three are to work the present short section. A 4–6–0 Side Tank
locomotive from the *Réseau Breton* has also been acquired and is
described under "4–6–0T, 1000mm Gauge".

FRANCE   0–6–6–0T   1000mm

CF du Vivarais No 403   [JFLC

No 403 and No 404 are Mallet compound 0–6–6–0 Side Tank locomotives
which were built in 1903 by SLM (works numbers 1492 and 1493) for the

229

Chemins de Fer Départmenteaux, Réseau du Vivarais. They are preserved in working order and are in use on the Tournon-Lamastre section of the *Réseau du Vivarais* now operated by the *Chemin de Fer Touristique de Meyzieu.*

No 414 is another Mallet Compound o-6-6-o Side Tank locomotive of later design than Nos 403 and 404 and which was built in 1932 for *Réseau du Vivarais* by Société Alsacienne (works number 7629). It is at present under repair but will later be working between Tournon and Lamastre.

Soon after the turn of the century the *Chemins de Fer Départmenteaux* obtained a concession to build an extension to their system from Cheylard, over hilly and difficult country, to Tournon on the Rhône. To work the line, they obtained from SLM, Winterthur, in 1901, a Mallet compound Side Tank locomotive, No 401. This locomotive gave complete satisfaction and seven more were purchased from SLM between 1902 and 1905. These were Nos 402–408. These engines were of the same design as No 401 but had direct spring loaded safety valves instead of the Salter type balanced safety valve on No 401. All the engines had round top boilers, and the coal bunkers were behind the side tanks and in front of the cab. Slide valves above the cylinders were operated by Walschaerts valve gear and the low pressure cylinders had long piston tail-rods. Live steam was automatically admitted to the low pressure cylinders on starting, and there was a modified form of Riggenbach counter-pressure braking. The principal brake was vacuum operated.

Dimensions: (*Nos 403, 404*)

    CYLINDERS: HIGH PRESSURE: 310 × 550mm
             LOW PRESSURE: 480 × 550mm
    COUPLED WHEELS: 1010mm
    GRATE AREA: 1.3m^2
    BOILER PRESSURE: 14kg/cm^2

In 1927 two further Mallet locomotives of the same type and of the same basic dimensions were obtained from Société Alsacienne and these were Vivarais Nos 409 and 410. They differed from the earlier engines in having coal bunkers behind the cab, Belpaire boilers, Coale safety valves, mechanical lubricators and Kylchap single blast pipes. These locomotives were followed in 1932 by four further Mallets from the same builder, Nos 411–414. These were identical with the 1927 engines except that they had larger side tanks and bunkers which resulted in an increase in weight from 44.3 tonnes to 46.1 tonnes.

Dimensions (of No 414): AS FOR NOS 403, 404

FRANCE
CHEMIN DE FER FORESTIER D'ABRESCHVILLER

700mm

In the forests east of Nancy and 15km south of Sarrebourg is the 5.2km-long 700mm-gauge forest railway of Abreschviller. This line is now operated as a tourist and museum railway and owns two locomotives in working order, both of which were built for the railway when it was a viable commercial enterprise.

CF Forestier d'Abreschviller No 3   [M. Geiger

An 0–6–0 Side Tank locomotive which carries the number 3, was built in 1928 by Decauville. Coal bunkers are in front of the cab and behind the side tanks. Slide valves above the cylinders are operated by Walschaerts valve gear.

Dimensions: CYLINDERS: 200 × 470mm
          COUPLED WHEELS: 600mm
          GRATE AREA: 0.39m²
          BOILER PRESSURE: 12kg/cm²

CF Forestier d'Abreschviller   Mallet 0–4–4–0 T   [Prèvôt

An 0–4–4–0 Mallet compound Side Tank locomotive was built in 1906 by
Heilbronn (works number 426). Coal bunkers are in front of the cab and
behind the side tanks. Slide valves above the cylinders are operated by
Walschaerts valve gear. The boiler has a round-top firebox and the dome,
surmounted by safety valves, is on the second ring of the boiler with sand
boxes in front and behind. This is the Mallet locomotive in its simplest
form.

Dimensions : CYLINDERS: HIGH PRESSURE: 210 × 570mm
                              LOW PRESSURE: 300 × 570mm
               COUPLED WHEELS: 700mm
               GRATE AREA: 0.58m^2
               BOILER PRESSURE: 12kg/cm^2

232

The German State Railway

The railways of the eight Federated German States came under the unified control of the Central Government in 1920 and they were combined to form the German State Railway, *Deutsche Reichsbahn*. In 1924, the railways were placed under the management of a State-owned corporation, the *Deutsche Reichsbahn-Gesellschaft*. In 1937, however, the railways, including those of the conquered countries, reverted to full State control.

After World War II, in 1945, and the division of Germany, the railways of Western Germany became known as the *Deutsche Bundesbahn*, German Federal Railway, while those of Eastern Germany retained the old title of *Deutsche Reichsbahn*.

For convenience, the German railways of 1920–45 will hereafter be referred to by the initials DRG, the railways of Western Germany by the initials DB and those of Eastern Germany by DR.

There is still a number of privately owned railways in Germany and these will be referred to by their titles.

Steam Locomotive Preservation in Western Germany

The majority of preserved steam locomotives of 1435mm gauge is in museums or is stored awaiting probable preservation in such museums.

The principal Railway Museums are three:

1. The *Verkehrsmuseum* at Nürnberg (Nürnberg Transport Museum) houses the major collection of models and of preserved locomotives. The present building was completed in 1925 and it replaced the Bavarian Railway Museum which had been opened in 1899, and which already had ensured the preservation of many interesting relics. At the present time, only about 45 per cent of the exhibition space of the museum is occupied; it is hoped, therefore, that a number of stored locomotives may ultimately be put on display there.

2. The Railway Department of the German National Museum in Munich (Deutsches Museum) was founded in 1903. It was badly damaged in World War II and much of it has been completely rebuilt. Now, in 1970, it is again being reconstructed and the splendid collection of models and preserved locomotives re-arranged. It is due to be re-opened in July 1970.

3. The *Verkehrsmuseum*, Berlin, was opened in 1906 and occupied the old station buildings of the Berlin-Hamburg Railway. Most of the exhibits survived World War II but the museum is now in East Berlin and is controlled by the *Deutsche Reichsbahn*. The site of the museum is,

however, required for other purposes and a new Transport Museum is being built in West Berlin near to the Heerstrasse S-Bahn station. A number of stored locomotives is earmarked for this museum.

All three museums have excellent and comprehensive libraries of books on transport. The large collections of locomotive models, mostly built to a scale of 1 : 10 are alone sufficient reason for a protracted visit to each museum.

Until recently there was a small transport museum at Karlsrühe but this has now been demolished. The steam locomotive preserved there, No 50.3163 has been scrapped. (The diesel locomotive which was also preserved, No V.140.001 is to go to Nürnberg.) At the Technical School in Karlsrühe an interesting relic is kept for instructional purposes. This comprises the front and rear ends of an outside-cylinder 2–4–2 express locomotive No 29 *KÖNIGIN MARIE* of the Pfalz Railway Class P² I. The ends are joined by steel girders; the coupled wheels, motion and most of the boiler are missing. For this reason it is not included in the schedule of preserved locomotives.

After the museums, the largest collection of preserved locomotives is in the hands of *Deutsche Gesellschaft für Eisenbahngesschichte EV*. This Company was formed exclusively for the preservation of railway locomotives and the study of railway history. It has its headquarters at Karlsruhe but the collection of about a dozen standard and narrow-gauge locomotives is located elsewhere, at Bochum-Dahlhausen and at Erndtebrück. Some of the standard-gauge locomotives are in good repair and will be used to work special trains from time to time on the line Achern-Ottenhöfen of the *Sudwestdeutschen Eisenbahn Gesellschaft* (SWEG).

Other standard gauge locomotives (at present only two) are owned by a society *"Eurovapor"*, which will use them to work special trains on the Haltingen-Kandern line of the SWEG.

Locomotives of 1435mm gauge owned by private collectors, are very few. A number of interesting engines is, however, displayed in various places—builders' works, playgrounds etc.

A considerable number of locomotives is in store, notably at the repair and maintenance works of the *Bundesbahn* at Schwerte. It is believed that many of these will be preserved and some may go to Nürnberg, others to Berlin. As in other countries, however, the position regarding preservation is very fluid and depends largely on available money and space.

Working replica of ADLER in the Verkehrsmuseum *at Nürnberg*   [P. R-W

The first locomotive in Germany was an inside-cylinder 2–2–2 with a four-wheeled tender built in 1835 by Robert Stephenson (works number 118) for the Nürnberg-Fürth Railway at a cost of £1,750. It was named *ADLER* (Eagle) and was said to have been a lighter edition of Stephenson's standard locomotives of *THE PATENTEE* class, and of which a large number were built from 1834 onwards. Warren, in *A Century of Locomotive Building* gives the weight of *ADLER* as 6 tons 12 cwt (6705.9kg) against 11 tons 9 cwt (11,633.7kg) of the original *THE PATENTEE*. German authorities, however, quote 14 tonnes for the locomotive of which 6 tonnes was available for adhesion. In *THE PATENTEE*, the dome was above the firebox whereas in the German engine it was on the first ring of the boiler.

ADLER had double frames and the inside horizontally-placed cylinders with slide valves were each operated by a moveable eccentric.

The inaugural train on December 7, 1835, from Fürth to Nürnberg was worked by *ADLER* amid scenes of great rejoicing but the *Ludwigsbahn* as the railway was known, soon obtained more locomotives. However, *ADLER* remained in service until 1857 when it was scrapped.

Two full-size replicas of the original engine exist. The first is an authentic working replica built in 1935 at Kaiserlautern Works for the Railway Centenary celebrations where it hauled a train of contemporary coaches. During the 125th birthday celebrations of the railway in 1960, this locomotive made a return journey between Nürnberg and Fürth travelling under its own power on the tracks of the tramways system. It is housed in the *Verkehrsmuseum* at Nürnberg.

The second is externally correct but it is not a working replica. It was built at Ingolstadt in 1950 for use as a static exhibit at processions and exhibitions. It is probably kept at Münich but is often "at work" in many different localities.

Dummy replica of ADLER on exhibition at Münich   [DB

Early references and paintings all refer to the name of the locomotive as *DER ADLER* and a model in the *Verkehrs museum* at Nürnberg also carries this name. Both the full-size replicas of the locomotive carry the name *ADLER* and most references now omit *DER*. One can assume that this is the correct form of the name.

Dimensions: *(of the original locomotive):*
    CYLINDERS: 229 × 406mm
    DRIVING WHEELS: 1371mm
    GRATE AREA: 0.48m^2
    BOILER PRESSURE: 3.3atm

Working replica of BEUTH at the Deutsches Museum, Münich. The sectioned 2–4–0 locomotive No 1000 is immediately behind   [P. R-W

BEUTH was an outside-cylinder 2–2–2 locomotive built in 1843 by Borsig (works number 24) for the Berlin-Anhalt Railway. It had a haycock firebox surmounted by a dome and a Salter-type safety-valve. The cylinders were inclined and the trailing axle was under the footplate behind the firebox. This locomotive embodied what was the best in English locomotive practice at that time.

A full size replica, containing parts of the original engine, was built by Borsig in 1921 and is in the Railway section of the Münich Deutsches Museum.

Dimensions: CYLINDERS: 330 × 560mm
    DRIVING WHEELS: 1524mm
    GRATE AREA: 0.83m^2
    BOILER PRESSURE: 5.5atm

Crampton 4–2–0 PHOENIX at Nürnberg [DB

PHOENIX is a 4–2–0 Crampton locomotive built by the Baden State Railways in 1863 at their own locomotive works in Karlsruhe. It is preserved in Nürnberg *Verkehrsmuseum*.

The Baden State Railways had 29 Crampton locomotives built between 1854 and 1863. Only three were built in the State Railways Works, the rest being constructed by Maschinenbau Gesellschaft Karlsruhe. The Baden Cramptons were all of the Maffei type with outside frames only (the original design had double frames) and with all bearings outside. The cranks were forged in one piece with the eccentrics; the valve gear was Stephenson link motion. Eight of the engines had leading bogies; in the others the carrying wheels formed a rigid wheel base. The steam dome was on the firebox and surmounted by a Salter type safety valve.

Dimensions: CYLINDERS: 405 × 560mm
DRIVING WHEELS: 2130mm
GRATE AREA: 1.1m^2
BOILER PRESSURE: 7kg/cm^2

Working replica of Crampton 4–2–0 DIE PFALZ which is to go to Berlin [DB

No 28, *DIE PFALZ*, was a 4–2–0 Crampton locomotive built in 1853 for the Palatinate Railway by Maffei (works number 134). It was one of four engines acquired by the railway for working a greatly accelerated express train service. These engines had domeless boilers but otherwise they conformed to the Maffei Crampton design already mentioned (page 238).

A full-size working replica of *DIE PFALZ* was built in 1923–24 under the supervision of Herr Carl Klensch and this is stored in the locomotive depot at Nürnberg. It is intended for the new Railway Museum at Berlin.

Dimensions: CYLINDERS: 381 × 612mm
DRIVING WHEELS: 1830mm
GRATE AREA: 1.0m^2
BOILER PRESSURE: 6.2kg/cm^2

LANDWÜHRDEN the first Krauss-built engine. At Verkehrsmuseum, *Nürnberg*   [DB

LANDWÜHRDEN is an 0–4–0 tender locomotive with outside cylinders which was built by Krauss in 1867 and it carries the works number 1 being the first locomotive to be built by the newly formed company. It became No II of the Oldenburg State Railways and was withdrawn from service in 1900. It is preserved and exhibited, without a tender, in the *Verkehrsmuseum* at Nürnberg. It is the only surviving locomotive of the Oldenburg State Railways.

Georg Krauss founded his firm for the construction of railway locomotives, in Münich in 1866. He was joined by two eminent engineers, Georg von Linde and Richard von Helmholz. In their early years these pioneers received much help and encouragement from the State of Bavaria and from the older firm of Maffei.

Their first locomotive, *LANDWÜHRDEN*, was exhibited in the Paris Exhibition of 1867 and obtained the highest award of the Gold Medal for excellence of design and workmanship. The 0–4–0 wheel arrangement was chosen for its simplicity and cheapness of construction but there were a number of original design features. The round-top firebox was radially stayed and a small "regulator box" containing a perforated steam collector pipe, replaced the dome. Special care was taken to obtain good proportions of grate and heating surface. The frames consisted of a "box" made up of riveted steel plates and the opportunity was taken to use this "box" as a well-tank for feed-water. The cylinders were horizontal with slide valves above and inclined. The valve gear was Allan link motion. The connecting and coupling rods were of fluted I-section steel, the first time that such a form had been used though Belpaire, in Belgium, was developing the same idea, independently, at the same time.

There is no doubt that this locomotive was, in many ways, an important "landmark" in the history of locomotive development in Europe.

Dimensions: CYLINDERS: 355 × 560mm
COUPLED WHEELS: 1500mm
GRATE AREA: 0.98m²
BOILER PRESSURE: 10kg/cm²

NORDGAU sectioned and in the Verkehrsmuseum *at Nürnberg*   [DB

NORDGAU is a two-cylinder simple 2–4–0 locomotive built in 1853 for the Bavarian State Railways as Class BV by Maffei (works number 151).

This locomotive has been sectioned and is preserved in the *Verkehrs-museum* at Nürnberg.

This was the last of five locomotives built by Maffei for the passenger train services of the Bavarian State Railways. The first, *DONAU*, went into service in 1846 and all the engines carried names except for the third which was BV 1050.

These locomotives had outside frames. They were of sound but unexceptional design and their speed was limited to 70km/h. The valve gear was Stephenson link motion, the eccentrics being on the leading coupled axle outside the frames but inside the cranks. The slide valves were on the inner sides of the cylinders.

Dimensions: CYLINDERS: 406 × 610mm
COUPLED WHEELS: 1462mm
GRATE AREA: 1.24m²
BOILER PRESSURE: 10kg/cm²

No 1000 is an outside-cylinder 2–4–0 locomotive with outside frames which was built in 1874 by Maffei (works number 1000) for the Bavarian State Railways as their Class B IX. This locomotive is sectioned and is exhibited in the Deutsches Museum, Münich. The coupled wheels can be revolved by electric power.

Between 1874 and 1891, 20 outside-cylinder 2–4–0 locomotives of Class B IX with outside frames were built for the Bavarian State Railways. They had horizontal cylinders and the slide valves were inside the frames. The valve gear was Stephenson link motion also inside the frames. An interesting feature of the design was the large compensating beams connecting the springs of the coupled wheels and with their fulcra suspended by the frames midway between the two coupled wheels on each side. The comparatively large diameter of the coupled wheels was also noteworthy.

Dimensions: CYLINDERS: 406 × 610mm
COUPLED WHEELS: 1870mm
GRATE AREA: 1.6m^2
BOILER PRESSURE: 10kg/cm^2

4–4–4 No 3201 which is exhibited at the Verkehrsmuseum, *Nürnberg*   [DB

Bavarian State Railways No 3201 Class S 2/6 is an experimental high speed four-cylinder compound 4–4–4 express locomotive built in 1906 by Maffei (works number 2519). It is preserved in the *Verkehrsmuseum* at Nürnberg.

This interesting locomotive is a four-cylinder balanced compound with all four cylinders in line and driving the leading coupled axle. The high-pressure cylinders are inside the frames and the low pressure outside. The four piston valves are above the cylinders and are driven by two sets of Walschaerts valve gear, the high-pressure valves being operated through rocking shafts. Bar frames carry a superheated boiler with a round top firebox having a wide grate and two fire holes. The trailing bogie is placed beneath the cab and entirely behind the firebox. The front of the double-windowed cab is wedge-shaped and there is wedge-shaped streamlining in front of both the dome and the chimney. The smokebox door is conical. The coupled wheels are 2200mm in diameter.

This locomotive was built largely as an advertisement for the constructors as it was an impractical machine for the Bavarian State Railways. Nonetheless, on July 2, 1907, with a train of 150 tonnes, No 3201 ran from Munich to Augsburg, a distance of 62km, during which it attained a speed of 154.5km/h and this remained the German railway speed record for steam until it was exceeded in 1935 by the three-cylinder 4–6–4 Class 05.

No 3201 was later transferred to the Pfalz Railway and it became Reichsbahn No 15.001 in 1923. In 1930 it was withdrawn for preservation in the Museum.

Dimensions: CYLINDERS: HIGH PRESSURE: 410 × 640mm
LOW PRESSURE: 610 × 640mm
COUPLED WHEELS: 2200mm
GRATE AREA: 4.7m²
BOILER PRESSURE: 14kg/cm²
SUPERHEATED

DB No 38.1639, KPEV Class P 8 which was the same type and class as the preserved locomotives Note latest type of smoke deflectors and tender from Series 52 locomotives [P. R-W

DB No 38.1444, Class P 35.17, is an outside-cylinder 4–6–0 locomotive of the Prussian State Railways' (KPEV) Class P8, built in 1913 by Linke-Hofmann and now preserved at that Company's works (Linke-Hofmann-Busch) at Salzgitter-Watenstadt.

DB No 38.3479 of the same class is at present stored at the Repair Shops of the *Deutsche Bundesbahn* at Schwerte and will probably be preserved.

It is probable that other examples of the Class P 8 will be preserved in Western Germany.

SNCB No 64.045 is a 4–6–0 locomotive of KPEV Class P 8, built by Henschel in 1916. It is in store in the Belgian State Railways' depot at Louvain awaiting preservation in the Belgian Railway Museum.

As a result of the Armistice of November 11, 1918 Germany provided Belgium with 2,000 steam locomotives and, of these, 1,959 were incorporated into SNCB stock. Of this number, 1,820 came from the Prussian State Railways and 168 of them were of Class P 8 which became SNCB Nos 6400–6567.

In 1906, the Prussian State Railways (*Königlich preussische Eisenbahn-Verwaltung*, KPEV) put into service the first units of what was to become one of the most famous and well-loved of all European steam locomotives. Classified P8, it was a simply, but soundly, constructed superheated

SNCB 64.097 was the same as the Class P 8 locomotive stored for preservation in Belgium. Note old type tender, boiler without top-feed dome, and standard SNCB chimney [P. R-W

outside-cylinder engine with piston valves above the cylinders and operated by Walschaerts valve gear. The maximum axle-load was 17.2 tonnes and the coupled wheel diameter was 1750mm. As a result, the P8 had a very wide availability and was a truly mixed traffic machine.

They had round-top fireboxes with long, narrow grates. During their lives they were fitted with, at least, three standard boilers in which the main dimensions remained the same but which varied in tube heating surface and in having different boiler mountings, e.g. two domes in the later engines,the first dome housing the top feed from the Knorr feed-water pump and heater.

The first of the class were built by Schwartzkopff and, between 1906 and 1921, no fewer than 3,370 were built for KPEV. In 1923–4, a further 101 were built for DRG. During the period 1914–22, similar locomotives were built for other German States railways (Mecklenburg, Oldenburg and Baden) and, between 1917 and 1925, a number of other European countries adopted the design as it stood. Thus, engines were built, partly or wholly in Germany for Rumania, Latvia and Lithuania; those for Poland numbered 100 but these engines had larger grates. The total number of engines of Class P 8 built, was about 3,950. As a result of both World Wars, most standard gauge railways of Europe received some of them and they were well liked wherever they worked.

Being efficient and economical machines, few alterations or modifications were made. On the DRG, DR and DB they were numbered in the series 38^{10-40} and were classified P 35.17. They carried no smoke deflectors when built but later were fitted with the standard DRG "side plates" and

247

then, most of them received the smaller smokebox deflector plates. As their tenders wore out, they were given semi-circular bogie tenders taken from Series 52 *Kriegsloks* as these engines were scrapped. Three engines of the 1923 batch ran for a time with poppet valves, one with Caprotti and two with Lentz.

After World War II, DB was very short of suburban tank locomotives and two engines of Class P 8, Nos 38.2919 and 2890, were equipped with four-wheeled tenders which were attached to them by a special form of draw-gear. The cabs were totally enclosed and the engines were classified as 4–6–4T and numbered 78.1001 and 1002. The transformation was carried out by Krauss-Maffei. A number of other engines of the class were equipped for push-and-pull working but retained their (second-hand) bogie tenders.

Many of those which are on the present *Reichsbahn* in East Germany, have been fitted with Giesl Ejectors.

On the SNCB, some had standard Belgian chimneys, some had ACFI feed-water pumps and heaters and a few had exhaust steam injectors.

Dimensions: CYLINDERS: 575 × 630mm
COUPLED WHEELS: 1750mm
GRATE AREA: 2.6m²
BOILER PRESSURE: 12kg/cm²
SUPERHEATED

SNCB No 6213 (old numbering) was a Prussian 3-cylinder 4–6–0 of Class S 10², identical with the preserved locomotive
[P. R-W

No 17.218 is a three-cylinder simple 4–6–0 locomotive which was built in 1914 by Schwartzkopff as Class S 10² of the Prussian State Railways. It has been sectioned and is at Mulheim (Ruhr).

Between the years 1911 and 1916 the Prussian State Railways took delivery of 530 multi-cylinder 4–6–0 express locomotives with combined plate and bar frames. The first 202 engines were four-cylinder simple machines of Class S 10. Two hundred and thirty-two similar engines were built contemporaneously as four-cylinder compounds of Class S 10¹, the first on de Glehn principles and the later engines with the four cylinders in line but maintaining the divided drive. These latter engines also had raised running plates which made them similar in appearance to the S 10 locomotives.

In 1914 the three-cylinder simple engines of Class S 10² were introduced and 96 were built during the next two years. They proved to be the last express locomotives to be built for KPEV. The three cylinders all drove on to the leading coupled axle and there were two sets of Walschaerts valve gear, the inside valve being driven by conjugated valve gear. Three of the class ran for ten years with Stumpff Uniflow cylinders and, in 1925, No 17.206 was converted to a three-cylinder compound with a Schmidt-Henschel ultra-high-pressure boiler. Two other locomotives (Nos 17.236 and 239) were, in 1932, also converted to the three-cylinder compound arrangement and had new conventional type boilers pressed to 25kg/cm². All these modified engines were ultimately re-converted to standard S 10². Some locomotives of all three S 10 classes went to other countries as reparations after World War I; others were built new for Poland and ten of Class S 10² were built for the German *Lubeck-Büchener Eisenbahn.*

Dimensions: (*Class S 10²*)

CYLINDERS (3): 500 × 630mm

COUPLED WHEELS: 1980mm

GRATE AREA: 2.86m²

BOILER PRESSURE: 14kg/cm²

SUPERHEATED

DRG Classification S 35.17.

No 18.451 was built in 1912 by Maffei (works number 3315). It has coupled wheels 2000mm in diameter. It has been restored to its original form as Bavarian State Railways No 3634 and is exhibited at the *Deutsche Museum* at Münich.

No 18.478 was built in 1917 by Maffei (works number 3520) as Bavarian State Railways No 3579. It has been completely restored by Herr Serge Lory and it is kept privately by him at Frauenfeld, Switzerland.

DB No 18.505 Bavarian Class S 3/6 in store at Minden [R. G. Farr

No 18.505 was built in 1924 by Maffei and was No 3706 of the Bavarian State Railways though, as it was delivered after the formation of the *Reichsbahn*, it never carried that number. It is in store at Minden for probable preservation.

No 18.528 was built for DRG in 1927 by Maffei (works number 5696) and was Class S 36.18. It is preserved in *Bundesbahn* livery at the works of Krauss-Maffei AG at München-Allach.

DB No 18.528 Bavarian Class S 3/6 exhibited at Krauss-Maffei works   [Gerhard Röder]

The Maffei four-cylinder compound Pacifics which were Class S 3/6 of the Bavarian State Railways were among the first of the type to appear in Europe. They were successful and very elegant machines and 159 were built between the years 1908 and 1930. The last 40 were built to the order of DRG and, of these, 18 came from Henschel—the only engines of the class not built by Maffei. These later engines, for many years, worked the Rheingold expresses.

On DRG (and later DB) they were Series 18$^{4-5}$ being numbered 18.401 to 18.548 but omitting Nos 18.435–40 and 18.459–60 which were blank. Nineteen engines went as reparations to France and Belgium after World War I leaving finally, 140 in DRG stock.

The Class S 3/6 locomotives were built in five batches as follows:

Batch 1. Built 1906–15: coupled wheels 1870mm; axle load 16.4 tonnes; boiler pressure 15kg/cm²; superheater heating surface 50m².
DRG Nos 18.401–424 and 18.461–465.

Batch 2. Built 1914 for the Pfalz Railway. Dimensions as for Batch 1.
DRG Nos 18.425–434.

Batch 3. Built 1912; coupled wheels 2000mm; axle load 17.5 tonnes; boiler pressure 16kg/cm²; altered boiler heating surface.
DRG Nos 18.441–458.

Batch 4. Built 1917–24; coupled wheels 1870mm; axle load 17.5 tonnes; boiler pressure 16kg/cm²; superheater heating surface 62m²; feed water heater.   DRG Nos 18.466–508.

Batch 5. Built 1926–30 for DRG; coupled wheels 1870mm; axle load 18.5 tonnes; boiler pressure 16kg/cm²; superheater heating surface 76.4m²; feed water heater.
DRG Nos 18.509–548.

DRG classification was S 36.16, S 36.17 and S 36.18 according to the axle load.

Benefiting from American design, all the engines had bar-frames, so being among the first European locomotives to adopt this form of construction. The boilers were superheated and had round-top fireboxes with wide grates, the ashpans being between the last coupled axle and the trailing axle which was beneath the cab.

252

The four cylinders, in line, all drove the middle coupled axle, the high pressure cylinders being between the frames and the low pressure cylinders outside. Except in 18 engines, the piston stroke of the high pressure and low pressure cylinders was unequal. Each cylinder had its own piston valve, the inside valves deriving their motion from the two sets of outside Heusinger valve gear. The cut-off for high pressure and low pressure cylinders was, therefore, in a fixed ratio. Live steam could be admitted to the low pressure cylinders for starting.

Between the years 1953 and 1956, 30 engines of the Series 18.509–548 were rebuilt with all-welded boilers with combustion chambers. These engines were Series 18[6] Class S 36.18 and the conversion raised their power output from 1830hp to 2250hp

Dimensions: CYLINDERS: HIGH PRESSURE: 425 × 610mm
                            LOW PRESSURE: 650 × 670mm
              COUPLED WHEELS: 1870mm (2000mm in Nos 18.441–458)
              GRATE AREA: 4.5m^2
              BOILER PRESSURE: 16kg/cm^2
              SUPERHEATED

DB No 18.316 Baden Class IVh as it appears to-day [R. G. Farr

No 18.316 was built in 1919 by Maffei (works number 5091) and was No 018–316–0 in the DB computerised numbering scheme. It is to be preserved by the College of Engineering at Offenburg.

No 18.323 was built in 1920 by Maffei and was given the number 018–323–6 under the latest DB scheme. It will be preserved by the Technical High School at Aachen.

Between 1918 and 1920 Maffei built 20 modern four-cylinder compound Pacifics for the Baden State Railways as their Class IVh. The engines were delivered in three batches:

$$\text{(DRG)} \quad \text{Nos 18.301–303 in 1918 (Class IVh}^1)$$
$$\text{,,} \quad 18.311\text{–}319 \text{ in } 1919 \text{ (,, } \text{IVh}^2)$$
$$\text{,,} \quad 18.321\text{–}328 \text{ in } 1920 \text{ (,, } \text{IVh}^3)$$

They were put into service between Basle and Mannheim but later were allocated to Bremen, Hamburg and Koblenz.

Maffei built the first German Pacifics for the Baden State Railways in 1907—superheated four-cylinder compounds with bar frames and with all four cylinders in line driving the second coupled axle. These engines, Class IVf, were the obvious prototype for the Bavarian Class S 3/6 (qv) but the later Baden engines differed very considerably from them. The most fundamental difference was that the drive was divided, the outside low pressure cylinders driving the second coupled axle and the inside, high pressure cylinders, the first. To achieve this, the inside cylinders

254

A works photo of Baden Class IVh showing original appearance [Krauss-Maffei

were placed ahead of the low pressure cylinders and also ahead of the smoke-box saddle. The high pressure piston valves were on the outside of their cylinders and were brought into line and ahead of the low pressure piston valves which were above their cylinders. By this means, one tandem valve spindle on each side was able to serve the two valves on each side of the engine and two sets of Walschaerts gear sufficed to operate the four piston valves. This arrangement was said to have the merit of simplicity in obviating the need for rocking shafts or similar moving parts, but it naturally prevented any variation in the ratio of the cut-off between high pressure and low pressure cylinders.

Class IVh had the distinguishing Maffei features of bar frames and boilers with round-top fireboxes and wide grates. They had coupled wheels of 2100mm diameter but were, at first, limited to a maximum speed of 130km/h. They became DRG Class S 36.17 though they are quoted by some authorities as being the first German locomotives to have a permitted axle load of 18 tonnes!

As built, they had stove-pipe chimneys, but these were later replaced by the graceful bell-mouthed chimneys which were also fitted to the Bavarian Pacifics.

Dimensions: CYLINDERS: HIGH PRESSURE: 440 × 680mm
LOW PRESSURE: 680 × 680mm
COUPLED WHEELS: 2100mm
GRATE AREA: 5.0m^2
BOILER PRESSURE: 15kg/cm^2
SUPERHEATED

No 01.207 of DR was of the same type and class as the preserved locomotive. It is shown in almost its original form with large smoke deflectors   [P. R-W

The following two-cylinder 4–6–2 locomotives are preserved or are in store for probable preservation:
No 01.220 Class S36.20 has been restored and is on display as a monument on the promenade by the River Altmühl at Treuchtlingen.

No 01.177 (new number 001–177–5) Class S36.20 was built in 1936 and was rebuilt with a large boiler in 1954. It is in store at *Bundesbahn Ausbesserung*, Schwerte for probable private preservation.

Another two-cylinder 4–6–2 of Series 01 Class S36.20 will probably be preserved by *Deutsche Gesellschaft für Eisenbahngeschichte EV*.

No 03.197 Class S36.17 is in store at *Bundesbahn Ausbesserung*, Schwerte for future preservation.

The following three-cylinder 4–6–2 locomotives are in store for probable preservation:
No 03.1001 Class S36.18 built in 1939 by Borsig and rebuilt with large boiler in 1958, is in store at the Hagen-Eckesey Depot of *Deutsche Bundesbahn*. It is almost certain that this will be the officially preserved locomotive of the Series but it is not known where it will go.

No 01.180 of DB was rebuilt with a large boiler and was identical with the stored locomotive
[P. R-W

DB No 03.211 was identical with the stored locomotive No 03.197　　　　　　　　　[P. R-W

DB No 03.1001 which is now in store for future preservation   [P. R-W

No 03.1013 Class S.36.18 built in 1939 by Borsig and rebuilt with large boiler in 1960 is in store at *Bundesbahn Ausbesserung*, Schwerte and will probably be preserved privately.

The Federated States Railways of Germany were amalgamated into the *Deutsche Reichsbahn* in 1920. Some 212 different classes of standard gauge locomotives were absorbed into the new system. It was obviously a matter of high priority to design and produce a series of new standard locomotives, and the matter was made urgent by the fact that, after World War I, many hundreds of German locomotives had been sent as reparations to other countries. A Locomotive Committee was set up, representing the railways and the leading German locomotive manufacturers. It was under the chairmanship and guidance of an eminent locomotive engineer, Dr. R. P. Wagner who was the equivalent of Chief Mechanical Engineer of the *Deutsche Reichsbahn* from its inception.

As a result of researches carried out by the Locomotive Committee, the 4–6–2 (Pacific) type was chosen for express passenger duties. During 1925–26 the first of the standard Pacifics went into service. Ten, built by Borsig (8) and AEG (2) were two-cylinder simples numbered 01.001–010 and ten others, built by Henschel (8) and Krauss-Maffei (2) were four-cylinder compounds numbered 02.001–010. No great advantages were obtained from the compounds and the two-cylinder simple design was adopted as standard, the ten compounds being rebuilt as simples in 1942, and re-numbered 01.011 and 01.233–241. As with all the DRG standard designs the appearance and much of the detail showed strong influence of the Prussian State Railways (KPEV).

Between 1925 and 1938, 231 locomotives of Series 01, Class S.36.20 were built. They had bar frames, horizontal outside cylinders and long-travel piston valves operated by Walschaerts valve gear. Adequate boilers were provided with round-top fireboxes, wide grades but no combustion chambers. There were three domes, the forward one being the inlet from the Knorr feed water pump and heater and the after one housing a Wagner regulator. The sand dome was between them. The engines had a complete system of electric lighting.

In 1929 a three-cylinder compound Pacific was built by Schwartzkopff. This locomotive, No H 02.001, was fitted with a Löffler-Schwartzkopff ultra-high-pressure boiler providing steam at a pressure of $120kg/cm^2$ to the two (outside) high pressure cylinders and re-heated exhaust steam at $15kg/cm^2$ to the (inside) low pressure cylinders.

The axle-load of the Series 01 was 20 tonnes and, in 1930, there appeared the first of the light-weight Pacifics of Series 03, Class S.36.17. These engines were very similar in appearance to those of Series 01 but they were less powerful and the axle load was reduced to 17.5 tonnes, giving them very wide availability. Two hundred and ninety-eight were built between 1930 and 1937, the later engines being slightly heavier and classified S36.18.

In 1932, two light-weight Pacifics with 18 tonnes axle load, were built by Krupp as four-cylinder compounds with boilers having a pressure of $25kg/cm^2$. These were Series 04, Class S.36.18.

The maximum speed of all the two-cylinder Pacifics was 130km/h. In the 1930s, train speeds were increasing all over the world and streamlining was the order of the day with convincing figures showing its efficacy (and publicity value) if not the delays and difficulties it created in repair work and day-to-day maintenance. Its introduction on the *Reichsbahn* has been briefly described on page 258. Its effect on the standard Pacifics began with the experimental semi-streamlining of No 03.154 in 1934 and the complete shrouding of No 03.193 the following year. The maximum speed of these engines was raised to 140km/h.

Dr. Wagner decided, however, that due to its better balancing, the three-cylinder locomotive was better suited to high speed running and in 1939 the first three-cylinder streamlined locomotive of Series o 1[10] Class S.36.20 was delivered by Schwartzkopff (works number 11000). The drive from the cylinders was divided and three sets of Walschaerts valve gear were provided.

In the next year, 54 further locomotives of the same series were built but without streamlining and, during the period 1939–41, 60 light-weight streamlined three-cylinder Pacifics of Series o 3[10] were built. These locomotives retained the 18-tonne axle load and were thus Class S36.18.

After World War II, streamlining was removed from all the Pacifics though the ten engines of Series o 3[10] which went to Poland as reparations, retained it until very recently.

From 1951 onwards, some locomotives of Series o 1, o 1[10] and o 3[10] which were working in Western Germany on the Bundesbahn were rebuilt with new boilers having larger diameter, slightly tapered, barrels and round-top fireboxes with combustion chambers. Their massive appearance was further enhanced by chimneys of wide external diameter. In these chimneys the extra width was due to the leading of the exhausts of the auxiliaries through the outer casing. The diameter of the chimney proper remained unaltered in the rebuilding.

Many of the rebuilt Pacifics were converted to oil burning and some of the rebuilt three-cylinder engines were fitted with roller bearing axle boxes and main bearings.

Dimensions:

	CYLINDERS	COUPLED WHEELS	GRATE AREA	BOILER PRESSURE
	mm	*mm*	*m^2*	*kg/cm^2*
Series o 1	600×660	2000	4.32	16
,, o 1 rebuilt	600×660	2000	3.95	16
,, o 1^{10}	(3) 500×660	2000	4.32	16
,, o 1^{10} rebuilt	(3) 500×660	2000	3.96	16
,, o 3	570×660	2000	3.97	16
,, o 3^{10}	(3) 470×660	2000	3.89	16
,, o 3^{10} rebuilt	(3) 470×660	2000	3.87	16

All series were superheated.

DB 3-cylinder oil burning 4–6–2 No 10.002 which is identical with No 10.001 stored for preservation [P. R-W

No 10.001 (finally renumbered 010–001–6) is a three-cylinder 4–6–2 locomotive built in 1956 by Krupp (works number 3351). It will be preserved in the Transport Museum in West Berlin.

The last two express locomotives to be built for the *Deutsche Bundesbahn* were Nos 10.001 and 002. They were three-cylinder machines with divided drive, the inside cylinder driving the leading coupled axle and the outside cylinders the second. Three sets of Walschaerts valve gear operated long-travel piston valves and the locomotives had double blast pipes and chimneys. Roller bearings were used for all axle boxes and for all main bearings. The maximum axle load was 22 tonnes. The frames were of I-section steel with transverse stiffening plates, the whole being fully welded.

The boilers had round-topped welded steel fireboxes with combustion chambers. No syphons or arch tubes were provided. Both locomotives were fitted for burning oil fuel though No 10.001 originally used the coal-oil system which originated in Germany but was most commonly used in Bulgaria and some other Eastern European countries. In this system, coal, hand-fired was used for all normal duties when the demands on the boiler were not excessive. On long gradients and with very heavy trains, the firebed was evenly maintained but oil was burned on top of the coal and the fireman's work was greatly lessened. The system did not find favour on No 10.001 and it was converted to burn oil fuel only.

The two Pacifics had many refinements such as marine-type revolving clear-vision screens in the driver's front spectacles, dual pressure braking, air-assisted reversers and very complete instrumentation. Provision was made for the injection of water into the superheater header if the pyrometer reading exceeded 450⁰ F.

The thought behind the construction of these locomotives was the ability of the steam locomotive to compete with the diesel in economical maintenance and maximum availability and these two Pacifics was each able to average nearly 20,000km per month with a fuel consumption of about 11 tonnes per 1000km.

Dimensions: CYLINDERS (3): 480 × 720mm
COUPLED WHEELS: 2000mm
GRATE AREA: 3.96m²
BOILER PRESSURE: 18kg/cm²
SUPERHEATED

DRG No 05.003 showing the appearance of the three 4–6–4s without streamline casing [DB

No 05.001 is a three-cylinder 4–6–4 locomotive which was built in 1934 by Borsig (works number 14552) for the *Deutsche Reichsbahn Gesellschaft.* It is one of three experimental high speed locomotives, the other two of which have been scrapped. It is preserved in the *Verkehrsmuseum* at Nürnberg where it has been since 1960.

The 1930s saw the railway systems of Western Europe (and elsewhere) reach their greatest heights of achievement. This period, the ten years before the outbreak of World War II, was undoubtedly the "golden age" of railways and the demands for passenger traffic were for higher speeds and greater comfort.

In Germany, in 1932, the high-speed diesel-electric train set made its debut with the two-car "Flying Hamburger" and thus began the serious challenge of this form of motive power.

Steam locomotive engineers took up the challenge and replied with high-speed streamlined locomotives, which, it was claimed, could haul a much greater payload than the diesel trains and at comparative speeds. Thus it came about that, in Germany, various high speed conventional locomotives were constructed, notably the Series 05, the larger stream-lined three-cylinder 4–8–4 of Series 06, the streamlined three-cylinder Pacifics of Series 01[10] and 03[10] and the two streamlined tank locomotives of Series 61. No 61.001 was a 4–6–4 Tank and was the only two-cylinder high speed locomotive. No 61.002 was a three-cylinder 4–6–6T.

The first two locomotives of Series 05 had bar frames and the maximum axle load was kept down to 19.2 tonnes. The three cylinders were in line and were horizontal, the middle cylinder driving the leading coupled axle and the outside cylinders the second. Three sets of Walschaerts gear were provided to drive the long travel piston valves; conjugated valve gear as used by Gresley in his Class A4 Pacifics, was not considered to be satisfactory at high speeds.

The boilers were of the same diameter as those of Series 01 Pacifics but were constructed of molybdenum steel plates. The inner firebox was of copper and the engines were hand-fired.

DRG No 05.001 re-streamlined, in the Verkehrsmuseum, *Nürnberg. It stands next to the 4-cylinder compound 4–4–4 No 3201* [Verkehrsmuseum, Nürnberg

Clasp brakes on each side of all the wheels of the locomotive were provided except for the leading bogie wheels which had trailing brake blocks only.

No. 05.003 appeared after the first two engines had been in service for two years. Frames, cylinders and motion were the same as for the earlier engines but the boiler was completely different and was equipped to burn pulverised fuel, the chimney being at the rear end of the engine. The driver's cab was in the front of the streamlined casing, with three large plate glass windows providing a view ahead normally obtainable only with electric or diesel locomotives. This experiment was not successful and a conventional boiler was later provided.

Many fast runs with heavy trains were credited to these locomotives and No 05.002 achieved a speed of 200.4km/h with a 200-tonne train on May 11, 1936.

After World War II, Series 05 lost their ugly streamlined casings but No 05.001 has been restored to its original streamlined form though on the Right hand side of the engine, the skirting over the wheels and motion has been omitted and part of the casing over the boiler and firebox has been removed.

Dimensions: CYLINDERS (3): 450 × 660mm

            COUPLED WHEELS: 2300mm

            GRATE AREA: 4.71m^2

            BOILER PRESSURE: 20kg/cm^2 (later reduced to 16kg/cm^2)

            SUPERHEATED

DRG No 55.4460 KPEV Class G 8¹, identical with the stored locomotive [P. R-W

Nos 55.4142 and 55.5041 are o–8–o freight locomotives of the Prussian State Railways (KPEV) Class G 8¹. These locomotives are in store at Schwerte and will probably be preserved.

At least one other locomotive of the same class will be preserved and will go to the *Deutsche Gesellschaft für Eisenbahngeschichte* EV at Karlsruhe.

The o–8–o freight locomotive was introduced on the KPEV in 1893. This was a two-cylinder simple of Class G 7¹ and a total of 1,200 engines were built during the following 24 years. Similar two-cylinder compounds of Class G 7² were also built during the period 1895–1911.

In 1902, Vulcan built for KPEV a two-cylinder simple o–8–o with outside Walschaerts valve gear, piston valves and a superheater. This was Class G 8 and more than 1,000 were supplied by various builders during the period 1902–13. These engines had a maximum axle-load of only 14.2 tonnes.

The final development of the Prussian o–8–o was the Class G 8¹ which was built, first by Hanomag and then by no fewer than 12 other locomotive builders between 1913 and 1921. In all, no less than 5,087 were built most of which went to KPEV but many of which were built for other countries.

As a result of two World Wars, these useful and economical machines were more widely scattered than even the ubiquitous 4–6–os of Class P 8 and all the standard gauge railways of Continental Europe operated them.

On the DRG, DB and DR they were numbered in the Series 55$^{25-57}$ Class G 44.17.

They were superheated engines with piston valves, Walschaerts valve gear, plate frames and a maximum axle load of 17 tonnes. They had round-topped fireboxes with narrow grates and embodied many of the features of the contemporary passenger locomotives of Class P 8. Very little alteration was made to them during their lives. Six hundred and eighty-eight were, however, rebuilt during the period 1933–41 with a leading truck. As 2–8–0s these engines were Prussian Class G 8^2, DRG Series 56$^{2-8}$ Class G 45.17. One of the many G 8^1 locomotives which worked on the Belgian Railways (SNCB) was equipped with a Giesl Ejector.

Dimensions: CYLINDERS: 600 × 660mm

               COUPLED WHEELS: 1350mm

               GRATE AREA: 2.66m^2

               BOILER PRESSURE: 14kg/cm^2

               SUPERHEATED

DB No 56.846 KPEV Class G 8² [P. R-W

A locomotive of KPEV Class G 8² (see page 266) rebuilt from 0–8–0 Class G 8¹ may be preserved and sent to the *Verkehrsmuseum* at Nürnberg. It would thus be the only preserved representative of the 1435mm-gauge 2–8–0 in Germany.

The identity of such a locomotive is unknown but it could be No 56.241 (new number 056–241–3) which was Class G 8¹ No 55.5452.

Dimensions: CYLINDERS: 600 × 660mm
COUPLED WHEELS: 1350mm
GRATE AREA: 2.66m²
BOILER PRESSURE: 14kg/cm²
SUPERHEATED

DRG No 39.090 was of the same type and class as the preserved locomotive but it is shown with the original smoke deflectors   [P. R-W

No 39.184 is a three-cylinder 2–8–2 locomotive built in 1924 by Linke-Hofmann and now preserved at the works museum of Messrs. Linke-Hofmann-Busch at Salzgitter-Watenstadt.

The three-cylinder 2–8–2 locomotives of DRG Series 39 Class P46.19 were designed by the Prussian State Railways (KPEV) as their Class P 10. However, the first locomotive was delivered by Borsig (works number 11000) in 1922 and the 262 locomotives of the Series 39 built by Borsig & Krupp over the next 5 years, were thus *Reichsbahn* engines.

The locomotives were required to haul trains of 600 tonnes up gradients of 1 per cent at a speed of 40 km/h and to have a maximum speed of 110 km/h. As constant, rather than high, speeds were required and as the locomotives would be needed to produce rapid acceleration from frequent stops, a three-cylinder design with eight coupled wheels of moderate diameter, was chosen. Bearing in mind the excellent riding qualities of the previous Saxon State Railways 2–8–2 with a Krauss-Helmholz leading truck, the KPEV engineers decided on a similar layout for the class P 10.

There were several interesting divergencies from previous Prussian design, the principal one being the adoption of a Belpaire, instead of a round-top, firebox. Of the three domes, the first contained the feed water inlet and the "purifying" trays; the second was the sand dome; the third dome contained the regulator valve. The three cylinders all drove the second coupled axle, the inside cylinder being inclined to enable the connecting rod to clear the first coupled axle. Three sets of Walschaerts valve gear were provided, all the eccentric rods being driven from outside return cranks on the third coupled axle: two were provided on the Left hand side for the Left hand and inside cylinders and one on the Right. That for the inside cylinder transmitted its motion by a double pendulum lever and shaft to the expansion link between the frames.

The Class P 10 were exceptionally quiet and smooth-running machines. In view of their 19-tonne axle-load they were never used as reparations engines but two of them went to Poland. Many of those which went to work on the *Reichsbahn* in East Germany were rebuilt with boilers having round-top fireboxes with combustion chambers. These engines became Series 22 of the DR, and they had Heinl feed water heaters.

Dimensions: CYLINDERS (3): 520 × 660 mm
　　　　　　　COUPLED WHEELS: 1750mm
　　　　　　　GRATE AREA: 4.0m^2
　　　　　　　BOILER PRESSURE: 14kg/cm^2
　　　　　　　SUPERHEATED

DB No 41.166 was identical with the stored locomotive [P. R-W]

No 41.297 is a two-cylinder 2–8–2 locomotive built in 1939 and rebuilt with large boiler. It is at present in store at *Bundesbahn Ausbesserung, Schwerte* and will probably be preserved.

The 366 locomotives of *Reichsbahn Gesellschaft* Series 41 Class G46.18 were introduced in 1936, the first engines being built by Schwartzkopff. During the next six years several other builders supplied them. They were classed as freight locomotives with a maximum speed of 90km/h although they were frequently to be found on passenger duties.

Two outside cylinders drove the third coupled axle (cf Series 39) and the piston valves were operated by Walschaerts valve gear. They had boilers of the standard DRG type with round-top fireboxes.

Between 1957 and 1961, the *Bundesbahn* rebuilt 103 of its Series 41 engines, including No 41.297, with larger boilers having combustion chambers and identical with those used for rebuilding the Pacifics of Series 03[10]. These rebuilt engines were Class G46.20.

In East Germany the rebuilding was with boilers identical with those used for the rebuilt engines of Series 22 (qv).

Dimensions: CYLINDERS: 520 × 720mm
            COUPLED WHEELS: 1600mm
            GRATE AREA: 3.89m^2
            BOILER PRESSURE: 16kg/cm^2
            SUPERHEATED

NSB No 3832 was identical with No 2770 which will be preserved. These were DRG Series 52
[P. R-W

No 2770, Class 63a of the Norwegian State Railways (NSB) is an outside-cylinder 2–10–0 built in 1944 as DRG No 52.2770 by Henschel (works number 28322). It is scheduled for preservation at Hamar.

In 1938, the *Deutsche Reichsbahn* introduced a powerful two-cylinder 2–10–0 freight locomotive with bar frames and a boiler with a round-top firebox having a wide grate but no combustion chamber. These locomotives of Series 50 were highly successful and, with a maximum axle-load only slightly in excess of 15 tonnes, they had a wide availability. They were among the last steam locomotives in Western Germany. Some 2159 were built, and it is hoped that one will be preserved. One was on display at Karlsruhe Museum but has now, unfortunately, been broken up.

In 1942 the first of 6,285 locomotives of Series 52 appeared. These engines were the war-time "austerity" variant of the Series 50. They were shorn of all embellishments and much of the running plate was omitted giving them a very stark appearance. Many had plate frames instead of bar frames but they were magnificent machines and, with their 15-tonne axle-load, the *Kriegloks*, as they were called, were to be found in the stock of most standard gauge European Railways, East and West. after World War II. Many were altered to run on the 1524mm gauge and sent to Soviet Russia.

No 2770 of the NSB is one of 74 of the Series 52 which were sent to Norway and which remained there to work both freight and passenger trains.

Dimensions: CYLINDERS: 600 × 660mm   GRATE AREA: 3.89m²
           COUPLED WHEELS: 1400mm   BOILER PRESSURE: 16kg/cm²
           SUPERHEATED

No 42.2708 of the Austrian Federal Railways (ÖBB) was built by Floridsdorf (works number 17591) in 1946. It is an outside-cylinder 2–10–0 and is at present in store at Vienna South Depot, reserved for preservation.

CFL No 5513 is now preserved at Bettembourg. This was one of the DRG Series 42, built in Austria
[P. R-W

No 5513, Class 150.55 of the Luxembourg National Railways Company (CFL) is an outside-cylinder 2–10–0 built in 1947 for the Austrian Federal Railways (ÖBB) as No 42.2721 by Floridsdorf (works number 17604). It was one of 20 such locomotives sold to CFL and it is preserved and on display in a park near the CFL workshops at Bettembourg.

An outside-cylinder 2–10–0 which was larger and more powerful than the Series 50 and 52 was introduced in 1943. This was Series 42 and in these engines the maximum axle-load was 17.6 tonnes. As they were essentially a war-time product, they were built to austerity standards and the DR regarded them as *Kreigsloks*. In all, 866 were built between 1943 and 1947, some in Poland and 266 by the Vienna Locomotive Works at Floridsdorf before 1945. These engines went to the *Reichsbahn*. Between 1945 and 1947 after the end of the World War II, a further 72 engines of Series 42 were built at Floridsdorf of which 33 were sent to Bulgaria, two to East Germany, five to Hungary, and Luxembourg received 20 of which the preserved locomotive No 5513 is one. The remaining 12 engines remained on the ÖBB in Austria and the preserved locomotive, No 42.2708 is one of these.

Dimensions: CYLINDERS: 630 × 660mm
COUPLED WHEELS: 1400mm
GRATE AREA: 4.7m^2
BOILER PRESSURE: 16kg/cm^2
SUPERHEATED

No 2100, Bavarian Class BBI is sectioned and exhibited in the Verkehrsmuseum *at Nürnberg* [DB

Bavarian State Railways No 2100 Class BB1 is a four-cylinder compound 0–4–4–0 Mallet tender locomotive built in 1896 by Maffei (works number 1802). It has been partly sectioned and is preserved, without a tender, in the *Verkehrsmuseum* at Nürnberg.

The four-cylinder compound articulated locomotive type designed and patented by Anatole Mallet, a well-known French engineer, was first built for service on narrow gauge railways having severe curvature and frequently very uneven track. The first Mallet locomotives went into service in 1888. The design was characterised by two sets of coupled wheels, the rear set being rigid in the frames while the leading set were in the frames of a Bissel truck whose centre of rotation was located in front of the rear set of wheels. The rear coupled wheels were driven by the two high pressure cylinders and the leading set by the two low pressure cylinders.

The first standard gauge Mallets were 0–4–4–0 Tank locomotives built by Maffei for the Swiss Central Railway in 1891. In 1896, the Pfalz Railway and the Bavarian State Railways put into service identical 0–4–4–0 Mallet tender engines of which No 2100 is the only survivor. These engines had slide valves for both high pressure and low pressure

273

cylinders. The valves were above the cylinders and were operated by Walschaerts valve gear.

On the Bavarian State Railways, the engines were used principally on the steeply-graded lines in the Black Forest.

Dimensions: CYLINDERS: HIGH PRESSURE: 415×630mm
LOW PRESSURE: 635×630mm
COUPLED WHEELS: 1340mm
GRATE AREA: 2.13m^2
BOILER PRESSURE: 14kg/cm^2

This opposed-piston 0–4–0T carries Maffei Works number 2499. It is preserved in the Verkehrs-museum *at Nürnberg*   [Verkehrsmuseum, Nürnberg

An outside-cylinder 0–4–0 Side Tank locomotive built in 1905 by Maffei for the Bavarian State Railways (KBSB) as their Class PtL 2/2 is preserved in the *Verkehrsmuseum* at Nürnberg. The works number of this locomotive is 2499: there is doubt as to its running number but it is one of the Series 4001–4024 of the KBSB (DRG 98.361–383). This locomotive is exhibited without cab, tanks and running plates.

No 4515 is an outside-cylinder 0–4–0 Well Tank locomotive built in 1908 by Krauss (works number 5897) for the Bavarian State Railways as their Class PtL 2/2. It is one of KBSB Series 4507–4535, the survivors of which became DRG 98.301–309. This locomotive has been sectioned and is on display in the *Verkehrsmuseum* at Nürnberg.

No. 98.307 is an outside-cylinder 0–4–0 Well Tank locomotive which was built in 1908 by Krauss (works number 5911), for the Bavarian State Railways as No 4529 Class PtL 2/2. It is at present in store at the DB

Bavarian No 4515, an 0–4–0WT is sectioned and exhibited in the Verkehrsmuseum *at Nürnberg*
[P. R-W

Locomotive Depot at Nürnberg and will go to the Railway Museum at Berlin.

During the period 1905–1913, the Bavarian State Railways put into service a number of 0–4–0 Tank locomotives for working light trains on branch lines and for operation by one man only (cf ÖBB locomotives, page 35).

There were two basic designs, one of which came from the State Railways' own workshops and examples of which were also supplied by Maffei. The other design came from Krauss but both Maffei and Krauss produced variants of the original designs. However, all the locomotives of Class PtL 2/2 had a number of common features.

    (i) they were all four-coupled tank engines with a comparatively long wheelbase,

    (ii) they all had Schmidt superheaters and piston valves operated by Heusinger valve gear,

    (iii) they all had hopper coal bunkers attached to the sloping backplates of the boilers and which were replenished from above.

At the base of each hopper was a manually operated sliding door-plate, the movement of which allowed controlled quantities of coal to be fed by gravity into the firebox. Provision was made for cleaning the fire through a small firehole in the Right hand side of the firebox in the Krauss engines and below the hopper feed plates in the Maffei engines.

The engines built in the Railway Workshops and by Maffei, of which works number 2499 is an example, are of great interest. The two outside cylinders were placed midway between the driving wheels and each cylinder had opposed pistons, the drive from one piston being to the leading axle and from the other to the trailing axle. Piston valves, above each cylinder, were operated by two sets of outside Heusinger valve gear. In No 2499, instead of return cranks, a single eccentric was used for each set of valve gear, this eccentric being located inside the leading driving crank on each side. The driving wheels were connected by a long coupling rod. In later Maffei engines the valve gear was driven from the trailing instead of from the leading axle, and return cranks replaced the eccentrics.

These locomotives were all Side Tanks and they had conventionally situated footplates and cabs.

The Krauss engines were quite different and there were three variants, but all had normal piston valve cylinders and none had opposed pistons.

    (i) The earliest Krauss engines, KBSB Nos 4501–4506, had inside cylinders driving an intermediate jackshaft from which two outside cranks drove each axle by means of connecting rods. These locomotives had end-tanks and the driving position was on the Right hand side of the boiler. There was an over-all cab.

    (ii) Later Krauss engines had outside cylinders driving on to the outside cranks of a jackshaft situated centrally across the engine. Connecting rods led from the jackshaft cranks to each driving wheel. The return cranks of the outside valve gear also derived their motion from the cranks of the lay shaft. These locomotives had Well tanks and the driving position was on the Right hand side of the boiler. A cab, with glass side windows, covered the extent of the boiler and from its appearance the little tank engines became known as the "glass box engines" (*glaskastenloks*). The preserved locomotives No 4515 and No. 98.307 are of this variant.

    (iii) The final Krauss design followed closely that described under (ii) above, the difference being in the motion. The jackshaft was omitted and the drive from the outside cylinders was directly on to the trailing coupled axle with a long coupling rod on each side of the engine connecting the two axles. In this conventional lay-out the return cranks of the valve gear also derived their motion from the trailing axle.

All those locomotives of Class PtL 2/2 which came into DRG stock became Series 98³ Class L 22.11.

Dimensions: Maffei No 2499

    CYLINDER DIAMETER: 265mm

    STROKE OF EACH OPPOSED PISTON: 280mm

    COUPLED WHEELS: 990mm

    GRATE AREA: $0.83m^2$

    BOILER PRESSURE: $12kg/cm^2$

    SUPERHEATED

Dimensions: Nos 4515 and 98.307

    CYLINDERS: $320 \times 400mm$

    COUPLED WHEELS: 1006mm

    GRATE AREA: $0.6m^2$

    BOILER PRESSURE: $12kg/cm^2$

    SUPERHEATED

No 88.7306 is an outside-cylinder 0–4–0 Well Tank locomotive which was built in 1892 by Maffei for the Pfalz Railways on which it was named *SCHEIDT*. It was withdrawn from stock in 1936 but was actually used as No 705.80.01 for departmental shunting until 1964. This locomotive was preserved and was on display at Ludwigshafen *Hauptbahnhof*, but with the opening of the new station, it has been put into store pending the decision on a new site.

From 1875—79, 86 of these shunting locomotives were built by Maffei for the Bavarian State Railways as their Class D IV. Between 1892 and 1897, 21 were built for the Pfalz Railways as their Class T 1. In all, 174 were built for the two railways, the later ones coming from Krauss. On DRG they were Class Gt 22.14.

These engines had round-top boilers with the dome on the first ring. Slide valves above the cylinders were operated by outside Allan link motion.

Dimensions: CYLINDERS: $266 \times 508mm$

    COUPLED WHEELS: 1006mm

    GRATE AREA: $0.75m^2$

    BOILER PRESSURE: $12kg/cm^2$

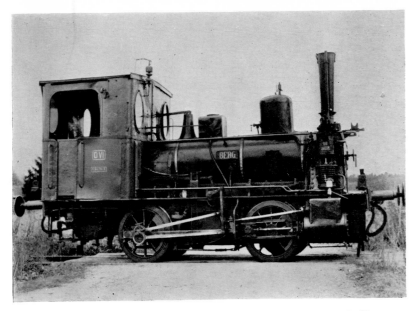

BERG ex Bavarian State Railways Class D VI   [Horst J. Obermayer

No. 98.7508 *BERG* is an outside-cylinder 0–4–0 Well Tank locomotive which was built in 1883 as Class D VI of the Bavarian State Railways by Krauss (works number 1222). It is now preserved in the ownership of *Deutsche Gesellschaft für Eisenbahngeschichte* EV.

Between the years of 1880 and 1894 Krauss of Münich built 45 0–4–0 Well Tank locomotives for working light local trains on the Bavarian State Railways. These were Class D VI and they had outside cylinders with slide valves on top and outside Stephenson link motion. Twenty-six of the engines came into the stock of the Reichsbahn on which they were Class L 22.9.

Dimensions: CYLINDERS: 266 × 508mm
COUPLED WHEELS: 976mm
GRATE AREA: 0.7m²
BOILER PRESSURE: 12kg/cm²

DB No 70.083 preserved at Mühldorf

[Brian Garvin

No 70.083 Class Pt 23.14 of the *Deutsche Bundesbahn* is an outside-cylinder 2–4–0 Side Tank locomotive built in 1912 by Krauss (works number 6733) for the Bavarian State Railways as their Class Pt 2/3. It is preserved and is on display at *Bundesbahnbetriebsamt*, Mühldorf.

No 770.86 of the Austrian Federal Railway (ÖBB) is an outside-cylinder 2–4–0 Side Tank locomotive which was built in 1913 as No 6086, Class Pt 2/3, of the Bavarian State Railways by Krauss (works number 6736). It is at Vienna South Depot but is to be put on display at Pochlarn.

Between 1909 and 1913, ninety seven 2–4–0 Side Tank locomotives were built for the Bavarian State Railways by Krauss. They were of peculiar appearance having the leading carrying wheel under the smokebox, and the driving wheels close together under the firebox and cab. Schmidt superheaters and piston valves contributed to their modern design but with their long and peculiarly spaced wheel-base, their stability was of some concern and the leading Bissel truck in some engines was replaced by a "fixed" axle.

In 1914 five identical engines were built for the Baden State Railways as their Class Ig[1]. Two years later this railway put 15 more into service but these had longer tanks and the axle-load was raised from 13.9 to 14.5 tonnes. That these little tank engines were very successful is evidenced by the fact that, in 1927–28, Krupp supplied eight more to DRG. These locomotives, however, were more powerful, the boiler pressure being raised from 12 to $14kg/cm^2$. The axle-load was increased to 15.2 tonnes as a result of a larger bunker, water tanks and a larger superheater. In these engines the leading axle was carried in the frames.

On trial, the original Bavarian engines were capable of maintaining a speed of 40 km/h up a gradient of 1 in 200 ($5^0/_{00}$) with a load of 320 tonnes.

Dimensions: (Class Pt 2/3)

CYLINDERS: $375 \times 500mm$	GRATE AREA: $1.22m^2$
COUPLED WHEELS: 1250mm	BOILER PRESSURE: $12kg/cm^2$
SUPERHEATED	

The following locomotives of Prussian State Railways 0–6–0 Well Tank locomotives of Class T3 are preserved or will probably be so:
No 89.7296 ex KPEV is preserved in a children's playground at Kassel.

No 89.7462 built for KPEV in 1904 by Hagans (works number 409) has been preserved in the children's playground at Cologne Zoo.

No 14 of the *Sudwestdeutschen Eisenbahn Gesellschaft* (SWEG) is of KPEV Class T 3 design. It is preserved in working order and works special trains on the SWEG line between Achern and Ottenhofen.

SWEG No 28 is typical of the several preserved locomotives of KPEV Class T 3
[Gerhard Richter

No 28 of SWEG is identical with No 14 (above). It also worked on similar duties but has now been withdrawn and will probably be preserved in the same area.

No 30 of SWEG is also of KPEV Class T 3 design and was built in 1904 by Borsig. It is owned now by a society called *Eurovapor* and was last noted at the DB Haltingen Depot at Basle prior to being put to work on the Haltingen-Kandern line of SWEG.

Also of KPEV Class T 3 design is No 1710 which was built for the Prenzlaner Kreisbahn
[Brian Garvin

No 1710 was built in 1901 by Freudenstein (works number 89) for the *Prenzlaner Kreisbahn* as their No 3. It later belonged to *Metallhuttenwerke*, Lübeck. It is of KPEV Class T 3 design and has been preserved by the *Freunde der Eisenbahn Klub*. Its present location is not known.

The much-loved little outside-cylinder 0–6–0 Well Tank locomotives of Class T 3 were first built for KPEV in 1881 and, from then until 1910, all the principal German locomotive builders were concerned in providing 1,345 of them for that Railway. Others were built for several private railways, a grand total of some 1,550 of the class being constructed.

Of the KPEV engines, 511 came into the stock of DRG and were Series 89.7001–7511, Class Gt 33.12.

The design embodied a round-top boiler with a large steam dome on the second ring. The sand box was behind the dome and the safety valves were in front of the cab. Coal was carried in two side bunkers. Slide valves above the cylinders were operated by Allan link motion; in engines built for various railways after 1910, Walschaerts valve gear was used. The bunker capacity also varied in engines built for private railways and the axle-load of some of these was only 11 tonnes.

Dimensions: CYLINDERS: 350 × 550mm
COUPLED WHEELS: 1100mm
GRATE AREA: 1.35m²
BOILER PRESSURE: 12kg/cm²

No 89.7531 is an outside-cylinder 0–6–0 Well Tank locomotive which was built in 1898 and was taken over by DRG in 1938 from its original

owners, the *Braunschweigische Landes-Eisenbahn* (BLE) and it received the computerised number 089–003–8 before being withdrawn. This little engine has an axle-load of only 10 tonnes and was DRG Class Gt 33.10. It is at present in store at Schwerte and it is believed that it may go to the *Verkehrsmuseum* at Munich.
Dimensions: NOT KNOWN.

No 89.7538 is an outside-cylinder 0–6–0 Well Tank locomotive which is one of ten engines of the same class, built between 1900 and 1907 for the *Braunschweigische Landes-Eisenbahn* (BLE). They became DRG Class Gt 33.12 in 1938.

No 89.7538 was intended for the Canadian Railway Museum at Delson, but it is not now to leave Germany. It is at present at Hannover on the DB and from there it is sent to various exhibitions from time to time. The future of this locomotive is uncertain.
Dimensions: NOT KNOWN. PROBABLY SIMILAR TO THOSE OF
      KPEV CLASS T 3

Ex Bremen Harbour Authority No 89.7513 is on display in Berlin   [DB

No 89.7513 is an outside-cylinder 0–6–0 Well Tank locomotive which was built in 1911 for the Bremen Harbour Authority (Hf Brm). It came into DRG stock and later came into the ownership of DB who withdrew it from service in 1964. It is now on display in the childrens' playground at Kreuzberg, West Berlin.

This was one of ten engines built for Hf Brm between 1911 and 1920. They were comparatively large and powerful machines with a 15-tonne axle load and they became DRG Class Gt 33.15. They had Walschaerts valve gear operating slide valves which were angled outwards above the cylinders. The boilers had round-top fireboxes.
Dimensions: NOT KNOWN

DB No 89.314 ex Württemberg State Railways preserved at Esslingen-Mettingen   [P. R-W

No 89.314 is an outside-cylinder Well Tank locomotive built in 1892 for the Württemberg State Railways by Esslingen. It is now preserved at the works of the former *Maschinenfabrik Esslingen* at Esslingen-Mettingen.

The Württemberg State Railways introduced their Class T 3 0–6–0 Well Tank locomotives in 1891 and from then, until 1910, Esslingen, Krauss and Heilbronn built 110 of them for shunting duties. They had outside Walschaerts valve gear and the coal was carried in side bunkers. The first 13 engines had an axle-load of only 10 tonnes but the remainder, including the preserved engine, had larger tank and bunker capacity and a 12-tonne axle load. Their DRG classification was Gt 33.12.

Dimensions: CYLINDERS: 380 × 540mm   GRATE AREA: 0.99m²
COUPLED WHEELS: 1045mm   BOILER PRESSURE: 12kg/cm²

284

BD No 89.854 was Bavarian Class R 3/3 and identical with the locomotive to be preserved [P. R-W

No 89.801 is an outside-cylinder 0–6–0 Side Tank locomotive built in 1921 by Krauss for the Bavarian State Railways as their Class R 3/3. It is at present stored at Schwerte for probable preservation.

The Bavarian State Railways shunting tank engines of Class R 3/3 were introduced in 1906 and 17 were built by Krauss between then and 1913. In 1921–22, the same builders supplied a further 90 engines with larger tanks and an axle-load increased from 15 to 16 tonnes. In all the engines, coal was carried in a hopper-type bunker above the Left hand side of the boiler, immediately in front of the cab. The boiler had a round-top firebox with a large dome on the second ring. The safety valves were on top of the dome. Walschaerts valve gear operated slide valves which were inclined outwards above the cylinders.

Dimensions: CYLINDERS: 420 × 610mm
          COUPLED WHEELS: 1216mm
          GRATE AREA: 1.61m^2
          BOILER PRESSURE: 12kg/cm^2

No 7270 is an outside-cylinder 0–6–2 Side Tank locomotive built in 1893 by Borsig (works number 4431) for the Prussian State Railways (KPEV) as their Class T 9^1. It passed into the ownership of Pfeifer & Langen who used it for shunting duties at their sugar factory. It is now preserved in working order by *Deutsche Gesellschaft für Eisenbahngeschichte EV.*

No 44 of the Kleinbahn–Frankfurt–Konigstein was of KPEV Class T 9^1 design   [Gerhard Röder

No 44 is also of KPEV Class T 9^1 design. It was built in 1913 for the *Kleinbahn Frankfurt-Königstein* by Henschel (works number 12478) and was withdrawn in 1963. It is now preserved in a childrens' playground in Hattersheim (Main).

Three hundred and twenty-eight 0–6–2 Side Tank locomotives of Class T 9^1 were built for the Prussian State Railways between 1892 and 1909 and 231 were taken into DRG stock to become Nos 90.001-231 Class Gt 34.14. A number of other locomotives of the same design were built during this period, and later, for various private railways.

The Class T 9^1 had round-top boilers with the steam dome on the first ring. Water was carried in side tanks which sloped towards the front and coal was in a bunker behind the cab. The trailing axle was in a backward extension of the main frame and had considerable lateral movement. Slide valves were inclined outwards above the cylinders and they were operated by outside Allan link motion. These were soundly designed, but unexceptional, engines which gave good service on branch line and shunting duties.

Dimensions: CYLINDERS: 430 × 630mm
COUPLED WHEELS: 1250mm
GRATE AREA: 1.73m^2
BOILER PRESSURE: 12kg/cm^2

No 98.507 is an outside-cylinder 0–6–2 Side Tank locomotive which was built in 1903 by Krauss (works number 4869) for the Bavarian State Railways as their No 2730 Class DX I. It has been restored and is on display, mounted on a plinth at Ingolstadt *Hauptbahnhof*.

The design of these Bavarian engines varied considerably from that of the Prussian Class T 9^1. The dome was placed just in front of the round-top firebox and was surmounted by Salter-type safety valves. The outside cylinders had slide valves above them but angled outwards at 45°. The valves were operated by Walschaerts valve gear. The trailing wheels were in a Bissel truck and a feature of the design was the unequal spacing of the coupled wheels, the middle and trailing wheels being located very close together. Coal was carried in a bunker at the rear of the cab.

Thirteen engines were built in 1895–97 and these engines had a 10-tonne axle load. Between 1897 and 1911 a further 127 were built with larger side tanks and an axle load of 11-tonnes. The engines were all designated for local and branch line passenger and freight duties and they became DRG Series 98$^{4-5}$ Classes L 34.10 and L 34.11.

Dimensions: CYLINDERS: 375 × 508mm
COUPLED WHEELS: 1006mm
GRATE AREA: 1.34m^2
BOILER PRESSURE: 12kg/cm^2

Bentheimer Eisenbahn *2–6–0T No 14*   [P. R-W Collection

A *Bentheimer Eisenbahn* outside-cylinder 2–6–0 Well Tank locomotive No 14, built in 1925 by Hanomag (works number 10416) is to be preserved at Nordhorn on the Netherlands-German frontier.

This locomotive is one which was designed by ELNA-*Engere Lokomotiv-Normenausschuss.* This was a committee of engineers from the Prussian, Saxon, Baden, Württemberg and Alsace-Lorraine railways, set up during World War I to produce standard locomotive designs for both the States and private railways. (The three-cylinder 2–12–0 freight locomotive of Prussian Class G 12 was their first design.) It remained actively in existence until a similar committee was set up by the *Deutsche Reichsbahn* to establish a number of standard locomotive designs for the new organisation.

Eight of these locomotives which were built for private railways were taken into DRG stock between 1938 and 1942. They fell into two classes, some having Well tanks only and being DRG Class Gt 34.14. Others had both Side and Well tanks and larger bunkers and were Gt 34.16.

Dimensions: NOT KNOWN

DB No 64.217 which was identical with the locomotive in store   [P. R-W

No 64.001 is an outside-cylinder 2–6–2 Side Tank locomotive built for DRG in 1928 by Borsig. It is at present stored at Schwerte and it will probably be preserved.

After the Locomotive Engineers Committee of the newly-formed *Reichsbahn* had provided adequate locomotives for the maintenance of heavy main-line express train services, they turned their attention to building modern, light-weight machines to work passenger and freight services on secondary lines laid with comparatively light-weight track.

In 1927 the elegant little 2–6–0 tender engines of Series 24 were introduced. These engines had outside cylinders, piston valves operated by Walschaerts valve gear and they were, of course, superheated. With an axle-load of only 15 tonnes they had a very wide availability.

In 1928 there appeared the first of Series 64, light-weight, passenger-tank locomotives. These engines were the tank locomotive version of Series 24 and the boiler, cylinders, motion, coupled wheels and many details, were identical in the two series. They were immensely popular and handy little machines. Between 1928 and 1940, 520 of them were built. The last ten engines were fitted with Krauss-Helmholz "bogies", all the others having Bissel trucks. They were Class Pt 35.15.

The trio of light-weight locomotive designs was completed by the introduction of the Series 86 freight tank locomotives (qv).

Dimensions: CYLINDERS: 500 × 660mm   GRATE AREA: 2.05m²
           COUPLED WHEELS: 1500mm   BOILER PRESSURE: 14kg/cm²
           SUPERHEATED

DB 2–6–4T No 66.001 was identical with the locomotive preserved   [Henschel & Sohn

No 66.002 (new number 066–002–7) is a 2–6–4 Side Tank locomotive built in 1955 for the *Deutsche Bundesbahn* by Henschel (works number 28924). It is preserved in working order by *Deutsche Gesellschaft für Eisenbahngeschichte EV.*

Two of these modern and handsome 2–6–4T locomotives were built in 1955, ostensibly to replace the Prussian 4–6–4T locomotives of Class T 18. As a result of the increasing use of diesel traction and the intended extension of electrification, Nos 66.001 and .002 remained the only examples of their class.

The leading radial axles and the leading coupled axles of these locomotives formed a modified Krauss truck which allowed a lateral displacement of 10mm each side of centre in the coupled axle and 105mm in the radial axle. The two cylinders had long-travel piston valves operated by Walschaerts valve gear. The boilers were welded with steel fireboxes and the engines had welded plate frames.

These two locomotives were each said to be capable of hauling 400-tonne trains at 100km/h on a level track, though with their maximum axle load of only 15.9 tonnes it is doubtful if this performance was ever achieved.

Dimensions: CYLINDERS: 470 × 660mm
                 COUPLED WHEELS: 1600mm
                 GRATE AREA: 1.95m^2
                 BOILER PRESSURE: 16kg/cm^2
                 SUPERHEATED

DB 4–6–4T No 78.371 was of the same type and class as the stored locomotive   [P. R-W

No 78.126 is a two-cylinder 4–6–4 Side and Back Tank locomotive of Prussian State Railways Class T 18. It is at present at Schwerte awaiting preservation.

More than 500 of these handsome tank locomotives of KPEV Class T 18 were built between 1912 and 1927, coming from the Vulcan Works and from Henschel. They were, obviously, the tank-engine version of the Class P 8 4–6–0 mixed traffic locomotive and, although the dimensions were not identical, all the leading characteristics of boiler, frames, cylinders etc., were in evidence. They proved to be reliable and economical machines and, at one time or another, handled a major part of the suburban traffic of all the great German cities.

These locomotives became Series 78⁰⁻⁵ Class Pt 37.17 of the DRG, DR and DB and they included in their number 20 which were built for the Württemberg State Railways and 462 which came from KPEV. Most of the remainder were built for DRG. One of those which went to DR in East Germany was fitted with a Giesl Ejector. A number of the engines went to Poland and to other European countries as reparations while eight were built new for the Turkish Railways in 1928.

Dimensions: CYLINDERS: 560 × 630mm
              COUPLED WHEELS: 1650mm
              GRATE AREA: 2.44m²
              BOILER PRESSURE: 12kg/cm²
              SUPERHEATED

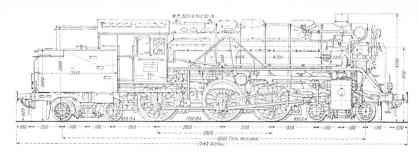

Side elevation of 4–6–4 Back Tank locomotive of Series 62   [P. R-W Collection

No 62.003 is a 4–6–4 Back Tank locomotive built in 1928 by Henschel for DRG. It is at present stored at Mulheim and will probably be preserved.

Fifteen of these heavy and powerful tank engines of Class Pt 37.20 were built for duties on busy suburban lines and, specifically, for working heavy trains in the Elberfeld district. No doubt, in view of the known instability of the 4–6–4 wheel arrangement with side tanks, such tanks were omitted from this design, the water being carried under the bunker. The design followed closely that of the standard Pacific locomotives of DRG and included such features as a round top boiler without combustion chamber, hollow axles, bar frames, Walschaerts valve gear operating long-travel piston valves above horizontal outside cylinders and piston tail-rods. All wheels were braked.

Eight of the 15 locomotives went to DR in East Germany, the remainder going to the *Bundesbahn*.

Dimensions: CYLINDERS: 600 × 660mm
            COUPLED WHEELS: 1750mm
            GRATE AREA: 3.5m^2
            BOILER PRESSURE: 14kg/cm^2
            SUPERHEATED

DB No 098 812–1, recently a prize in a competition　　　　　　　　　　[DB

No 098–812–1 (ex 98.812) Class L 44.11 is an outside-cylinder 0–8–0 Side Tank locomotive which was built in 1914 by Krauss (works number 6911) for the Bavarian State Railways as their No 2562 Class GtL 4/4. It was recently offered by *Deutsche Bundesbahn* as a prize in a publicity competition and it was won by Herr Manfred Moser. The locomotive is at present at Schweinfurt Locomotive Depot of the DB, but is likely to go on permanent loan to *Deutsche Gesellschaft für Eisenbahngeschichte EV.*

This locomotive is one of 53 which were first built in 1911 for the *"lokalbahn"* services of the Bavarian State Railways. They introduced a new concept in the design of locomotives for service on lightly laid and often rough track. With superheated boilers and piston valve cylinders, it was a remarkable achievement to keep the maximum axle-load down to 10.8 tonnes and the total weight to 43 tonnes. The wheelbase was kept short by arranging the last two coupled axles as close together as possible but provision was made for lateral movement in the first and fourth axles. Drive was to the third axle, necessitating fairly long connecting rods.

Dimensions: CYLINDERS: 460 × 508mm　　GRATE AREA: 1.36m^2
　　　　　　　COUPLED WHEELS: 1006mm　BOILER PRESSURE: 12kg/cm^2
　　　　　　　SUPERHEATED

293

DB No 098 886–5 which is stored pending preservation [Gerhard Richter

No 098–886–5 (ex 98.886) is an outside-cylinder 0–8–0 Side Tank loco-motive built in 1924 by Krauss (works number 8275) for the Bavarian State Railways as their No 2636 Class GtL 4/4. It is stored at Schweinfurt pending preservation.

This is one of 63 locomotives of the same design as No 098–812–1 (above) but having larger tanks and bunkers, and weighing 46.3 tonnes. They were DRG and DB Class L 44.12 and were built 1923–28. *Dimensions:* AS FOR NO 098–812–1

DB No 92.739, KPEV Class T 13 awaiting preservation at Kassel [R. G. Farr

No 92.739 is an outside-cylinder 0–8–0 Side Tank locomotive built in 1917 for KPEV as their Class T 13. It is at present on display at Stadt Allendorf.

Five hundred and sixty-two non-superheater 0–8–0 Side Tank loco-motives of Class T 13 were supplied by various builders to KPEV between the years of 1910 and 1923. The outside cylinders drove the second axle and Walschaerts valve gear operated slide valves above the cylinders.

With a 15-tonne axle load, they had wide availability but they were not scattered widely outside Germany, being found only in Poland, Austria, Saar and Czechoslovakia. They became DRG Class Gt 44.15.

Dimensions: CYLINDERS: 500 × 600mm
          COUPLED WHEELS: 1250mm
          GRATE AREA: 1.73m^2
          BOILER PRESSURE: 12kg/cm^2.

No 81.004 is an 0–8–0 Side Tank locomotive with outside cylinders which was built for DRG by Hanomag in 1928. It is at present in store at Oldenburg awaiting preservation in the *Verkehrsmuseum* at Berlin.

Ten powerful 0–8–0 Side Tank locomotives for shunting duties were built by Hanomag in 1928. Twelve years later it was intended to build 60 more of these engines but, probably because of the outbreak of World War II, the order was cancelled.

The locomotives were Class Gt 44.17 and they had outside cylinders driving the third axle with Walschaerts valve gear operating piston valves above the cylinders. The boilers had superheaters and round-top fire-boxes and there were four domes—the first for top feed, the second for sand, the third contained the regulator valve and the fourth was another sand dome.

Dimensions: CYLINDERS: 500 × 550mm
          COUPLED WHEELS: 1100mm
          GRATE AREA: 1.78m^2
          BOILER PRESSURE: 14kg/cm^2
          SUPERHEATED

ÖBB No 86.070 was one of DRG Series 86 which had leading and trailing Bissel trucks. No 86.491, which is stored, has Krauss-Helmholz "bogies" but is otherwise identical   [P. R-W

No 86.491 is an outside-cylinder 2–8–2 Side Tank locomotive, built in 1942, as DRG Class Gt 46.15, and which was withdrawn in November 1967. It is at present in store at *Bundesbahn Ausbesserung*, Schwerte and will probably be preserved.

Following on the successful introduction of the light-weight 2–6–0 of Series 24 and the 2–6–2T of Series 64 (qv) the 2–8–2T locomotives of Series 86 Class Gt 46.15 were introduced late in 1928, and between then and 1943 a total of 775 were built by all the principal German locomotive works. They were intended for the many secondary lines in hilly and often mountainous districts and the design at once proved its value. Many of the mechanical parts were standard with those of the Series 24 and 64 but the boiler dimensions were not the same. As in the cases of these two previous classes there was considerable difference of opinion as to whether the engines should have Bissel trucks or Krauss-Helmholz "bogies". The former were much cheaper to construct, the latter were claimed to give much greater lateral stability. Although all early engines of Series 86 had Bissel trucks, the majority had the Krauss-Helmholz arrangement.

After World War II, engines of Series 86 were ceded to Austria, Czechoslovakia and Poland while East and West Germany divided the remainder.

Dimensions: CYLINDERS: 570 × 660mm   GRATE AREA: 2.38m²
           COUPLED WHEELS: 1400mm   BOILER PRESSURE: 14kg/cm²
           SUPERHEATED

DR No 94.818 was identical with DB No 94.816

[P. R-W

No 94.816 is an outside-cylinder 0–10–0 Side Tank locomotive built for the Prussian State Railways in 1917 and at present stored at Schwerte for future preservation.

Twelve hundred and fifty 0–10–0 Side Tank locomotives of Class T 16¹ were supplied to KPEV and DRG by various builders between the years 1913 and 1924. They had a 17-tonne axle load and were DRG Class Gt 55.17.

They were typically Prussian engines, obvious kinsmen of the P 8, G 8¹ and G 10 classes. Two outside cylinders, Walschaerts valve gear, Schmidt superheaters and round-top boilers with long narrow grates were common features. Unlike the preceding class (T 16) the drive was to the third and not to the fourth, axle.

They had a very short wheelbase and side play was provided in the leading and trailing axles. As such, they were ideal for heavy shunting duties and they were in demand in West and East Germany and in other countries whence they were sent as reparations after both World Wars.

Dimensions: CYLINDERS: 610 × 660mm
      COUPLED WHEELS: 1350mm
      GRATE AREA: 2.3m²
      BOILER PRESSURE: 12kg/cm²
      SUPERHEATED

DRG No 85.004 was of the same type and class as No 85.007　　　　[DB

No 85.007 is a three-cylinder 2–10–2 Side Tank locomotive which was built in 1932 by Henschel. It was withdrawn from service in June 1961 and is at present preserved at the School of Engineering at Constance but may ultimately go to the *Verkehrsmuseum* at Nürnberg.

Ten heavy tank locomotives of Series 85 were built for duties on the Höllental lines in the Black Forest. They were designed to work, unaided, 560-tonne trains on a continuous 1 per cent gradient at 40km/h, but they were also extensively used for banking purposes. When the Black Forest line was electrified in 1960, the ten engines were redundant and, after working for a short period at Wuppertal and elsewhere, they were withdrawn.

Series 85, with a 20-tonne axle-load, were the heaviest German tank locomotives. They were the tank-engine version of the three-cylinder 2–10–0 freight locomotives of Series 44. They had bar frames and the leading radial axle formed a Krauss-Helmholz bogie with the leading coupled axle. The two outside cylinders were placed horizontally and drove the third coupled axle while the steeply inclined inside cylinder drove the second. The three cylinders were of slightly greater diameter than those of the Series 44. There were three sets of Walschaerts valve gear. The boilers were of the standard *Reichsbahn* pattern but the pressure was reduced from 16kg/cm² to 14kg/cm². They were Class Gt 57.20.

Dimensions: CYLINDERS (3): 600 × 660mm
　　　　　　　　COUPLED WHEELS: 1400mm
　　　　　　　　GRATE AREA: 3.5m²
　　　　　　　　BOILER PRESSURE: 14kg/cm²
　　　　　　　　SUPERHEATED

No 97.502 of DRG is preserved at the builders' works at Esslingen-Mettingen   [P. R-W

No 97.502 is a four-cylinder compound rack and adhesion 0–10–0 Side Tank locomotive which was built for the Württemberg State Railways but delivered to DRG in 1922 by Esslingen (works number 4057). It is preserved at the builders' works, Maschinenfabrik Esslingen at Esslingen-Mettingen, now owned by the Mercedes-Daimler-Benz combine.

No 97.504 is another locomotive, identical with No 97.502 but it was built for DRG in 1925 by Esslingen (works number 4142). It will be preserved in the *Verkehrsmuseum* at Berlin.

In 1923 two powerful rack and adhesion 0–10–0 Side Tank locomotives were built for the Württemberg State Railways by Esslingen. They were delivered to DRG and were Class Z 55.15. They were followed by two more for DRG in 1925. No 97.503 was destroyed during World War II.

The locomotives were four-cylinder compounds, the high pressure cylinders driving the third coupled axle of the adhesion wheels and the low pressure cylinders, situated above the high pressure cylinders, drove the two coupled rack pinions through reduction gear wheels. The high pressure and low pressure cylinders were identical in size and each cylinder had its own piston valve. A change valve enabled the locomotive to be worked on the rack sections either as a compound or as a four-cylinder simple. The rack engine could be cut out and the locomotive worked as a two-cylinder simple on the adhesion sections of the line. Both engines could be used for Riggenbach counter-pressure braking.

Cylinders and motion of the rack and adhesion 0–10–0 T No 97.502   [P. R-W

The locomotives were used on the 100°/₀₀₀ (1 in 10) gradient of the Württemberg line from Honau up to Lichtenstein, a distance of 2.2km. This section is operated by the Riggenbach-Klose rack system and, on the locomotives, a single rack pinion, able to withstand a force of 16,000kg, was all that was necessary. However, as a measure of safety and also to increase the effectiveness of the counter-pressure brake, a second pinion, coupled to the first, was provided.

The locomotives were withdrawn in 1962 and the section is now operated by diesel-rack railcars.

Dimensions: CYLINDERS: ADHESION: 560 × 560mm
                     RACK: 560 × 560mm
          COUPLED WHEELS (ADHESION): 1150mm
          GRATE AREA: 2.5m²
          BOILER PRESSURE: 14kg/cm²
          SUPERHEATED

Narrow Gauge Steam Locomotive Preservation in West Germany

A considerable number of narrow gauge locomotives exists, many of them being kept as monuments in parks, playgrounds etc. Most of these are industrial locomotives and, therefore, outside the scope of this book.

Deutsche Gesellschaft für Eisenbahngeschichte EV owns several narrow gauge locomotives but at present has no intention of working them as it has the 1435mm-gauge locomotives which it owns.

The most important German narrow gauge railways were laid to a gauge of 1000mm. The narrow gauge lines of the former Saxon State Railways and of the former Württemberg State Railways which were of 750mm-gauge also formed a large part of the total narrow gauge railway systems, while the Prussian State Railways owned some 785mm-gauge lines and there were some smaller 900mm-gauge systems.

Narrow gauge steam locomotives were all in the DRG 99 Series, various types and classes being given numbers between 99.001 and 99.7843 with many blanks and, including in the Series, locomotives of the narrow gauge railways of Austria, Czechoslovakia, Jugoslavia, Luxembourg and Poland.

In the following pages, descriptions are given of what are probably the most important German preserved narrow gauge steam locomotives but, it is realised, that there may be others which should be included in this account.

GERMANY   1000mm
DEUTSCHE EISENBAHN VEREIN (DEV)
(GERMAN RAILWAY ASSOCIATION)

This amateur society operates passenger train services at week-ends over the 1000mm-gauge freight branch line of the *Verkehrsbetriebe Grafschaft Hoya Gmbh* (VGH) between Bruckhausen Vilsen and Asendorf, near Bremen in North Germany.

Motive power to work the line is provided by:

(i) an outside-cylinder 0–4–0 Well Tank locomotive built in 1927 by Henschel for an industrial concern,

(ii) an outside-cylinder 0–6–0 Side Tank locomotive built in 1899 by Hanomag (works number 3341) as No 31 *HOYA* of the *Hoya Syke Asendorfer Eisenbahn Gmbh*, (HSA),

(iii) a similar outside-cylinder 0–6–0 Side Tank locomotive built in 1899 by Hanomag (works number 3344) as No 33 *BRUCKHAUSEN* for VGH,

(iv) an outside-cylinder 0–6–0 Side Tank locomotive built in 1911 by Hohenzollern (works number 2798) as No 15 of the *Kreis Altenser Eisenbahn* (KAE).

Dimensions of the two HSA locomotives:
      CYLINDERS: 320 × 300mm
      COUPLED WHEELS: 920mm
      GRATE AREA: 1.3m^2
      BOILER PRESSURE: 12kg/cm^2
Details of other locomotives not known.

Dates and times at which trains are operated by DEV have not been communicated, but this Museum Railway carries mails on Sundays between Bruckhausen Vilsen and Asendorf. For the purpose, an old postal van has been restored and is staffed on a voluntary basis by members of the Association.

Chiemsee-Bahn *0–4–0 Tram locomotive and train at Prien*   [R. G. Farr

Still at work after 83 years on the 2½km-long *Chiemsee-Bahn* between Prien and the lakeside at Stock, is an outside-cylinder 0–4–0 Tram locomotive built in 1887 by Krauss (works number 1813). It is identical with locomotives built for Bavarian Local Railways such as the *Walhallabahn*. This locomotive will inevitably be preserved one day, and this seems to be sufficient justification for including it herein.

It has been little altered during its long service, the greatest innovation being the provision of a turbo-generator and electric lighting. Slide valves operated by outside Allan link motion are inclined on top of the outside cylinders. Water is carried in side tanks. As the railway is not laid alongside a road, there is no skirting around the wheels of the locomotive and no condensing arrangements are provided.

Dimensions: CYLINDERS: 225 × 350mm
           COUPLED WHEELS: 800mm
           GRATE AREA: 0.56^2
           BOILER PRESSURE: 13kg/cm^2

OEG 0–4–0 Tram locomotive No 102

[Helmut Röth

No 102 is an inside-cylinder 0–4–0 Tram locomotive with side tanks and the usual overall cab and wheel skirting. It was built in 1891 by Henschel (works number 3618) for the *Oberheinischen Eisenbahn* (OEG) and it worked on their line between Heidelberg and Mannheim via Weinheim. The Company presented the locomotive and two passenger coaches to *Deutsche Gesellschaft für Eisenbahngeschichte EV* in 1968. As this Company has no plans to operate trains on the 1000mm gauge, the two coaches were given by them to *Deutsche Eisenbahn Verein EV* for service on their line between Bruchhausen Vilsen and Heiligenberg.

No 102 has outside frames and two inside cylinders with slide valves operated by inside Walschaerts valve gear. The driver's position is on the Right hand side of the boiler.

Dimensions: CYLINDERS: 250 × 300mm
COUPLED WHEELS: 600mm
GRATE AREA: 0.6m²
BOILER PRESSURE: 12kg/cm²

MEG o–4–o Tank locomotive No 46 [H. Urselmann

No 46 is an inside-cylinder 0–4–0 Side Tank locomotive built in 1898 by Graffenstaden (works number 4805) for the *Mittelbadischen Eisenbahn AG*. It was acquired, in 1969, by *Deutsche Gesellschaft für Eisenbahngeschichte EV* and it will be displayed in their projected Railway Museum.

This rather odd-looking machine has outside frames: the wheels, cylinders, valves and valve gear are inside the frames but coupling rods are outside. A single buffer is placed centrally at each end of the loco-motive. The large dome, surmounted by two safety valves, is on the first ring of the boiler and the two short side-tanks are placed well forward. A small turbo-generator on the left of the smokebox, supplies electric current for lighting.

Dimensions: CYLINDERS: 260 × 320mm
COUPLED WHEELS: 880mm
GRATE AREA: 0.61m²
BOILER PRESSURE: 12kg/cm²

OEG 0–4–0WT No 56 [M. A. Schmann

No 56 is an outside-cylinder 0–4–0 Well Tank locomotive which was built in 1886 by Karlsrühe (works number 1167) for the *Oberrheinischen-Eisenbahn-Gesellschaft* (OEG). It is preserved on a plinth at Mannheim Neckarstadt.

This little engine has slide valves above the cylinders and outside Allan link motion. Coal is carried in bunkers in front of the cab.

Dimensions: NOT KNOWN

No 11 and No 12 are 0–4–0 Tank locomotives built in 1913 for the *Wurttembergische Nebenbahn*. This is the *Hartsfeldbahn* which operated between Aalen, Neresheim and Dillingen. No 11 (Esslingen works number 3710) is preserved at the station at Neresheim. No 12 is preserved in Dillingen.

Further details are not known.

306

Zell Todtnau 0–6–0T No 74   [Krauss-Maffei

No 74 is an outside-cylinder 0–6–0 Side Tank locomotive built in 1888 by Krauss (works number 2024) for the Zell-Todtnau Railway. It is now preserved in the collection of *Deutsche Gesellschaft für Eisenbahngeschichte, EV*, being one of the first two locomotives acquired by this concern.

This is a straightforward narrow-gauge tank engine design. The slide valves are angled outwards on top of the outside cylinders and the valve gear is Walschaerts. The drive is to the third coupled axle.

Water is carried in two short side tanks and the coal bunkers are immediately behind the tanks.

Dimensions: CYLINDERS: 300 × 500mm
             COUPLED WHEELS: 935mm
             GRATE AREA: 0.82m²
             BOILER PRESSURE: 12kg/cm²

No 99.211, Class K 33.6, is an 0–6–0 Side Tank locomotive which was built in 1929 by Henschel (works number 21443) for the 1000mm-gauge lines of the former Oldenburg State Railways on the North German island of Wangerooge where it is preserved.

This was the first six-coupled tank engine to work on the island's railway and was a great improvement upon the previous four-coupled engines. It has a short wheelbase, the drive being to the third coupled axle. Walschaerts valve gear operates piston valves above the outside cylinders and the locomotive is superheated. Coal bunkers are behind the side tanks.

It was originally intended to preserve this locomotive in the new Railway Museum in Berlin. However, when it was replaced by diesel traction in 1960, the islanders insisted on its retention as a monument at Wangerooge.

Dimensions: NOT KNOWN

Ex LAG 0–6–2T No 99.253   [Brian Garvin

No 99.253 is an outside-cylinder 0–6–2 Tank locomotive with small Side tanks. It was built in 1908 by Krauss (works number 5929) for *Lokalbahn, AG.,* München (LAG) and later was taken over by DRG and subsequently DB, being Class K 34.5. This locomotive is now preserved as a monument outside the Divisional Headquarters of the *Bundesbahn* at Regensburg.

This was one of three locomotives built for LAG between 1902 and 1908. Slide valves, angled outwards, above the cylinders are operated by Walschaerts valve-gear. A lipped chimney gives the locomotive a pleasing appearance.

Dimensions: CYLINDERS: 300 × 400mm
COUPLED WHEELS: 800mm
GRATE AREA: 1.03m²
BOILER PRESSURE: 12kg/cm²

0–10–0T No 99.193   [R. Gottschall

No 99.193 is an 0–10–0 Side Tank locomotive built in 1927 by Esslingen (works number 4183) for DRG. It is now preserved in working order on the Blonay-Chamby Museum Railway near Vevey in Switzerland.

Four of these 1000mm-gauge tank engines were built for the Nagold-Altensteig line of the former Württemburg State Railway where they replaced some ancient Klose locomotives. With a maximum axle-load of 9 tonnes, they were DRG and DB Class K 55.9. In their design, provision was made for some lateral and radial movement of the first and fifth coupled axles. The drive is to the fourth axle. Walschaerts valve gear operates piston valves above the cylinders.

Dimensions: CYLINDERS: 430 × 400mm
          COUPLED WHEELS: 800mm
          GRATE AREA: 1.6m²
          BOILER PRESSURE: 14kg/cm²
          SUPERHEATED

BEG 0–4–4–0T No 11/SM   [Gerhard Röder]

No 11/SM of the *Brohltal-Eisenbahn-Gesellschaft* was built in 1906 by Humbolt (works number 348). It is now preserved by *Deutsche Gesellschaft für Eisenbahngeschichte EV.*

This is a Mallet four-cylinder compound 0–4–4–0 Side Tank locomotive in which the coal bunker is on the left-hand side of the engine in front of the cab and abaft the side tanks. Four sets of Walschaerts valve gear operate the slide valves above the cylinders.

Among the most interesting features of this locomotive is the arrangement of the buffers. A single centrally placed buffer dealt with 1000mm-gauge stock, while two buffers at a higher level and off-set to the right, enabled the locomotive to propel standard-gauge vehicles while running on three rail two-gauge track.

Dimensions: CYLINDERS: HIGH PRESSURE: 350 × 500mm
                      LOW PRESSURE: 500 × 500mm
       COUPLED WHEELS: 1000mm
       GRATE AREA: 1.5m²
       BOILER PRESSURE: 14kg/cm²

Zell Todtnau 0–4–4–0T No 105

[R. Gottschall

No 105 is a Mallet compound (0–4–4–0 Side Tank locomotive which was built in 1918 by Karlsruhe (works number 2051) for the Zell-Todtnau line in the Black Forest. This line was operated by the *Mittelbadischen Eisenbahn* AG (MEG). No 105 is now the property of the Blonay-Chamby Museum Railway and works on their line near Vevey in Switzerland.

In 1896 a Mallet locomotive with Belpaire boiler was purchased from Société Alsacienne to work on the Zell-Todtnau line which abounds in severe curves and steep inclines. In 1918, No 105 was built for the railway and, apart from having a round-top boiler, was identical with its predecessor. Both high and low pressure cylinders have slide valves operated by Walschaerts valve gear. Coal is carried in bunkers in front of the cab and behind the side tanks.

Dimensions: CYLINDERS: HIGH PRESSURE: 250 × 450mm
LOW PRESSURE: 380 × 450mm
COUPLED WHEELS: 900mm
GRATE AREA: 0.75m²
BOILER PRESSURE: 12kg/cm²

Zell Todtnau 0–6–6–0T No 104   [R. Gottschall

No 104 is a Mallet compound 0–6–6–0 Side Tank locomotive which was built in 1925 by Hanomag (works number 10437) for the Zell-Todtnau line in the Black Forest. This locomotive is now preserved in working order on the Blonay-Chamby Museum Railway near Vevey, Switzerland.

This locomotive is one of two identical machines built by Hanomag, the other going to the *Brohtalbahn.* They were very powerful machines of handsome appearance with lipped chimneys. Coal is carried in a bunker behind the cab and both locomotives originally had feed-water heaters. Steam distribution is by Walschaerts valve gear operating piston valves above high-pressure and low-pressure cylinders. However, neither locomotive was ever superheated.

Dimensions: CYLINDERS: HIGH PRESSURE: 400 × 450mm
                       LOW PRESSURE: 620 × 450mm
        COUPLED WHEELS: 900mm
        BOILER PRESSURE: 14kg/cm^2

0–10–0T No 99.716

No 99.716 Class K 55.9 is an outside-cylinder superheated 0–10–0 Side Tank locomotive which was built for DRG in 1927 by Hartmann (works number 4673). It is preserved outside the *Bundesbahn* station at Guglingen.

For service on the considerable 750mm-gauge systems of the former Saxon and the Württemberg State Railways, the *Reichsbahn* ordered a considerable number of powerful 0–10–0T locomotives. The design was a modernisation of previous Saxon engines and the new engines which first appeared in 1923, incorporated a system providing for lateral and radial displacement of the first and fifth coupled axles. The drive is to the fourth coupled axle and Walschaerts valve gear operates piston valves above the cylinders.

Dimensions: CYLINDERS: 400 × 450mm
COUPLED WHEELS: 800mm
GRATE AREA: 1.6m²
BOILER PRESSURE: 14kg/cm²
SUPERHEATED

RSE 2–8–2T No 53   [Hartmut Born

No 53 is a superheated, outside-cylinder 2–8–2 Side Tank locomotive built for the *Rhein Sieg Eisenbahn* in 1944 by Jung (works number 10175). It is at present preserved by *Deutsche Gesellschaft für Eisenbahngeschichte EV*.

This is a modern locomotive with the boiler surmounted by three domes for top-feed, steam and sand respectively. It is even provided with smoke deflectors. Piston valves above the cylinders are operated by Walschaerts valve gear and the drive is to the trailing coupled axle. This locomotive was converted for oil-firing in 1957.

Dimensions: CYLINDERS: 400 × 450mm
COUPLED WHEELS: 900mm
GRATE AREA: 2.0m²
BOILER PRESSURE: 15kg/cm²
SUPERHEATED

Appendix 1

Locomotive Manufacturers

Abbreviated Name	Full Name

Aarau = Maschinenfabrik der Internationalen Gesellschaft fur Berg-bahnen, Aarau, Switzerland.

AB Atlas = AB Atlas, Stockholm, Sweden.

AEG = Allgemeine Elektricitats-Gesellschaft, Berlin-Grünewald.

Alco = American Locomotive Company, Schenectady, NY, USA.

Ansaldo = Società-Ansaldo-Armstrong, Sampierdarena-Genova, Italy.

Ateliers d'Oullins = PLM Company's Works at Oullins, France.

Avonside = Avonside Engine Company, Bristol, England.

Babcock & Wilcox = Sociedad Española de Constructiones Babcock & Wilcox, Sestro-Bilbao, Spain.

Baldwin = Baldwin Locomotive Company, Philadelphia, Penna, USA.

Batignolles-Châtillon = Batignolles-Châtillon-Bacalan, Bordeaux, France.

Berlin = Berliner Maschinenbau AG, Vormals L. Schwartzkopff, Berlin.

B.P. = Beyer Peacock & Co, Gorton, Manchester, England.

Blanc-Misseron = (ANF) Ateliers de Constructions du Nord de la France, Crespin-Blanc-Misseron (Nord), les Mureaux.

Borsig = A. Borsig, Berlin-Tegel, Germany.

Boussu = S.A. des Ateliers de Construction du Boussu, Boussu, Belgium.

Breda (Italy) = Ernesto Breda, Milan, Italy.

Breda (Netherlands) = Machinefabriek Backer & Rueb, Breda, Holland.

Buddicom = Allcard Buddicom, Chartreux, Rouen, France.

Cail = J. F. Cail = Société Française de Constructions Mecaniques, Denain, France.

Canada Works = Peto, Betts & Brassey, Canada Works, Birkenhead, England.

Canadian = Canadian Locomotive Works, Montreal, Canada.

Chaplin = Alex. Chaplin & Co, Cranston Hill Engine Works, Glasgow.

Chemnitz = Sachsische Maschinenfabrik, vormals Richard Hartmann, Chemnitz, Germany.

Cockerill = John Cockerill, Seraing, Belgium.

Corpet Louvet = Société Corpet Louvet et Cie, La Courneuve, France.

Couillet = Société Anonyme des Usines Metallurgiques du Hainaut, Couillet, Marcinelle, Belgium.

Decauville = Société Anonyme Decauville, Corbeil, France.

Dübs = Dübs & Co., Scotland.

Erste Böhmische-Marische Maschinenfabrik = First Bohemian-Moravian Engine Works, Prague, Czechoslovakia.

Esslingen = Maschinenfabrik Esslingen-Mettingen, Esslingen am Neckar, Germany.

Est = Est Railway Works, Epernay, France.

Euskalduna = Compañia Euskalduna de Construction y Reparaçion de Buques SA, Bilbao, Spain.

Fairbairn = W. Fairbairn & Sons, Canal Street Works, Manchester, England.

Falun = Vagn & Maskinfabriks AB, Falun, Sweden.

Abbreviated Name	Full Name

F.A.M.H. = Compagnie des Forges et Aciéries de la Marine d'Homé-court, France.

Fives = Compagnie de Fives-Lille pour Constructions Mecaniques et Enterprises, Fives-Lille, France.

Fletcher Jennings = Fletcher Jennings & Company, Lowca Works, Whitehaven, England.

Floridsdorf = Wiener Lokomotivfabrik, AG, Wien-Floridsdorf, Austria.

Fox Walker = Fox, Walker & Co., Bristol, England.

Franco-Belge = Societe Franco-Belge de Matériel de Chemins de Fer, La Croyère, Belgium.

Freudenstein = Freudenstein AG, Berlin, Germany.

Frichs = A/S Frichs, Maskinfabrik, Aarhus, Denmark.

Gouin = Ernst Gouin, Etablissement Gouin, Paris, France.

Graffenstaden = Société Usine de Graffenstaden, Graffenstaden, France.

Hagans = Christian Hagans, Erfurt, Germany.

Haine-St. Pierre = Société Anonyme des Forges, Usines et Fonderies, Haine-St. Pierre, Belgium.

Hallette = Alfred Hallette, Arras, France.

Hamar = Jernstöper & Maskinfabrik, Hamar, Norway.

Hanomag = Hannoversche Maschinenbau AG vormals Georg Egestorff, Hannover-Linden, Germany.

Hartmann = Maschinenfabrik Richard Hartmann, Chemnitz, Germany.

Haswell = John Haswell Lokomotivfabrik (later StEG), Wien, Austria.

Heilbronn = Maschinenfabrik, Heilbronn, Germany.

Henschel = Henschel & Söhn, Cassel (later, Henschel-Werke GmbH, Kassel, Germany).

Helsingfors = Railway Works, Helsinki, Finland.

Hohenzollern = Hohenzollern AG fur Lokomotivbau, Dusseldorf-Grafenberg, Germany.

Hudswell Clark = Hudswell Clark & Company, Railway Foundry, Leeds, England.

Henry Hughes = Henry Hughes, Falcon Works, Loughborough, England.

Humboldt = Humboldt Lokomotivbau, Köln-Kalk, Germany.

Hunslet = The Hunslet Engine Works, Leeds, England.

Jones & Potts = Jones & Potts, Newton-le-Willows, Lancs., England.

Jones = Jones, Turner & Evans, Warrington, England.

Jung = Arn. Jung Lokomotivfabrik GmbH, Jungenthal bei Kirchberg, Germany.

Kalmar = Kalmar Verkstads AB, Kalmar, Sweden.

Karlsruhe = See Kessler.

Kessler = Maschinenfabrik von Emil Kessler, Karlsruhe, Germany.

Koechlin = Lokomotivfabrik André Koechlin & Cie, Mulhouse, France.

Krauss = Lokomotivfabrik Krauss & Co., München, Germany.

Krauss-Linz = Lokomotivfabrik Krauss & Co., Linz an der Donau, Austria.

Krauss-Maffei = Krauss-Maffei AG, München-Allach, Germany.

Kristinehamn = Kristinehamns Mekaniska Verkstad, Kristinehamn, Sweden.

Krupp = Fried. Krupp, Maschinenfabriken, Essen, Germany.

Abbreviated Name	Full Name

Lima = Lima Locomotive Company, Lima, Ohio, USA.

Linke-Hofmann = Linke-Hofmann Werke, Breslau, Germany.

Lokomo = Lokomo Oy, Tampere, Finland.

Longridge = R. B. Longridge & Co., Bedlington Iron Works, Northumberland, England.

Macosa = Material y Construcciones SA, Valencia, Spain.

Maffei = J. A. Maffei AG, München, Germany.

Manning Wardle = Manning Wardle & Co. Ltd., Boyne Engine Works, Leeds, England.

Maquinista = La Maquinista Terrestre y Maritima, Barcelona, Spain.

Merryweather = Merryweather & Sons, Greenwich, England.

La Meuse = S.A. des Ateliers de Construction de la Meuse, Sclessin-Liège, Belgium.

Montreal = Montreal Locomotive Works, Montreal, Canada.

Motala = Motala Mekaniska Verkstad, Motala, Sweden.

Munktells = Th. Munktells, Mekaniska Verkstad, Eskilstuna, Sweden.

Neilson = Neilson & Co., Glasgow, Scotland.

NOHAB = Nydquist & Holm AB, Trollhättan, Sweden.

Nord = Chemin de Fer du Nord Railway Works, La Chapelle, Paris, France.

Norris = Norris Works at Wien (affiliated to Norris Locomotive Works, Philadelphia, USA).

NBL = North British Locomotive Company, Glasgow, Scotland.

Nydquist = Nydquist & Holm (see NOHAB, above).

Olten = Swiss Central Railway Works at Olten, Switzerland.

OM = Officine Meccaniche, Milan, Italy.

Oullins = Parent & Schaken, Oullins, France.

Orenstein = Orenstein & Koppel, Berlin-Drewitz, Germany.

Parent = Société Parent, Schaken, Caillet et Cie, Fives, Lille, France.

PLM = Works of the P.L.M. at Arles, France.

Postula = Postula & Cie, Renaud Works, Brussels, Belgium.

Richmond = Richmond Locomotive Works, Richmond, Va., USA.

Saronno = Costruzioni Meccaniche Saronno, Italy.

Sentinel = Sentinel Wagon Works Ltd., Shrewsbury, England.

Schneider = Schneider & Cie, Le Creusot, France.

Schwartzkopff = L. Schwartzkopff AG, Berlin, Germany (see also Berlin).

Sharp Stewart = Sharp Stewart & Co., Ltd., Glasgow, Scotland.

Skoda = Skoda-Werke, Pilsen, Czechoslovakia.

Slaughter-Grüning = Slaughter-Grüning & Co., Fishponds, Bristol, England.

SLM = Swiss Locomotive and Machine Company, Winterthur, Switzerland.

Société Alsacienne = SACM = Société Alsacienne de Constructions Mécaniques, Graffenstaden, Mulhouse, France.

St. Leonard = Société Anonyme des Ateliers, St. Leonard, Liege, Belgium.

Robert Stephenson = Robert Stephenson & Co., Newcastle-upon-Tyne, England.

StEG = Wien-Gloggnitz Railway Works, Wien, Austria (later became

Abbreviated Name	Full Name

Maschinenfabrik der k.k.priv. österreichischen staats-eisenbahnen Gesellschaft, Wien).

Tampereen = Tampereen Pellava Oy, Tampere, Finland.

Tayleur = Charles Tayleur & Co., Newton-le-Willows, Lancs., England.

Thunes = Thunes Mekaniske Verkstad, Oslo, Norway.

Tubize = Société Générale d'Exploitation, Morel-Zaman, Tubize, Belgium.

Turin = FS Railway Works, Turin, Italy.

Vulcan = A/S Vulcan Works, Maribo, Denmark.

Werkspoor = Nederlandsche Fabrik van Werktuigen en Spoorwegmaterieel, Amsterdam, Holland.

Wiener-Neustadt = Lokomotivfabrik, vormals G. Sigl, Wiener-Neustadt, Austria.

Yorkshire = Yorkshire Engine Company Ltd., Sheffield, England.

Appendix 2

Location of Preserved and Stored Locomotives

Austria

Location	Number		Type
Budapest, Railway Museum	674	GKB	o–6–o
Graz-Andritz, Andritritzer Schleppbahn	98.703		o–6–oT
Graz, Depot GKB	671	GKB	o–6–o*
	56.3115	GKB	2–8–o*
	1851	GKB	o–6–oT*
	30.114		2–6–2T*
Hohenau, Sugar Factory	494.62		o–6–oT
Linz, Depot ÖBB	77.66		4–6–2T*
	78.603		4–6–4T*
Linz, ÖBB Garden	106		o–6–o
	852		o–6–o
	LICAON		2–4–oT
Münich, East Depot DB	680	GKB	o–6–o*
Murzzuschlag, Depot ÖBB	95.107		2–10–2T*
Rome, Smistamento Depot FS	180.56		o–10–o*
	97.99		o–6–oT*
Vienna, East Depot ÖBB	01.032		2–6–2*
	392.2512		o–8–oT*
Vienna, Franz-Joseph Depot ÖBB	372	GKB	4–4–o*
	333.002		o–6–o*
	310.23		2–6–4*
	214.10		2–8–4*
	69.02		2–2–2T*
	91.32		2–6–oT*
	2 *SULM* GKB		2–6–2T*
Vienna, South Depot ÖBB	60.115		2–6–o*
	38.4101		4–6–o*
	73.79		o–8–o*
	270.125		2–8–o*
	113.02		4–8–o*
	80.988		o–10–o*
	258.902		2–10–o*
	81.44		2–10–o*
	088.01		o–4–oT*
	ILSE		o–4–oT*
	3071.07		2–4–2T*
	92.2220		o–8–oT*
Vienna, Stadlau Depot ÖBB	175.817		2–6–2T*
	95.107		2–10–2T*

* *The locomotive is stored and, therefore, the location given is not permanent.*

Location	Number	Type
Vienna, Technical Museum	*AJAX*	0–4–2
	STEINBRUCK	4–4–0
	254	4–4–0
	180.01	0–10–0
	4 *GMUNDEN*	4–4–0T
Vordernberg	97.201	0–6–2RT*
	197.301	0–12–0RT*
	297.401	2–12–2RT*

Austria—Narrow Gauge

Location	Number	Type
Bad Ischl	SKGLB 4	0–6–2T
Garsten	298.51	0–6–2T
Haag	698.01	0–4–0T
Innsbruck	ZB I	0–6–2T
Kuhnsdorf	199.02	0–8–2T
	399.01	0–8–4T
Mondsee	SKGLB 9	0–6–2T
Murau	2	0–4–0WT
Obergrafendorf	298.102	0–6–2T
	398.01	0–6–2T
	498.07	0–6–2T
	699.01	0–8–0TT
Ruprechtshofen	298.205	0–6–2T
Vienna, Technical Museum	I	0–4–0RT
Waidhofen	Yv I	0–6–4T
Welshpool	699.01	0–8–0TT

Belgium

Location	Number	Type
Brussels, Railway Museum	*PAYS DE WAES*	2–2–2T
Brussels, Midi Depot, SNCB	*LA BELGE* (rep.)	2–2–2*
	L'ELEPHANT (rep.)	2–4–0*
Louvain, Depot SNCB	1805	4–4–0*
	12.004	4–4–2*
	7.039	4–6–0*
	10.018	4–6–2*
	1.002	4–6–2*
	29.013	2–8–0*
	16.042	4–4–2T*
	1152	0–6–0T*
	53.320	0–8–0T*
	615	0–8–0T*
Schepdaal, Tramways Museum	813	0–6–0 Tram
Steamtown, Bellows Falls, Vt., USA	*PRINCE DE LIEGE*	0–4–0T

* *The locomotive is stored and, therefore, the location given is not permanent.*

Belgium—Narrow Gauge

Location	Number		Type
Schepdaal, Tramways Museum	303		0–6–0 Tram
	979		0–6–0 Tram
	1066		0–6–0 Tram
Tramways de L'Aisne	1075		0–6–0 Tram
	1076		0–6–0 Tram

Denmark

Location	Number		Type
Aalborg, Vesterkaerets Skøle	34	FFJ	2–6–0
Bramminge, Depot DSB	908		4–6–2*
Brande, Depot DSB	1		0–4–2*
	802		2–6–0*
Copenhagen, Depot DSB	602		0–6–0*
Esbjerg, Depot DSB	273		2–4–0*
	937		4–6–0*
Frederikshavn, Depot DSB	783		2–8–0*
Helsingor, Technical Museum	40		0–4–2
	L2		0–4–0T
Helsingor, HHGB Depot	1	SVJ	2–4–0T*
	7	ØSJS	2–6–0T*
Kolding, Locomotive Club	12	TKVJ	2–6–0
Lunderskov, Depot DSB	942		4–6–0*
Mansion Egeskov, Funen	3	NFR	2–6–0T
Mariager Handset Veteran Railway—Danish Railway Club	7	LTJ	2–4–0T
	L106	HOJ	2–6–0T*
	L107	HBS	2–6–0T*
	14	OKMJ	2–6–2T
Maribo, Danish Railway Club	5	OHJ	0–6–0
	19	LJ	2–6–0
	564		4–4–0
	1	KB	0–4–0T*
	4	SB	0–4–0T*
	20	LR	0–4–0T
	3	ØSJS	0–6–0T
	2	ØSJS	0–6–0T
	6	ØSJS	0–8–0T*
	11	GDS	4–6–0T
Naestved, Depot DSB	715		4–4–0*

The locomotive is stored and, therefore, the location given is not permanent.

Location	Number		Type
Odense, Depot DSB	263		2–4–0*
	159		4–4–0*
	931		4–4–2*
	78		0–6–0*
	363		0–4–0T*
	385		0–4–0T*
	125		0–4–4T*
	318		2–4–2T*
Padborg, Depot DSB	428		0–6–0T*
Randers, Depot DSB	885		2–6–0*
	900		2–6–0*
Roskilde, Depot DSB	582		4–4–0*
Ryomgard, Depot DSB	45		2–4–0*
Skanderborg, Depot DSB	563		4–4–0*
Slagelse, Depot DSB	368		0–4–0T*
Struer, Depot DSB	246		0–4–2*
Tollose, Private owner	3	SNNB	0–6–0T
Viborg, Depot DSB	871		2–6–0*
	958		4–6–0*

Locomotives of Private Railways are indicated by the numbers followed by the Company's initials.

Finland

Location	Number	Type
Hyvinkaa, Depot VR	400	2–6–0*
	451	4–6–0*
	1319	2–10–0*
Hyvinkaa, Works VR	135	2–6–0
	489	2–6–4T*
	1800	4–6–4T*
Kaipianen, Depot VR	58	4–4–0*
	21	0–6–0*
	110	0–6–0*
	124	2–6–0*
	132	0–4–4T*
	9	0–4–2T*
Kuopio, Works VR	68	0–4–0T
Kouvola	859	2–8–0
Lastenlinna Linnankeskenkatu Hospital	419	2–8–0
Myllymaki, Depot VR	407	2–8–0*

* *This locomotive is stored and, therefore, the location given is not permanent.*

Location	Number	Type
Pasila, Depot VR	742	4–6–0*
	895	2–8–0*
Pieksamaki Museum	852	2–8–0
Riihimaki, Depot VR	554	4–6–0*
Sysmajarvi, Depot VR	497	4–6–0*
Tampereen Works	315	2–6–0
Vaasa, Depot VR	456	2–6–4T*

Finland—Narrow Gauge

Location	Number	Type
Forssa Depot, Jokioisten Railway	HFR 4	2–6–2T
Humpilla-Forssa	HFR 5	2–6–2T
	HKR 5	2–8–2T
Karkilla, Bus Station	HKR 3	2–8–2T
Lahti, Railway Station	LLR 7	2–8–0
Loviissa, Railway Station	LLR 6	2–6–0
Riihimaki-Loppi, Fire Station	RLR 3	0–6–2T
Tampere, Public Park	HKR 2	0–6–2T

France

Location	Number	Type
Delson, Montreal, Railway Museum	030 C 841	0–6–0
Lakeside Railway, Carnforth, England	231 K 22	4–6–2
Montpellier, Railway Station	81 Herault Rly.	0–8–0T
Mulhouse, Railway Museum (Locomotives at present in store at various places)	3	2–2–2*
	5 *SEZANNE*	2–2–2*
	6 *L'AIGLE*	2–2–2*
	120 A 36	2–4–0*
	121 A 340	2–4–2*
	701	4–2–0*
	C.145	4–4–2*
	221 A 30	4–4–2*
	030 A 1	0–6–0*
	030 C 815	0–6–0*
	3486	0–6–0*
	230 B 114	4–6–0*
	230 C 531	4–6–0*
	230 B 614	4–6–0*
	230 D 9	4–6–0*

* *The locomotive is stored and, therefore, the location given is not permanent.*

Location	Number	Type
	231 A 546	4–6–2*
	231 E 22	4–6–2*
	231 C 78	4–6–2*
	231 H 8	4–6–2*
	231 D 596	4–6–2*
	3.1102	4–6–4*
	232 U 1	4–6–4*
	040 A 51	0–8–0*
	040 B 9	0–8–0*
	140 A 908	2–8–0*
	140 A 259	2–8–0*
	140 C 344	2–8–0*
	241 A 1	4–8–2*
	241 P 17	4–8–2*
	150 A 65	2–10–0*
	150 P 13	2–10–0*
	030 TA 628	0–6–0T*
	032 TA 312	0–6–4T*
	040 TC 90	0–8–0T*
	141 TA	2–8–2T†
	141 TD 740	2–8–2T†
	242 TA 6	4–8–4T
Palavas, Railway Station	70 Herault Rly	0–8–0T
Paris, Noisy-le-Sec Depot	80 *LE CONTINENT*	4–2–0
Pithiviers, Museum of Transport	103	0–6–0T
Saint Pierre des Corps, Depot SNCF	230 G 352	4–6–0
Thoringy, Private Garden	*RIMANCOURT*	0–6–0T
Zürich, Sihlwald Depot	241 A 65	4–8–2*

It is understood that Chapelon Pacific 231 E 41 is undergoing a general repair and may be used to work special trains.

France—Narrow Gauge

Blonay Chamby	E 332	4–6–0T
C.F. Forestier d'Abreschviller	3	0–6–0T
	—	0–4–4–0T
Jouy	13	2–6–0T
	15	2–6–0T
Le Mans	51	0–6–0 Tram
Melle	3	0–6–0 Tram
Paris, Malakoff Museum	75	0–6–0T
	4	0–6–0T

* *The locomotive is stored and, therefore, the location given is not permanent.*
† *The identity of this locomotive is not certain.*

Location	Number	Type
Pithiviers, Museum of Transport	1	0–6–0T
	2 JACQUELINE	0–8–0T
	3	0–6–0T
	4 LA MARTROY	0–6–2T
	5 LE MINIHIC	0–6–0T
	8 COLETTE	0–6–0T
	9 LES FONTENELLES	2–6–0T
	10	0–4–0T
	12 PITHIVIERS	0–8–0T
	—	0–4–0T
Portmadoc, Wales	3–23 MOUNTAINEER	2–6–2T
St. Brieuc	36	0–6–0T
C.F. Touristique de Meyzieu	1 COQUETTE	0–4–0T
	2 CHAMPAGNE	0–6–0T
	3 BEAUJOLAIS	0–6–0T
	7	0–6–0T
	8 CHABLAIS	2–6–0T
	4 BOURGOGNE	0–8–0T
	4–13 RHONE	0–8–0T
	5 LOIRET	0–4–4–0T
Towyn, Wales	Cambrai	0–6–0T
Verneuil, Museum	3714	0–6–2T
	77	2–6–0T
	1 AISNE	2–6–0T
C.F. du Vivarais	E 327	4–6–0T
	403	0–6–6–0T
	404	0–6–6–0T
	414	0–6–6–0T

West Germany

Location	Number	Type
Aachen, Technical School	18.323	4–6–2*
Achern-Ottenhofen	14	0–6–0T
	28	0–6–0T
Berlin, Kreuzberg	89.7513	0–6–0T
Bettembourg, Luxembourg	5513	2–10–0
Bucholz, Depot DB	1710	0–6–0T*
Cologne Zoo	89.7462	0–6–0T
Constance, Engineering School	85.007	2–10–2T
Deutsche Gesellschaft für Eisenbahngeschichte EV	unknown	4–6–2
	98.7508	0–4–0T*
	7270	0–6–2T*
	66.002	2–6–4T*

* The locomotive is stored and, therefore, the location given is not permanent.

Location	Number	Type
Frauenfeld, Switzerland	18.478	4–6–2*
Hagen-Eckesey, Depot DB	03.1001	4–6–2*
Haltingen (Basle), Depot DB	30	0–6–0T
Hamar, Norway	2770	2–10–0
Hannover, Depot DB	89.7538	0–6–0T*
Hattersheim (Main)	44	0–6–2T
Hohenbudberg, Depot DB	56.241	2–8–0*
Horb, Depot DB	97.504	0–10–0RT
Ingolstadt	98.507	0–6–2T
Kassel, Children's Playground	89.7296	0–6–0T
Kassel, Depot DB	10.001	4–6–2
Krauss-Maffei, München-Allach	18.528	4–6–2
Linke-Hofmann, Busche, Salzgitter-Watenstadt	38.1444	4–6–0
	39.184	2–8–2
Louvain, Belgium, Depot SNCB	64.045	4–6–0*
Ludwigshafen, Depot DB	88.7306	0–4–0T*
Mercedes-Benz, Esslingen-Mettingen	89.314	0–6–0T
	97.502	0–10–0RT
Minden, Depot DB	18.505	4–6–2*
Mühldorf, Bundesbahnbetriebsamt	70.083	2–4–0T
Mulheim (Ruhr)	17.218	4–6–0*
	62.003	4–6–4T*
München, Deutschesmuseum	*BEUTH* (rep.)	2–2–2
	1000	2–4–0
	18.451	4–6–2
Nordhorn	14	2–6–0T
Nürnberg, Depot DB	28 *DIE PFALZ* (rep.)	4–2–0*
	98.307	0–4–0T*
Nürnberg, Verkehrsmuseum	*ADLER* (rep.)	2–2–2
	PHOENIX	4–2–0
	LANDWUHRDEN	0–4–0
	NORDGAU	2–4–0
	3201	4–4–4
	05.001	4–6–4
	2100	0–4–4–0
	4515	0–4–0T
	2499 (works number)	0–4–0T
Offenburg, Engineering College	18.316	4–6–2*
Oldenburg, Depot DB	81.004	0–8–0T*
Schweinfurt, Depot DB	098–812–1	0–8–0T*
	098–886–5	0–8–0T*
Schwerte, Bundesbahn Aussbesserung	01.177	4–6–2*
	03.197	4–6–2*

* *The locomotive is stored and, therefore, the location given is not permanent.*
(rep.) = Replica.

Location	Number	Type
	03.1013	4–6–2*
	55.4142	0–8–0*
	55.5041	0–8–0*
	41.297	2–8–2*
	89.7531	0–6–0T*
	89.801	0–6–0T*
	64.001	2–6–2T*
	78.126	4–6–4T*
	86.491	2–8–2T*
	94.816	0–10–0T*
Stadt Allendorf	92.739	0–8–0T
Treuchtlingen	01.220	4–6–2
Vienna, South Depot ÖBB	42.2708	2–10–0*
	770.86	2–4–0T*

West Germany—Narrow Gauge

1000mm GAUGE

Location	Number	Type
Blonay-Chamby	99.193	0–10–0T
	ZTE 105	0–4–4–0T
	ZTE 104	0–6–6–0T
Chiemsee-Bahn	—	0–4–0 Tram
Deutsche Gesellschaft für Eisenbahn-geschichte EV	MEG 46	0–4–0T
	OEG 102	0–4–0 Tram
	ZTE 74	0–6–0T
	BEG 11/sm	0–4–4–0T
Deutsche Eisenbahn Verein (DEV)	3	0–4–0WT
	HSA 31	0–6–0T
	HSA 33	0–6–0T
	KAE 15	0–6–0T
Dillengen	WN 12	0–4–0T
Mannheim	OEG 56	0–4–0T
Neresheim	WN 11	0–4–0T
Regensburg	LAG 99.253	0–6–2T
Wangerooge	99.211	0–6–0T

750mm GAUGE

Location	Number	Type
Guglingen	99.716	0–10–0T

785mm GAUGE

Location	Number	Type
Deutsche Gesellschaft für Eisenbahn-geschichte EV	RSE 53	2–8–2T

Appendix 3

Alterations and additions to December 31, 1970

AUSTRIA   1435mm

Sudbahn 0–6–0 Class 29 No 852 at Linz will go to Innsbruck for the museum there.

Krauss Dampftramway (Vienna) 0–6–0 Tram No 11 built in 1884 by Krauss Linz (works number 1482) is now stored at Vienna, Franz Josef Depot ÖBB.

Mahrisch-Schlesische Landesbahn 0–6–0T No 3 which became CSD No 310.906, is preserved privately in Austria. It was built in 1905 by Wiener Neustadt (works number 4598) and was kkStB No 197.40.

No 92.2231 ÖBB 0–8–0 Side Tank locomotive built by Krauss Linz in 1909 (works number 6213), is now in use on the *Montafonerbahn* (Bludenz-Schruns). It is restored with its old kkStB number 178.84.

Austrian locomotives to be preserved in Czechoslovakia

CSD 4–4–0 No 252.008 ex kkStB No 301.09 built by Wiener Neustadt in 1881 (works number 2586) is in Prague Museum.

CSD 2–6–0 No 344.142 ex kkStB 760.42 built by Steg in 1909 (works number 3615).

CSD 2–6–2 No 354.7152 built in 1916 by *Erste Böhmisch-Mährische Maschinenfabrik* (works number 657) was kkStB 429.1996 and a two-cylinder compound. It is now a simple and is preserved at Nimburg.

CSD 2–6–4 No 375.007 ex kkStB No 310.15 built in 1911 by *Erste Böhmische-Mährische Maschinenfabrik* (works number 390) is in Prague Museum.

CSD 0–8–0 No 411.019 ex kkStB No 171.20 built by Wiener Neustadt in 1873 (works number 1740).

CSD 0–8–0 No 414.404 ex kkStB No 175.04 built by Steg in 1894 (works number 2416).

CSD 0–8–0 No 414.096 ex kkStB No 73.368 built by Steg in 1906 (works number 3282) is preserved at Budweis.

CSD 2–8–0 No 434.2296 ex kkStB No 170.145 built by Steg in 1914 (works number 3964). Rebuilt as two-cylinder simple from compound.

CSD 0–6–0T No 310.001 ex kkStB No 97.02 built by Wiener Neustadt in 1883 (works number 2782) is preserved at Olmutz.

CSD 0–6–0T No 310.0118 was built by *Erste Böhmische-Mährische Maschinenfabrik* as kkStB No 97.227 in 1903 (works number 108). It is in Prague Museum.

CSD 0–8–0T No 422.0103 ex kkStB No 178.205 is a two-cylinder compound built in 1918 by Krauss Linz (works number 7315). It is preserved at Budweis.

CSD 0–8–0T No 403.303 ex kkStB No 378.02 was built in 1880 by Steg (works number 1619) and is preserved at Nimburg.

CSD 0–8–2 rack and adhesion Tank locomotive No 404.003 was kkStB No 169.52 and is preserved at Nimburg.

760mm

No 11.810, a Styrian Railways 0–6–0 Tender-Tank locomotive, was built in 1944 by Jung (works number 10120) for the *Heeresfeldbahn*. It has been sold to the *CF Forestier d'Abreschviller* in France.

No Z6, an 0–6–0T of the Styrian Railways, built in 1893 by Krauss (works number 2855) is at Kapfenberg for restoration by "Klub 760".

Zillertalbahn 0–6–2T No 1 *RAIMUND* is now at Innsbruck for the local museum.

No 298.14 ÖBB 0–6–2T built in 1898 by Krauss Linz (works number 3816) has been bought by *Eurovapor* for working steam special trains in the *Waldenburger Bahn* in Switzerland.

No U47.001 of CSD was No 391 of kkHB (*Heeresbahn*) built in 1907 by Henschel (works number 7930). It is a four-cylinder Mallet compound 0–4–4–0T and is now in the museum at Prague.

No Kh 111 of the *Murtal-bahn* (Unzmarkt-Mauterndorf) is an 0–10–0 Side Tank locomotive with outside cylinders and Caprotti valves which has been restored to work special steam trains. It was built in 1930 by Krauss Linz (works number 1519).

BELGIUM

Pays-de Waes is No 2 and is believed to have been withdrawn in 1896 and not in 1890. It is understood that the gauge of the Antwerp-Ghent Railway was 1140mm and not 1150mm.

1435mm

No 7.039 4–6–0 carries works number 1326.

No 10.018 4–6–2 was built in 1911 by Cockerill (works number 2818).

No 808 of SNCV was built in 1894 by St. Leonard (works number 941). It belonged to the Groenendael-Overijssche Tramway and is now stored at Louvain.

No 813 0–6–0 Tram carries works number 1468.

No 1152 0–6–0PT was built in 1879 (not 1884) by Everard (works number 316).

1000mm

0–6–0T No 24 *LA SCARPE* built in 1907 by Corpet Louvet (works number 1087) is at Schepdaal for use on the *Tramway de l'Aisne*. It probably came from a French light railway.

DENMARK   1435mm

Hong Tollose Railway will operate trains with No 625 0–6–0 Class G now named *GERDA*, built in 1898 by Breda (works number 402). This engine was obtained from DSB in 1957.

DSB 4–6–0 Class R–1 No 937 built in 1913 by Borsig (works number 8583) is stored at Esbjerg Depot DSB for preservation.

Vemb Lemvig Thyboron Railway No 5, a 2–6–0 Side Tank locomotive built in 1911 by Henschel (works number 10557), is on loan to the Mariager Handset Veteran Railway.

Odsherreds Railway (OhJ) from Holbaek, will operate trains with a 2–8–2 Side Tank locomotive No 38, built in 1917 by Henschel (works number 14299) as Svendborg Faaborg Railway No 33. It became DSB Class Df No 130 in 1949, went to Troldhede Kolding Vejen Railway in 1959 and to OhJ in 1968.

FINLAND   600mm

An 0–6–0 Side Tank locomotive built in 1920 for the Ojakkala-Olkala Railway by Orenstein (works number 7325) is preserved outside the museum at Vihdin.

FRANCE   1435mm

Etat 2–4–0 No 3029 *PARTHENAY* is at Laval Depot and has been restored for exhibition.

Ouest 0–6–0 No 030 C 815 is now in working order at Laval.

Sud-Ouest 4–6–0 No 230 G 353 is at Noisy-le-Sec Depot restored in full working order. It will probably replace No 80 *LE CONTINENT* for working special trains.

SNCF four-cylinder compound 4–8–2 No 241 P 30 has gone to Switzerland for preservation and is now at Vallorbe.

CF Avricourt à Blamont et Cirey No 2 *CIREY* has been acquired by the *CF Forestier d'Abreschviller* as a static exhibit. It is an 0–4–4–0 Mallet compound Side Tank locomotive built in 1911 by Henschel (works number 10416).

Examples of the following classes will be preserved at Mulhouse:
    PLM   2–8–2 Class 141 F
    SNCF 2–8–2 Class 141 R
    Est   2–8–2T Class 141 TB

1000mm

Mulhouse Tramways 2–4–2 Tram No 7 built in 1882 by SLM (works number 316) is being restored for use on the Blonay Chomby Railway in Switzerland.

CFE 0–6–2 Side Tank locomotive No 3714 built by Robatel and Buffault in 1910, is to go to Florac to work on the *Ligne de Lozère*.

CFTA P-O Corrèze No 101 is an 0–4–4–0 Mallet compound Side Tank locomotive built in 1906 by Blanc Misseron (works number 337) and Tubize (works number 1473). It is to work on the *Reseau du Vivarais*.

Pithiviers à Toury 2–6–2 Side Tank locomotive No 3.23 built in 1916 by ALCO (works number 57156) is now in service on the Festiniog Railway in Wales, the gauge of which is almost identical. It has been named *MOUNTAINEER*.

GERMANY   1435mm

No 28, an 0–6–0T of SWEG was built in 1900 by Borsig (works number 4788).

It now seems probable that those locomotives stored at Schwerte, Mulheim (Ruhr) and Hohenbudberg will be scrapped.

The following locomotives will be reserved:

4–6–0 SNCB No 64.045 ex KPEV Class P 8 is at Louvain and may be preserved. It was built in 1916 by Henschel (works number 13855).

No 45.010, a DB 2–10–2 is at present stored at Neuenmarkt Wirsberg and will most probably be preserved at Nürnberg.

0–4–0T No 1B *ANNE* ex *Julicher Kreisbahn*, which was built in 1910 by Humboldt (works number 735). The locomotive is owned by Otto Straznicky at Kottingen and will run on the DEG-operated Duren-Baal line west of Cologne.

0–4–0T No 7 ex SWEG *Nebenbahn* which runs from Bad Krozingen to Sulzburg and Untermunstertal. It is located at Staufen (on the SWEG line) not far from Bad Krozingen, south of Freiburg.

0–4–0T No 2 is to be preserved by Frankfurt Tramways. They obtained it in 1955 from the *Frankfurter Lokalbahn*.

0–6–0T No 89.7005 Class T 3 is at present at Wuppertal Langerfeld Depot DB and it carries the number 004.

0–6–0T No 53 ex *Delmenhorst Harpstedter Eisenbahn*, built in 1925 by Hanomag (works number 10431) is preserved by Tramway Stichting at Enschede, Holland.

2–6–0T No 146 (ELNA) ex *Butzbach Licher Eisenbahn* is now at Bochum Dalhausen and owned by DGEV. It was built in 1941 by Henschel (works number 24932). The line is now operated from Butzbach to Bad Nauheim by DEG.

No 75.1118, and 75.435 Baden 2–6–2 Side Tank locomotives will probably be preserved. They are at Constance.

4–6–4T No 78.510 ex KPEV Class T 18, built in 1924, is preserved at Witten Hauptbahnhof.

No 78.468 ex KPEV Class T 18 is preserved on a plinth at Hamburg to commemorate some of the suburban services.

Schwartzeck, an 0–8–0T belonging to *Lokalbahn Lam Kotzing* is preserved at Straubing.

No 7, a 2–8–2 Side Tank locomotive of the *Tegernsee Bahn* operates trains between Schaftlach and Tegernsee during the summer in association with DEGB. No 7 was built in 1936 by Krauss Maffei (works number 15582). There is probably another similar locomotive in use on the line.

1000mm

The following locomotives are to be preserved:
No 56 0–4–0T ex *Oberrheinische Eisenbahn* is preserved at Mannheim Neckarstadt.

No 60 0–4–0T ex *Kleinbahn Giessen Bieber* is preserved at Krofdorf.

No 1 0–6–0T ex *Kleinbahn Bremen Tarmstadt* is preserved at Bremen.

No 35 *BUCKEN*, an 0–6–0T built in 1912 by Hanomag (works number 6612) will probably be preserved by *Hoya Syke Asendorfer Eisenbahn*.

No 16, an 0–6–0T built in 1900 by Henschel (works number 5575) for the *Nassauische Kleinbahn*, is preserved at Limburg.

No 13, *CARL*, an 0–6–0T ex *Kreis Altenser Eisenbahn* is preserved at Altena.

No 22, an 0–6–0T ex *Kreis Altenser Eisenbahn* is preserved in the Heimat-museum, Ludenschied.

No 2s, an 0–6–0T built in 1901 by Borsig (works number 4871) for the *Wurttemburgische Eisenbahn*, is preserved at Laichingen.

No 2, an 0–6–2 Rack and Adhesion Tank locomotive belonging to the *Drachensfelsbahn*, is preserved at Königswinter.

750mm

No 2 0–4–0T of the *Kleinbahn Phillipsheim Binsfield* is preserved at Binsfield.

No 24 0–6–0T ex SWEG *Mochmuhl Dorzbach* is preserved at Krautheim.

No 99.651, an 0–10–0T is preserved at Steinheim. This locomotive is Saxon State Railways Class VIk No 220. It was built in 1918 by Henschel (works number 16132).

No 99.604, an 0–4–4–0 Mallet Tank locomotive has been bought by *Deutsche Gesellschaft für Eisenbahngeschichte EV* and is at Bochum. This locomotive was built in 1914 by Hartmann (works number 3792) and was Saxon State Railways No 194 Class IVk.